W0036033

ADVANCE PRAISE

Naren Nath's book, *The Consumer Revolution*, does an amazing job of tying together the history of mankind's development, political systems, methods and places of commerce, creation of forums to stores, impacts of the industrial and nuclear revolutions, and development of media, printing press and modes of entertainment such as music, plays, film, radio and TV to the tremendous impact of the Internet. He explains why power has shifted from the producer and marketer to the consumer.

It's a fascinating read for everyone, but is essential for students of marketing and those in business, entertainment, media and control of sports franchises who want to stay relevant and not be left behind.

Tom Kalinske, *Former CEO of Mattel,*
Sega of America, LeapFrog

The Consumer Revolution is a gripping saga of how today's consumer has become more empowered than ever before, tilting the balance of power away from producers, corporations, media empires and politicians for the first time in human history. This has created a profound disruption in the make-up of human society with far-reaching impacts, portrayed in a very engaging fashion by Naren in this book.

Shailesh Mehta, *Former Chairman of Providian Financial, Board of Directors at PayPal and Mastercard, Eponym of the Shailesh J. Mehta School of Management at Indian Institute of Technology Bombay*

Naren's long experience in e-commerce has created a unique view of its history and the game-changing future technologies that are changing retail forever.

Terry Jones, *Founder of Travelocity.com and Founding Chairman of Kayak.com*

The Consumer Revolution is a fascinating narrative of how technology empowered the consumer, how it redefined the rights and duties of producers and consumers, and how social change is ignited by the consumer exercising this power with every new disruption in the modern age. Other than business, the book makes us think deeply on its effect on poverty alleviation, education and healthcare, and the manner in which it is going to change the way we think about products and services. This book deserves a scientific sequel that will chart out the fundamental principles that have redefined the consumer.

Partha Pratim Chakrabarti, *Former Director of Indian Institute of Technology Kharagpur*

The Consumer Revolution tells one of the most captivating tales of today—how 'the common (hu)man' came to harness uncommon power and influence in the world. It is a must-read for anyone trying to make sense of some of the biggest current events and trends in the world, gaze into the crystal ball of where human society is headed and activate in order to thrive in it.

Jill Lublin, *Bestselling Author, International Speaker, Master Publicity Strategist*

Naren paints a detailed picture of consumer quality of life and business evolution leading to re-distribution of power and wealth from the industrial revolution to the technology revolution and beyond! Not just consumers, there are implications for businesses, lawmakers, media and others. Fasten your seat belts for what's coming!

Latif Nathani, *Former CEO of eBay India, Executive at Microsoft Corporation*

The Consumer Revolution is a remarkable story of how everyday consumers are becoming dramatically more empowered today. Naren provides a truly unique context and perspective on this revolution, and illustrates why consumers should feel incredibly inspired to express their will and shape their world unlike ever before.

Captain Shalini Singh, *Former Indian Army, TEDx Speaker, Life Coach, Social Activist*

This book will fundamentally change material culture scholarship. It challenges the way social, cultural and economic historians think about consumer behaviour, and will quickly become the book that everyone interested in the meaning of everyday things must read to participate in the lively discussions that will follow its publication.

Priyanka Shetty, *Times of India*

The
Consumer
Revolution

The
Consumer
Revolution

Tipping
the
Balance of
POWER

Naren Nath

Los Angeles | London | New Delhi
Singapore | Washington DC | Melbourne

First published in 2020 by

SAGE Publications India Pvt Ltd
B1/I-1 Mohan Cooperative Industrial Area
Mathura Road, New Delhi 110 044, India
www.sagepub.in

SAGE Publications Inc
2455 Teller Road
Thousand Oaks, California 91320, USA

SAGE Publications Ltd
1 Oliver's Yard, 55 City Road
London EC1Y 1SP, United Kingdom

SAGE Publications Asia-Pacific Pte Ltd
18 Cross Street #10-10/11/12
China Square Central
Singapore 048423

Published by Vivek Mehra for SAGE Publications India Pvt Ltd. Typeset in 11/14.5 pt Adobe Caslon Pro by Fidus Design Pvt. Ltd, Chandigarh.

Library of Congress Cataloging-in-Publication Data Available

ISBN: 978-93-5328-753-5 (PB)

SAGE Team: Manisha Mathews, Mahira Chadha and Sudeshna Nandy

The Consumer Revolution is dedicated to my parents, Dr Lalit Kishore and Mrs Lalita Kishore, who are and will always be my gold standard of intellect and humanity.

CONTENTS

PREFACE

We live in a time of unprecedented velocity and change. There are now 4.2 billion people on the Internet. Five billion people on mobile phones. Social media and artificial intelligence are racing ahead. #MeToo. #BlackLivesMatter. #NeverAgain. Harvey Weinstein. Matt Lauer. Bill Cosby. Arab Spring. Ferguson unrest. Siri, Alexa and Cortana. Blockchain and Bitcoin. Fake news. Foreign interference in elections. Facebook user data scandals. European Union's General Data Protection Regulation. Plummeting fortunes for newspapers and magazines. Decline in television viewership, even for the National Football League (NFL) and the Oscars. Netflix, Hulu, Amazon Prime. Video games, sports betting, fantasy sports. Ad blockers. Turmoil in advertising. Retail apocalypse. Skyrocketing power and wealth at Apple, Amazon, Google, Microsoft, Facebook. Shared economy and Uber, Lyft and Airbnb. Student debt. Rabid polarization in politics.

How do you make sense of these turbulent times? How do you comprehend their underlying reasons? How do you fathom their trajectories? What do these seemingly isolated events have to do with each other? Everything, as it turns out.

Up to this point, there has been no framework or treatise put forth that weaves these global events into one common fabric that explains them all. There has been no doctrine of empowerment for the everyday consumer that puts them in charge of these global events, as the instigators of these events, rather than merely be subject to them. Until 'The Consumer Revolution'.

The book is borne out of years of study and pattern matching of a wide range of social, cultural, political, economic and interpersonal phenomena, starting with my time at Stanford University. While I learnt many invaluable lessons from many exceptional faculty members and fellow students, one experience that really stood out for me was a course taught by Andy Grove, then CEO of Intel Corporation. From his incredible vantage point, Andy gave profound lessons on strategy and market dynamics, which have influenced my thinking to this day.

After Stanford, my insights into consumer empowerment got further refined during my time at Microsoft, through interactions with the likes of Bill Gates and Nathan Myhrvold. My learnings were massive, and I got a bird's eyes view to the shaping of the high-tech industry from the number one source in the world. During this time, I began to observe technologies such as video on demand, time-shifted television and the genesis of the World Wide Web (WWW), and how they were enabling consumer behaviour in unusual yet entirely logical ways.

My observations and explorations around consumer empowerment continued to get refined through my time at Trilogy and cFares, and led to the founding of MetaRail, specifically to address the needs and preferences of consumers in the era of rampant advertising and privacy concerns. *The Consumer Revolution* is thus borne out of decades of learnings and insights in the company of some of the world's smartest and most successful executives and professors.

The book attempts to address the core anxiety amongst readers about the state of the world as it begins to go through rapid and disruptive change. It demystifies some of the intangibles behind change, weaves seemingly random events—sometimes thrilling and sometimes frightful—into a universal framework that reassures readers that there is a method to the madness. It comforts readers who feel powerless and helpless in the face of these larger-than-life events and personalities over which they perceive to have no influence or control.

At its core, the book is meant to share a perspective and encourage you to grasp the phenomenal power you are now bestowed with, and to engage and make a stand wherever you deem fit. Hopefully, you will agree with me that a profound revolution is now underway with you at the heart of it, and unlike ever before, you have a voice, have a say, can take action and make a real difference in your own lives and in the world at large.

I would like to thank the innumerable teachers, colleagues, family members and friends that guided my journey in coming up with the subject matter of the book. In particular, I want to express my sincere appreciation to Lt. Col. R. K. Srivastava (retd.), Arti Srivastava, Sarah Triolo, Hailey Buddenberg, Rajesh Grover and Manisha Mathews for their contribution in helping the book come to life and finding its way to you!

1

REVOLUTIONS

There are inventions. There are innovations. And then there are revolutions.

It is all really a matter of scale. Think of all the transformative revolutions in human history. They were all truly momentous, truly monumental, truly metamorphosizing.

FIRE!

The discovery of controlled fire—the first great revolution to light up human civilization—ignited a transformation of truly epic proportions. Imagine a world without fire. Darkness besetting civilization after sunset. Icy weather and frigid storms raging against cowering, defenceless humans. No semblance of cooked food, and nothing but raw flora and fauna to subsist on. Tools and implements requiring herculean efforts to fashion and shape at room temperatures. Severe limitations in what humans could construct, create, cure, contain and craft. An abysmal standard of living and abject living conditions to survive through.

And then, during the Early Stone Age around 1.6 million years ago, a few of our *Homo erectus* ancestors got inspired by a flash of lightning striking a forest in the Lake Turkana region of modern-day Kenya. The lightning flash started a small natural-born forest fire, not unlike others that this group had seen before. Having experienced the manifold benefits of natural-born fires, this enterprising group discovered a way to extend this fire with the use of a small piece of wood—a substance the group had astutely observed was slow to burn. They were then able to place this controlled, slow-burning piece of wood in a safe location, a shallow patch of earth, and begin to enjoy its myriad benefits. This very same shallow, oxidized patch of earth has in fact been discovered, providing evidence of the first known instance of controlled fire in the world!

Other similar oxidized patches of earth have since been found in the region, providing further evidence of controlled fire migrating to central Kenya around 1.4 million years ago, and to Ethiopia and South Africa around 1 million years ago. From Africa the use of controlled fire spread around the world as its benefits had such universal appeal. Evidence of fire hearths have been found in Israel dating back to 790,000 years ago, followed by China and the United Kingdom around 400,000 years ago.

The controlled fires of this era were still opportunistic extensions of natural fires, however, bringing bounty when nature so bestowed it upon humans, and misery when it didn't. The first signs of the habitual use of controlled fires didn't appear until 300,000 years ago, confirmed via both direct evidence and indirect indicators or references. As an example, there is evidence that this is the era when our ancestors began to have larger brains, distinctive sleep patterns and habitation of cooler geographies, all indicative of the effective control of fire. Also, in this era there is evidence of our ancestors developing smaller mouths, teeth and guts, again pointing to the greater efficiency achieved by consuming cooked food all year long. Not only is the tracing of these historical associations fascinating in and of itself, but the implications on human behaviour and even human evolution prompted by the use of fire is positively mind-boggling. Harnessing fire was so impactful that it prompted a change in basic human physiology and biological makeup! This was a true revolution for humankind.

So profound was the impact of fire on human life that early humans considered it nothing short of divine. In fact, right around 300,000 years ago, coincidentally, humans believed the legendary Prometheus stole fire from the gods and gifted it to humans. According to Greek mythology, Prometheus was a Titan engaged in battle with the Olympian gods led by Zeus for control of the heavens and the Earth. The gods had fire, which gave them an insurmountable advantage over petty humans. Prometheus proceeded to steal fire from the gods and bring it to humans to enable them to survive and thrive. Zeus was so infuriated by this grand larceny that he punished Prometheus by chaining him to a rock, and having an eagle eat at his liver every day until he was rescued by Hercules eons later.

But here on Earth, humans rejoiced. They had fire. There was heat. There was light. There was healthy and delectable food. There was nutrition and healthcare. There were remedies for common ailments. There was life and living after dark. There was the ability to venture out into caves and crannies. There was defence against predators. There was unprecedented safety, warmth and comfort.

And all this was just the beginning. The advent of controlled fire set off a chain reaction of unprecedented transformations that affected nearly every aspect of human life. It spread like wildfire! Everywhere it reached, humans harnessed it, fashioned it for their purposes, and benefitted from it. The impact was truly powerful and far-reaching, and everywhere humans basked in its glow. The arrival of fire altered the course of human history and human development forever.

WHEELS

So did the next great revolution to turn up for human civilization—a whopping 295,000 years later. Up until that time, humans were very limited in their mobility and transportation capabilities. They could travel only as far and as fast as their own feet could carry them. This was all the more limiting for their young and their infirmed. Furthermore, there was no way for humans to transport anything, except on their own feet, and their own arms, and their own shoulders and backs. This limited severely how much they could transport, and how far.

These limitations eased in an appreciable way with the adoption of pets and beasts of burden by humans. The domestication of pets in society had just begun by this time, and the use of horses and donkeys for transportation just initiated; so humans could harness their capabilities to some degree for these purposes. But every step of movement still required physical effort from a biological creature. Transporting anything had to be done by using biological legs, one laborious step after the other, resulting in dramatically slower productivity and pace of life compared to the era to follow.

Then around 3500 BC, an enterprising potter in Mesopotamia came up with the notion of a rotating circular platform of clay to facilitate the shaping of clay pots more evenly and efficiently while keeping hands stationary on the clay. Up until this point, potters would keep the clay itself stationary and move their hands around it to fashion pottery and other wares. This technique was clearly not able to achieve the same levels of symmetry and regularity that rotating clay platforms were, leading to clear benefits in pottery.

The trend of rotating clay platforms caught on quickly as other potters started to take advantage of the same technique, finding it easier and better to leverage the physics of rotation to facilitate their tasks. Without even fully comprehending its precise nature, the merits of rotation and angular momentum had begun to permeate the human psyche.

This led to humans starting to experiment with other applications of angular momentum, such as rolling round logs to achieve some semblance of mobility and transportability around the same era. This innovation, coupled with pottery wheel enhancements directly led to the invention of the wheel, somewhat contemporaneously in Mesopotamia, the Caucasus region and Eastern Europe. Although the exact origins of the invention are not precisely known, the impact on human society could not possibly be overstated. This was the second bona fide revolution to dramatically impact human society.

As inventions go, the wheel was a unique one in that it was the result of completely home-grown ingenuity. Most major innovations up to this point, such as fire, were inspired by nature—by observing and replicating a phenomenon created by cosmic forces. But the wheel had no direct analogue in nature. It was a direct product of human intelligence and enterprise.

In the grand scheme of things, it took humans a long time to adapt the wheel for use in its primary purpose today—transportation. The hard part wasn't the rolling cylinder making up the wheel. It was the connection between a rotating wheel and a non-rotating platform that could be used to transport things or people. This was such a complex problem for its time that it is unlikely that the wheel could have been implemented through multiple incremental advancements, like many other famous inventions. It was more likely invented by a stroke of genius by one inspired inventor who is an anonymous hero in the development folklore of human society today.

The first use of a wheel for transportation was likely a wheel barrow using one solitary wheel. This subsequently evolved into single-axle and double-axle wagons, and chariots with wheels on either side for greater stability. And the rest, of course, is history.

The arrival of the wheel completely transformed mobility and transportation. Human beings were suddenly able to move around over much greater distances with much greater ease. They were able to transport heavy loads of material or equipment easily and efficiently. This was because the wheel brought into play the physics of angular momentum—the natural tendency of a circular object to continue rotating on its own accord, unless hindered by a countering force such as friction or braking. This made it supremely efficient for transportation on land.

This revolution also set the wheels in motion for other major innovations such as chariots, carriages, wagons and other modes of transportation. Many new machines were invented that relied on the unique characteristics of the wheel, such as pulleys and watches. Entirely new forms of projecting power arose leveraging the capabilities of the wheel, whether for military or law enforcement purposes. The ability to roll things rather than carry them around was truly transformative and far-reaching, and it touched human lives and society in countless ways.

EXPLOSIVES

The next major revolution of this magnitude, one might argue, was the invention of explosives in China in the 10th century AD. Prior to explosives, every kinetic movement required expending physical energy and force by a biological creature. That placed severe limitations on what level of force and impact was feasible and available, and in what time frame. Terrain had to be cleared by hand. Rocks had to be carved manually. Armies had to be defeated by manual force and weaponry. All of this placed significant restrictions on the order of magnitude of force that could be applied to any problem or situation, for any purpose.

Then, by concocting a mixture of saltpetre, sulphur and charcoal, Chinese inventors were able to create a reaction that released vast amounts of gas and energy in a very condensed amount of time— in other words, an explosion. This mixture, called black powder, was likely first used for signals and fireworks. Over the next three centuries, many variations of this technology were developed for use in disparate situations and for different purposes. Chinese inventors were able to put black powder in bamboo tubes and shoot out stones at others. Arab inventors came up with something similar around the same period that shot out iron arrows. Also during that era, Roger Bacon, an English scholar, first documented precise instructions for making black powder.

In the 14th century AD, a German monk named Berthold Schwarz invented a mechanism to pack black powder into iron tubes to create the predecessor to today's guns. These firearms proliferated rapidly thereafter around Europe and the world as a very efficient implement to apply and project force, primarily by military troops. Guns and other derivates like canons developed into the weapons of choice for armies around the world.

By the 17th century AD, human society had also discovered how to use black powder for peaceful purposes. The initial uses were for mining in Germany, Hungary and Czechoslovakia, followed by civil engineering applications in France.

Explosives and explosions continued to get larger and more controlled over the next few decades, enabling greater and greater applicability in different usage scenarios. The combination of explosive power coupled with effective control of it made for a very potent mix that benefitted society in many ways.

This all took a major step forward with the invention of nitroglycerine by an Italian chemist named Ascanio Sobrero in 1847. There were several risks to handling nitroglycerine however, until Alfred Nobel refined its manufacturing techniques, and invented the blasting cap, a device for detonating explosives in a significantly safer way. Nobel then went one better with his invention of dynamite, a still more powerful and controllable form of explosive that brought yet more utility to human society.

One of the most significant derivatives of controlled explosions was, of course, the internal combustion engine and its use in automobiles invented by Karl Friedrich Benz in 1885. The ability to move at great speed and over great distances without expending any physical energy was truly transformative. The impact on human society and human productivity was profound, as the significantly expanded mobility led to dramatic gains in collaboration and productivity from human efforts.

Gasoline-powered internal combustion engines were soon powering automobiles of all shapes and sizes, as well as boats and ships. And then in 1903 Wilbur and Orville Wright famously achieved the first powered flight near Kitty Hawk, North Carolina, leading to the invention of airplanes. The effect of this invention on human society was truly dramatic as flying substantially reduced the transportation time between two locations and ushered in a new era of productivity and convenience. Airplanes also enabled many other forms of peaceful as well as wartime capabilities, extending the reaches of human endeavour wherever deemed appropriate.

NUCLEAR ENERGY

The quest for more and more powerful forms of explosions, and the ensuing vast amounts of kinetic energy released from them led humankind to nuclear explosions. The wheels for this were set in motion in 1938, when Otto Hahn, Lise Meitner and Fritz Strassmann discovered nuclear fission in a nuclear physics laboratory in Berlin. They discovered that when an atom of a radioactive material split into lighter atoms, it released a vast amount of energy. From such a minuscule atomic level discovery, a fearsome new form of explosions and power was to emerge.

A few months later, Frederic Joliot, H. Von Halban and L. Kowarski discovered neutron multiplication in uranium, the key phenomenon behind a nuclear chain reaction. In a nuclear chain reaction, a single reaction produces one or more subsequent reactions, leading to the self-propagating and self-compounding nature of nuclear explosions. Each single reaction releases vast amounts of energy that in turn triggers vast amounts of nuclear reactions, compounding the overall scale of the explosion.

Concerned about the head start German scientists might have had towards building a nuclear weapon, in 1939, the US President Franklin D. Roosevelt authorized the formation of the Manhattan

Project, a unique endeavour to bring together leading physicists and weaponry experts around the country to develop a nuclear weapon. The project was spearheaded by J. Robert Oppenheimer, who was in charge of the Los Alamos Laboratory in New Mexico where much of the work was performed.

Oppenheimer and his team accomplished their mission on 16 July 1945 with the successful explosion of the first atomic bomb in a remote desert location near Alamogordo, New Mexico. And the world would never be the same again.

A mere three weeks after the first atomic explosion test, the United States dropped the first atomic bomb from a B-29 bomber called Enola Gay on the Japanese city of Hiroshima, to follow up on US President Harry Truman's surrender ultimatum to Japan. The bomb killed 80,000 people instantly, and tens of thousands more from radioactive effects over time. When the Japanese still did not surrender, the United States dropped a second atomic bomb on the city of Nagasaki, killing another 40,000 people instantly. Such was the death and destruction wrought by these two bombs that Emperor Hirohito of Japan surrendered, bringing a definitive end to the years long Second World War.

Having seen the fearsome power of atomic weapons at work and the political power they wielded, other nations raced ahead trying to build atomic bombs and stockpiling weapons in order to project power on the global stage. The United States and the erstwhile Soviet Union amassed the largest number of weapons and political power, followed by the United Kingdom, France and China, and subsequently by India, Pakistan and others. Nuclear weapons continue to be a fearsome force, with extensive negotiations, treaties and tests in the global community to strike the right balance between power, checks and balances.

While the world was busy developing and deploying nuclear explosives for military purposes, it was also busy trying to harness nuclear power for peaceful purposes. In 1951, electricity was generated for the first time by a nuclear reactor at an experimental station near Arco, Idaho. The key to a sustained, controlled nuclear reaction was to ensure that one and only one neutron was allowed to strike another uranium nucleus. If more than one neutron were to strike, it would lead to an explosion, and if less than one neutron were to strike, it would lead to the reaction dying out. The number of neutrons striking uranium nuclei could be regulated through control rods—rods made of materials such as cadmium, indium and boron which could absorb neutrons without undergoing nuclear fission themselves.

From this point on the use of nuclear energy for power-generation purposes grew in leaps and bounds. In 1954, the Soviet Union commissioned the Obninsk Nuclear Power Plant, the world's first power plant to generate electricity for a power grid. In 1955, the United States launched the USS Nautilus, the first nuclear-powered submarine in the world.

Nuclear fission subsequently led to the discovery of an even more powerful form of nuclear explosion called nuclear fusion. Unlike nuclear fission, where vast amounts of energy are released from the loss of mass when atoms are split, in nuclear fusion, vast amounts of energy are released from the loss of mass when two atoms fuse together. In 1952, Edward Teller supervised the test of the first nuclear fusion bomb on the island of Elugelab in the Pacific Ocean, demonstrating the ferocious power and fury of nuclear fusion at work. In 1961, the Soviet Union detonated the most powerful bomb in the history of mankind with the Tsar Bomba, which yielded over 50 megatons of TNT, more than 3,000 times the power of the bomb dropped on Hiroshima. The blast radius of this test explosion was so large that the entire city of Paris and its outskirts would have been razed to the ground in an instant. Nuclear fusion, which is responsible for the incredible amounts of energy produced and released by the Sun was now a force to be reckoned with here on Earth!

The energy from explosives has been channelled for countless purposes, including generating sufficient kinetic energy and force to move or destroy objects. Explosions and their controlled versions have made their way around the world, and taken many forms of human use, such as warfare, guns, demolitions and transportation. The effort and costs to perform these actions came down dramatically relative to the astronomical levels prior to the invention of explosives. And the ability for people to travel great distances in a fraction of the time brought about tremendous productivity gains to the human race. The net results, again, were revolutionary and worldwide.

THE INDUSTRIAL REVOLUTION

After explosives, the next major revolution to galvanize the world on a global scale was the Industrial Revolution, born in the thick of the agrarian, rural heartland of 18th century England. Prior to the Industrial Revolution, production and manufacturing in England and the rest of the world were done with manual tools and labour. There was little upfront investment or planning, and minimal use of manufacturing equipment and mechanized production. The bulk of the effort and time went in the creation of products one at a time by manual means. Production capacities were limited to what a human being could physically produce, one product unit at a time. There were large product variances as each product was manually created and subject to the natural variations of manual production. Industry was very fragmented as there were no real economies of scale. There was minimal standardization, and artisans laboured to produce products from their crafts as best and as fast as they could. The scale of output was very limited, nearly every product was bespoke, and a very limited number of people were able to benefit from each artisan's production.

The inefficiencies of producing goods manually led to severe limitations in manufacturing capacities required to keep pace with the needs of a growing market. This problem was particularly exacerbated for England by its colonial conquests, and the burgeoning demand in its newly colonized markets, despite the abundant supply of raw materials that came with them. One industry that felt the production shortages most acutely was the textile industry. Up until this point, textiles were primarily made in people's homes or cottages with rudimentary equipment and inconsistent management processes. The result was an inefficient and unreliable infrastructure for producing textiles at scale.

Then in 1764, James Hargreaves invented the spinning jenny, an engine that spun and produced multiple spools of threads simultaneously as a way to scale up the textile manufacturing processes. The machine produced significant efficiencies in textile manufacturing and quickly caught on around England. Other refinements followed, leading up to the invention of the power loom by Edmund Cartwright in the 1780s to mechanize cloth weaving. Productivity and output soared from the use of these larger scale automated machines that required a larger upfront investment, but then generated significant volume and cost efficiencies once manufacturing got underway.

Other industries started to go through similar transformations, ushering in their own equivalents of spinning jennies and power looms to scale up and automate production. The iron industry had earlier discovered a cheaper and easier method to produce cast iron, using coke fuelled furnaces. In the 1850s, Henry Bessemer invented an inexpensive process for mass manufacturing steel. This was a critical accomplishment as iron and steel became staples for the Industrial Revolution, and core to most of the machinery developed to automate the production of goods.

Also critical to the Industrial Revolution was the development of the steam engine by Thomas Newcomen in 1712. A cheap and scalable source of power was fundamental to the growth of industrialization, and steam engines were instrumental in powering this revolution. Besides operating manufacturing machines, steam engines also became the primary power generators used in trains and steam boats—both critical to the transportation advancements that went hand in hand with the Industrial Revolution. The ability to transport vast quantities of goods from manufacturing centres to customer centres was as core to the Industrial Revolution as the manufacturing ability itself.

Manufacturing was thus transformed from using manual tools and labour to using manufacturing machinery, factories and mass production assembly lines during the Industrial Revolution. New materials such as iron and steel were used to create machines with high production capacities. New energy sources such as petroleum and electricity were used to power these large machines along with steam engines. Factories emerged, along with new management models focused on division of labour and specialized skill sets. Special purpose machines were built for specialized tasks, requiring upfront investments, but thereafter being able to automate production at high volumes once deployed. And large-scale transportation modes were developed to move high volumes of products across great distances. There was a heightened application of science and technology to the manufacturing process. These tools and technologies lead to larger capital investments, a giant increase in productivity and output and a giant appetite for natural resources.

The Industrial Revolution brought a dramatic increase in productivity, and economic and political influence to England. It powered England's further ascension as the largest global super power that could colonize nations far and wide into a colossal British Empire, leading writer John Wilson to famously say 'His Majesty's dominions, on which the sun never sets'.

From England, the Industrial Revolution spread to Belgium and France, although not always with the full cooperation of the British who had realized and held on to its enormous competitive advantage. The draw for its efficiencies was too strong however, and gradually more and more European countries started to embrace it, most notably Germany which had the vast reserves of

natural resources necessary to become the leader of the manufacturing pack in Europe. From Europe, the Industrial Revolution
gradually spread to other parts of the world, with dramatic improve-
ments and gains seen by Japan, and more recently, by China.
The Industrial Revolution had a profound effect on manufacturing and production, and on its centrality in modern societies.
Raw materials were able to be processed much more efficiently
and fashioned at scale into finished products. Standardization
became de rigueur and massive economies of scale were created.

The Industrial Revolution clearly led to dramatic efficiencies
and scale in manufacturing. But it also led to giant creation and
re-distribution of wealth in humankind. Enterprises that were
able to take advantage of the efficiencies of the Industrial
Revolution were able to extract extraordinary returns. They were
able to outcompete other manufacturers in markets, capture huge
swaths of customers and reinforce their position by making further
investments, thereby creating dynasties of business success that
ruled much of the world for decades. The self-reinforcing nature
of competitive advantage ensured that the rich got richer, and the
strong got stronger. It became more and more difficult for new
entrants to establish a beachhead and penetrate the market as
the threshold to compete just got a whole harder. Innovation
became the privilege of the industrial behemoths for the most
part. These industrial giants could afford to move at a leisurely
pace, secure within the fortress walls of their colossal enterprises
and shut out innovative new entrants purely on the basis of their
scale and capital investments.

In the concentration of power that ensued from the Industrial
Revolution, not only was power usurped from weaker and non-
modernized competitors but also from consumers. Post-Industrial
Revolution corporate behemoths were empowered to dictate the
terms to their customers, given the paucity of choices afforded in
the market. This attitude was best embodied in Henry Ford's now
epic quote 'Any customer can have a car painted any colour that he
wants so long as it is black'.

This accumulation of power by leading merchants at the expense of consumers had profound ramifications on the state of the world. Producers were able to determine and dictate to consumers what would be made available to them and by when. They were able to train consumers on the range of features and choices that would be made available to them that they had to pick from. They were able to set value-based pricing, based on utility functions of consumers rather than the cost of producing things. Such was the power of these post-Industrial Revolution giants that they were even able to roam and colonize entire continents, acquiring consumers and capturing new markets at will, devouring natural resources, destroying indigenous cottage industries along the way just as they did in their native habitats. The more the scale of their reach, the more power these corporate behemoths accumulated, the more surplus they extracted, and the more terms they dictated to consumers around the world. Of course, the most benevolent of these corporate powers did bring in a wide array of reforms and services to help their consumers enjoy a steadily improved standard of living, but on their terms, and in furtherance of their own corporate or colonial objectives.

Not only did the post-Industrial Revolution super powers dictate the product selection and the pricing to consumers, they began to dictate the perception and positioning of their products and services as well. In June 1836 the French newspaper *La Presse* published the first paid advertisement in its pages as a way to offset publishing costs. The trend caught on very quickly as the perfect symbiosis between heavyweight merchants and manufacturers on the one hand, and premier newspapers, magazines and publishing outlets on the other. Or simply put, between advertisers and publishers.

Advertising afforded corporate behemoths a whole new platform to message to consumers and to train them on how to think about their products, their propositions, their pricing, their positioning and their brand. Such was the scale and concentration of power at major brands and major media outlets that they were able to dictate not only what consumers were able to buy, but what they were able to think about them, and how they felt before, during and after spending their money on it. One of the branding powerhouses of our times, Proctor & Gamble started its corporate journey in Cincinnati in 1837, and became the bluest of blue chips in consumer marketing. Others such as Unilever, Coke, Pepsi and Nestle followed suit in North America and Europe.

Shortly after the first advertisement was published, the culmination of the work of several inventors led to Samuel Morse inventing and patenting the telegraph in 1837. This ushered in a whole new era of telecommunication, where humans were able to communicate with one another around the globe without someone needing to physically travel the distance to deliver the message. The effects were transformative, and all of society benefitted tremendously from this. Information could now travel briskly, communication became global, and significant efficiencies were realized around the world.

This trend accelerated further in 1876 with Alexander Graham Bell's invention of the telephone. People could now speak with one another around the world in a live conversation, resulting in even greater societal benefits. The social, business and military benefits of real-time communication were enormous. There were still relatively few providers for these communication services however, so the terms of service were still dictated by these behemoth providers, and consumers had to learn to live and communicate within the confines of the formats afforded to them.

In 1879, Thomas Edison invented the light bulb by harnessing electricity. This unleashed a fresh round of innovation, effectiveness and productivity around the world. A whole new source of energy was uncovered that was cleaner and more transportable than coal and gasoline. Industrial production soared yet again, and whole new classes of consumer products and services were born. And yet, the tradition of the Industrial Revolution continued.

Electricity was generated and distributed by a small number of producers who were again able to dictate product pricing and positioning to consumers. And other corporate goliaths in other categories were able to leverage the power of electricity to further reinforce their already established advantages, further cementing their competitive standing and power over consumers.

In 1895, Guglielmo Marconi invented the radio in Italy. In 1927, at the culmination of the work of several inventors, Philo Taylor Farnsworth invented the television. Together, these two inventions revolutionized entertainment. Prior to these inventions, people were limited to live entertainment, which placed severe restrictions on how many people could watch or hear an entertainer perform at a given time and location. The effects on society of extending entertainment beyond physical proximity barriers were far-reaching. Cultures emigrated and co-mingled. People were influenced by arts and styles, and talents they had not previously been exposed to.

And yet some fundamental traits of the Industrial Revolution persisted. Radio and television became domains of a few large corporations which were able to use their positions of power and scale to further reinforce their market positions. Companies such as CBS, NBC, ABS, BBC, New York Times Company, Washington Post, Telegraph Media Group, Sony and Universal were able to extract the lion's share of economic value from artists as well as from consumers, of course. They were able to dictate what entertainment was presented to consumers, when, in what formats, at what times, and consumers were programmed to alter their listening or viewing habits, in fact their very lives around what radio and television companies decided to broadcast to them. Radio and television companies thus accumulated phenomenal power of influence and suggestion over consumers—more shades of the Industrial Revolution.

Radio and television led to the reinforcement of the Industrial Revolution in another fundamental way. They provided large corporations and businesses yet another platform to reach out to consumers, articulate their value propositions, describe their products, and communicate and convey to consumers how to think and feel about their products. In other words, advertise.

Advertisers wielded the power of the purse over media companies to great effect. They were able to dictate when and how their products or brands would be promoted and marketed. They were able to incorporate psychological research to determine when and how to target consumers at their most receptive in order to achieve their corporate profitability goals. This led to trends such as advertising toys and fast foods during children's programming, beer and men's products during sporting events, and detergent and beauty products during daytime shows—ironically called soap operas for the tight integration between media and advertising.

Together, advertisers and media companies collaborated to produce a remarkable training of consumers. People were trained to eat pizza and chips during sporting events. They were trained to eat cupcakes and bonbons during daytime soap operas. They were trained to acquiesce with whatever was on offer on radio or television, because someone else was calling the shots. They were trained to watch or listen to entertainment in producer-defined chunks of time, rather than time slots convenient to them. They were even trained to compartmentalize their time for basic bodily functions around commercial breaks!

This led to a few advertisers and media companies accumulating massive power over consumers. Consumers became the targets of their strategies rather than the audiences they served. Consumers were at the receiving end of what was on offer, with no say in it. And there wasn't even a way for consumers to easily congregate with each other to develop a voice, except in forums mediated by the same media and advertising companies, further accentuating the power asymmetry that existed.

The Industrial Revolution and its derivatives thus accomplished dramatic productivity gains in human society, but also produced a massive concentration of power and wealth, and influence among the largest and most entrenched corporate powers. It dramatically altered the power balance between producers and consumers, and dramatically expanded wealth inequities around the world. The effect on society was thus transformative, and deem the Industrial Revolution worthy of being considered a true global revolution.

COMPUTERS AND THE INTERNET

The next major revolution of this scale to arrive on the global scene was the computer revolution, capped by the advent of the Internet in the 20th century. Before the arrival of the personal computer, countless complex and repetitive tasks had to all be done by human beings, leading to severe waste of human resources. Trillions of hours were spent writing and re-writing letters, articles and papers. Trillions of hours were spent computing numbers, and inputting and outputting them in various formats. Every piece of paperwork—reports, news articles, financial summaries, taxes, letters, homework—had to be done by manual means and required an expert at hand to get it done. Every student had to learn math, spelling and grammar, and multiple languages to compete on the global stage, rather than learn about intrinsic thought processes and creativity, and production and expression that were much more integral to their growth and value proposition to the world.

That all began to change with the invention of the computer. The seeds to this were sown by an English mathematics professor named Charles Babbage who designed the first analytical engine in the 19th century. In 1937 John Atanasoff and Clifford Berry invented the first electronic digital computer. This was followed by the ENIAC, the first general-purpose computer in 1946, known to have dimmed the lights in parts of Philadelphia with its extreme levels of power consumption!

In 1951, the first transistor-based computer was created, called the UNIVAC. In 1953, IBM introduced the first general-purpose computers for commercial use. The advent of integrated circuits ushered in an era of compounding computing power at progressively miniaturizing form factors, leading to the invention of the personal computer by IBM, Microsoft and Intel in 1981. Three years later, Apple introduced its Macintosh computer featuring graphical icons for the first time.

Computers changed the rules of the game in far more substantial ways than anyone could have originally envisioned. Information could now be stored and retrieved in far more efficient ways, obviating the need for people to memorize vast amounts of information and recount them as one of their competitive advantages. Simple but repetitive problems could be solved far faster and with more accuracy than what humans were capable of. Many more productivity tools could be created that made human lives better and easier in most walks of life. Writing letters and papers became a breeze because you could edit so efficiently. Spell checkers did away with the need to be a spelling champion just to get your point across. Spreadsheets made painful repetitive arithmetic processes a thing of the past. Drawing and painting tools made it far easier to draw pictures and edit them at will, rather than starting over each time.

As computer algorithms got better, more and more complex problems became solvable with computers. Patients could be diagnosed, weather could be forecast and financial models could be projected far easier and better than before. The developments in artificial intelligence and machine learning have now provided a further shot in the arm to what computers are capable of. Not only are they able to solve many complex problems better than humans, they are beginning to approximate human cognizance and responsiveness in less quantifiable domains like emotions too. Harnessed correctly, they are beginning to provide a tremendous boost to human productivity.

With the advent of the personal computer, the power of computing was suddenly available to the mass consumer, rather than being the competitive advantage solely of the privileged few. Everyone was able to benefit from the storage and computation power and tools afforded by the computer, and creativity and productivity sky-rocketed. The computer democratized knowledge and productivity around the world.

Computers had many unique qualities and characteristics but benefitted in particular from two unique traits that made them explosive in use and adoption relative to other major inventions. The first was the intrinsic nature of the semi-conductor itself, the foundational material used in most digital devices today. Thanks to Gordon Moore at Intel, the technology community came to understand and harness the fundamental power of semiconductors and integrated circuits. Moore's Law stated that with the state of technology available, the number of transistors in an integrated circuit was doubling every two years. This meant a doubling of computing power at the same or even declining costs every two years. This level of compounding productivity gain was simply unheard of for mankind. No other technology or invention before this had such a trajectory of relentless performance gains ever before. This enabled greater and greater functionality enhancements at lower and lower costs and response times. The impact on human productivity was nothing short of mind-boggling.

The second fundamental characteristic of computers that led to dramatic growth and adoption was the modular, building-block nature of software, mastered by the software powerhouses of the world such as Microsoft, Oracle and IBM. For the first time in its history, technologists were able to lay one computational brick on top of other computation bricks, compounding productivity gains by building incremental modules on top of earlier ones. No other invention before this had the ability to accelerate product development capabilities on the backs of earlier ones—literally. This meant a ferocious pace of new product developments and creations that could usher in dramatic advances at lightning speed. Software companies were able to unleash whole new applications and tools at faster and faster rates, advancing human productivity at unprecedented rates.

Together, these two characteristics of computing led to an explosion in creativity and output unlike any other seen before. The rate of innovation in the world began to accelerate, with ever more advancements in every field happening at an increasingly rapid rate, with no end or cap in sight.

As if the computer wasn't transformative enough by itself, in 1983 ARPANET transformed to become today's Internet, and in 1989 Tim Berners-Lee invented the World Wide Web (WWW). The world would never be the same again.

The seeds of the modern-day Internet were sowed all the way back in 1962 by J. C. R. Licklider at the Massachusetts Institute of Technology (MIT). Licklider came up with a series of memos describing his 'Galactic Network' concept that got the scientific community going on the idea of a global network of computers. He then became the first head of the computer research programme at the US Defense Advanced Research Projects Agency, or DARPA, and further espoused his vision. His colleagues at DARPA and a researcher from MIT named Lawrence Roberts put together plans for the ARPANET. This led to a phase of increasing collaboration between DARPA, other research institutes in Europe and the United States, and universities such as MIT, Stanford, UC Los Angeles and UC Santa Barbara to refine the building blocks, networking implementations and protocols for computer-to-computer communication. These efforts culminated in ARPANET switching its core communication protocol to TCP/IP on 1 January 1983, giving birth to the Internet.

This fledgling network received a major shot in the arm in 1989, courtesy of Tim Berners-Lee. Berners-Lee was a software engineer at CERN, the premier particle physics laboratory near Geneva. He noticed that scientists were having a difficult time sharing information across networks and computers, often requiring laborious integration or translation processes to transfer information. He thought it would be ideal to have one common language, addressing system and protocol for all his lab computers. By 1990, he wrote specifications for the Hypertext Markup Language, the Uniform Resource Locator and the Hypertext Transfer Protocol, which became the anchors of the modern-day WWW. Berners-Lee also wrote the first web browser and the first web server using his specifications, and the modern-day web was born.

The web enabled anyone on the network to publish information using Berners-Lee's specifications, and anyone on the network to view it with browsers based on the same specifications. This spurred an incredible explosion of creativity and productivity unlike anything the world had seen before. The developments since then have been nothing short of breathtaking. The Internet is transforming our lives in very fundamental ways.

At its core, the Internet is a network. It is about connecting people, companies and processes around the world. This simple connectivity is a source of tremendous power for everyone on the network. For the first time in human history, anyone in the world can connect with anyone else, collaborate with anyone, find any information and buy anything within seconds. For the first time in human history, there is a central nervous system for all of humanity and it is in the cloud. The cloud stores all knowledge for and about all humans on the planet. The cloud draws its power from all the computers on the network and gets more and more powerful and competent every day. The cloud can analyse vast reams of data about people on the network, draw conclusions and assist individuals on the network in brilliant new ways. Layer on to this the advances that are now being made in machine learning by analysing and deriving knowledge and even wisdom out of the information contained in the cloud, and you have a very potent force that can be channelled for incredible societal benefits.

The Internet has become a significant force for democratizing information. There are remarkable levels of information available on the Internet. The cost to producing and publishing information has become minuscule. This is leading to an explosive growth in information available for instant access to all. The content universe is expanding exponentially every moment.

This ability to access any information anywhere in an instant has brought about a transformative change in the world. In the farthest reaches of society, a user can hop on the Internet and access any piece of information in a flash. Prior to the Internet, acquiring information required substantial time and resources. People had to go to libraries or universities or well-informed friends or family members to acquire knowledge and information. The world was divided into information haves and have-nots. Those with information wielded significant power over those who did not. That information gap has now been all but eradicated, and the world is becoming a level playing field for all when it comes to the realm of information.

The Internet has also opened up unprecedented avenues for people to connect with each other. Prior to the Internet, there were significant costs and overheads for consumers to find, connect and communicate with each other. This included actual physical communication costs—be it via postal mail or telegraph or telephone. But there were even more substantial searching and contacting costs—finding old friends or distant family members, and simply getting in touch with them when many did not have the telecommunication resources or equipment necessary to connect.

The ability to connect and communicate afforded by the Internet has seen incredible advancements in the state of human society worldwide. People can communicate with whoever they choose in new mediums, formats and delivery methods, unencumbered by the limitations imposed on them by earlier communication mechanisms. Networks can form at rapid speed. News can travel people-to-people, no longer limited by what media companies choose to convey using their limited channels. Causes can be conceived and brought alive faster than previously imaginable.

People can discover long-lost friends and family with the greatest of ease. They can keep in touch and share their daily lives with each other minute-by-minute like never before.

A corollary of instant, universal connectivity is its far-reaching impact on interpersonal relationships. The history of social structures since the dawn of human civilization is rich and varied, with many implications for personal human relationships. These relationships have well-defined patterns from the past and underlying reasons why these patterns exist. In particular, social patterns and relationships have almost always been defined in the context of physical proximity, and of authority and power dynamics prevalent in societies at different times in human history.

These long-standing relationship models are evolving significantly in today's digital world. In particular, Millennials and Gen Zers are redefining personal relationships and social structures in unforeseen ways, with implications for traditional authority-based relationships. This has the potential to fundamentally reshape human relationships in a fashion dramatically different from past patterns.

The combination of universal information access coupled with deep connectivity has given humans the unique ability to congregate or band together with others, giving rise to a fundamental new dynamic in the political process and in government itself. Consumers are no longer dependent on carefully packaged political messages and broadcast mediums to consume them through. They are able to get their own information, make their own assessments and connect with other consumers who share their beliefs. They can still be influenced by packaging and positioning of course, but that influence is now tempered by independent corroboration and triangulation. Consumers can now hold the political system and political representatives accountable to a much greater degree. They can initiate an agenda to a much greater degree, rather than merely be subject to what is dished out to them. The value of true performance and actual track record among politicians is rising in the political arena, and the value of positioning and posturing is plummeting—trends unimaginable a mere 50 years ago.

The Internet has also unlocked tremendous consumer potential when it comes to the world of entertainment. Prior to the Internet, all entertainment was controlled by a few publishers and broadcasters. Consumers had very limited choice and were essentially subject to the programme selections of broadcasters and publishers when choosing entertainment. The amount and range of programming was carefully selected by broadcasters to meet their business objectives. Not only were consumers constrained by the parameters put in place by broadcasters, but artists and actors were also constrained by the exact same entities. The flow of entertainment was severely controlled and managed by large profit-making enterprises.

Since its arrival, the Internet has heralded in substantially heightened levels of consumer choice and control in the world of entertainment. Consumers can now select from a dizzying array of entertainment choices. They can consume entertainment when they want it, where they want it, how they want it, with whom they want it, at will. They can also turn producer, and publish and distribute their own entertainment out to a worldwide audience at will. The lines between consumers and producers of entertainment are increasingly blurring.

And of course, the Internet has also unlocked massive potential for consumers when it comes to transacting with merchants. The entire model for shopping and purchasing is now changing. Consumers now have incredible choice and convenience to shop for products and services over the Internet. They have independent sources of information they can rely on for making purchase decisions. They are able to cross-check claims made by merchants in a flash. They can read product reviews by other consumers to vet out quality products. They can compare products and prices across competing merchants with ease. They can find matching complementary products and other related products easily and efficiently. They can return products they don't like with ease, and they can reward or punish merchants with reviews based on their satisfaction or dissatisfaction.

The Internet has also given consumers entirely new levels of control over advertising. In the perpetual tug of war between advertisers and consumers for control of screen real estate, the consumer is now starting to win. Whereas consumers earlier had no control over what was advertised and where, now they are able to turn on ad blockers to block out ads completely. Or they are able to shut down a video ad or pop-up ad as soon as it comes up, getting faster and faster at the draw. As the battle royale rages between consumers and advertisers, centuries of training are starting to come undone as consumers are starting to demonstrate who is really in charge in the digital era.

In its gestalt, the computer and Internet revolution have transformed the lives of people in breathtaking ways. It is a fitting successor to the long and storied history of the revolutions our human race have achieved to date.

WHAT'S NEXT?

Are we done with major revolutions for a while?

The answer, as it turns out, is no! The technological, political, social and economic advances of the last century have sown the seeds of what might well be the biggest revolution of them all. We can see early indications of a gigantic revolution brewing and barrelling down our way. One that has the potential to remake the fabric of human society and restructure the commercial and political landscape beyond recognition.

Look at the major news headlines and trends of today. Technology is becoming pervasive, and human connectivity is like never before in history. What impact is that going to have on human society? Facebook, Twitter, Instagram, WhatsApp and Snapchat have become household names. Siri, Alexa and Cortana have registered on our social psyche. Hashtags like #MeToo, #BlackLivesMatter and #NeverAgain have become stunningly powerful. So much so that they have toppled legendary stars and power brokers such as Harvey Weinstein, Bill Cosby, Charlie Rose and Matt Lauer. Arab Spring happened, ousting governments in a way that was unimaginable only a decade ago.

As if staying abreast of all the real news wasn't daunting enough, fake news happened. Cyber espionage and cyber terrorism happened. Allegations of foreign government intervention in the US presidential elections are still going on. Facebook's data scandal happened, leading to serious concerns about data privacy and the European Union's General Data Protection Regulation. In the midst of this all, Bitcoin and blockchain technology showed up, looking for trust and security in the same environment where others lost it.

We are seeing plummeting fortunes at famed newspapers and magazines. And actual declines in television viewership after decades of growth, including for high profile programmes such as American football and the Oscars, previously thought to be impervious to audience ebbs and flows. Netflix, Hulu, Amazon Prime, Spotify, video games and sport betting are in their ascendancy, replacing the declines in traditional media. Ad blocking usage is soaring even as the advertising industry goes through turmoil.

The retail apocalypse is upon us. Stores are closing in record numbers, especially in the United States. Famed retailers are going out of business at astonishing rates, customer loyalties are on the decline, and it's getting tougher and tougher to win their business. At the same time, shipping and delivery services are thriving more than ever before, and entire new generations of delivery innovations such as delivery drones are starting to make appearances.

Some of the most legendary companies in the world are starting to buckle and quake or entirely capitulate. Organizations are working harder than ever to court their customers, to engage with them and to seek their approvals in myriad ways. Yet in the thick of it all, behemoths such as Amazon, Apple, Facebook, Google and Microsoft are more valuable and more powerful than ever, reaching market values of a trillion dollars and above for the first time in human history.

We are in a time of unprecedented velocity and change. These are monumental changes in the makeup of human society. How do you make sense of these turbulent times? How do you fathom their underlying reasons? What do these seemingly isolated events have to do with each other?

Everything, as it turns out.

There is a common theme behind these seemingly disparate sweeping changes. There is a common thread, a common backdrop, a common narrative. There is a Category 5 hurricane brewing. The outer bands are just about starting to show up, and current events are just the tip of the iceberg.

This revolution at full tilt will be something spectacular to behold. Even more tantalizingly, this revolution will include us all in its throes—not merely as spectators and observers, but as full-fledged principals and participants. We, the people, are the engine and the raw energy that are fuelling this revolution. It is feeding on itself, it is drawing its power from empowering each and every one of us to fling ourselves into it, and it has the potential to unleash more energy and motion than anything seen before. The perfect storm for the human race is here!

2

TECTONIC POWER SHIFT

There are 7.7 billion people in the world today. 7.7 billion unique lives, unique perspectives, unique worlds of our own and unique value propositions within them. Despite the significant variations amongst us—in location, background, circumstances, age, gender, ethnic background, education levels, income levels and even IQ, each of the 7.7 billion of us has something of unique value to offer to someone else in our own worlds.

However, for most of us humans, this unique value has been limited in scope and impact only to our own little worlds. To our own micro-local or familial or social environments, rather than to anything remotely approaching national or global scope. This is because for the vast majority of us, there has been no forum or platform to connect, convey and project our perspectives to others at scale. No wonder we have been called the silent majority. It is not that the majority is silent. But rather for the overwhelming majority of us humans, our voices simply cannot be heard through the layers of societal barriers and natural friction muffling our sounds.

THE STARS!

There are only a select few leaders of our societies who are able to break through the clutter and establish a voice on the global stage. And as a result, the select few garner the attention of the silent majority when it comes to the nationwide and worldwide stages. We have and continue to concentrate vast amounts of our public attention on our leaders and champions who sit at the top of the proverbial totem pole. On kings and queens, presidents and prime ministers, corporate chief executive officers, movie stars, rock stars and sports stars. For good reason, one might argue. After all they represent the most successful, the most talented, the most powerful, the best-connected and the most influential representatives of our tribe.

However, the fact remains that the overwhelming majority of our public attention is showered on a minuscule minority of humans. We are exceedingly over-indexed on our stars. In the process, we are inadvertent enablers of the vast amounts of power, wealth, influence, impact and superior quality of life our stars have accumulated. We are enablers of the very inequities we protest against.

Why is this so? How did this come about? Is this a chance occurrence or is there something systemic about human society that creates this effect?

As it turns out, in the historical set-up of human society, this outcome was always an inevitability. There was too much societal friction, and there were too many chasms in information and connection for most of us to amplify our voices and impact things at a global level. So the vast majority of us made our peace with influencing and participating in our immediate communities and surroundings, and letting our stars rule the roost on the global stage.

As humans, we all operate at a macro level and at a micro level. The macro level encompasses large-scale national or global events, personalities and phenomena. The micro level entails our immediate family, friends, work colleagues and service providers, and events that pertain to them.

At the macro level everything is all about the champions and the leaders of our societies. It is they who break through the noise clutter and rise above the masses to the levels of prominence that make the rest of us take note. There is an incredibly arduous process that these leaders have to go through to rise to pre-eminence. This might entail years of toil, strategy and persistence, not to mention the innate talent needed to rise to the top. The friction to get through this journey is severe, and only the most competent, and perhaps the luckiest, make it through. The barriers to ascension are extremely high. They weed out all but the most exceptional amongst us.

However, we all also operate at a micro level. In fact, it is this micro level that consumes most of our lives. In our everyday lives, we are mothers and fathers, brothers and sisters, spouses and children, friends and members of our local communities. We are doctors, engineers, lawyers, accountants, construction workers, farm hands and endless other varieties of professionals that provide a valuable service in society. We live, we love, we battle, we grieve, we rejoice, we savour and we celebrate, every day.

We might not be world leaders like Franklin Roosevelt or Winston Churchill or Mahatma Gandhi, but in our micro lives we take those in our charge and lead them through mazes and blazes every day. We might not score goals like Cristiano Ronaldo or centuries like Virat Kohli or baskets like Stephen Curry, but in our micro lives we are champions to those around us every day. We might not be business tycoons like Bill Gates or Jack Ma or Mukesh Ambani, but in our micro lives we provide for our loved ones every day. We might not dazzle the silver screen like Leonardo DiCaprio or Jennifer Lawrence or Shah Rukh Khan, but in our micro lives we shine like stars that get brighter every day.

At the micro level, there are triumphs and disasters, there are heroes and villains, there are smiles and tears for 7.7 billion people—every day. Mount Everest is scaled, and the Marina Trench is dived into—every day. Life is lived at the micro level—every day. We witness countless things, we learn countless things and we create countless things in the course of our daily lives. Those in our immediate circles bear witness to those, can participate in those, share those and benefit from those. The rest of humanity doesn't. It can't, because it has minimal visibility to individual acts of accomplishment in our micro lives.

The macro level of existence and consciousness which occupies so much of the public mind share actually takes up a tiny portion of our individual mind shares. We might make the time to follow a world event, or listen to a classical masterpiece, or watch a movie, or attend a sporting event, but then we go back to our daily lives. The vast amount of our time and attention is spent on our own micro lives.

And yet, the social, political and economic order of the world is dictated by macro events and characters. The collective attention of the world is overwhelmingly directed at these phenomena and personalities. A tiny fraction of our human race is massively over-represented, and the vast majority is massively under-represented at the global level. A tiny fraction of humanity wields massive power over the vast majority that is subject to it. A tiny fraction of humanity possesses vast amounts of the wealth and resources of our world, while a vast majority simply supports them while getting by with much less.

FRAUGHT WITH FRICTION

For the rest of us, there has always been tremendous friction in-built in our day-to-day lives. Friction in access to information, friction in connecting with other like-minded individuals, friction in impacting policy or governance, friction in finding entertainment or leisure activities, friction in finding the best shopping or business transaction to be had.

Take information. All through human history, information and knowledge beyond the very basic levels have been the domain of the privileged few. You had to have gone to the right schools and colleges, or to the right teachers and gurus, or to be born in the right families to have access to higher knowledge. The rest of humanity was plain out of luck. The friction to get information on your own accord was exorbitant. It required access to learned experts to educate you about a topic. Or access to a library with the information you sought, if one even existed close to you. Learning was further challenged by the various languages of the world, and the need to find information that you could actually comprehend and assimilate. These natural barriers limited access to information to what was locally available, within someone's physical proximity and with associated time delays.

A similar dynamic existed when it came to connecting with other individuals. Since the dawn of human society, there has been tremendous friction in finding and connecting with other like-minded people. The day-to-day lives of most people have been filled with interactions in their micro circles—immediate family, close friends, daily job colleagues and members of their immediate communities. You learnt to find common ground with those in your immediate surroundings, and make peace with the compromises you needed to make. There were only a few dozen connections to work with, so you learnt to make do with them the best you could. There was simply no possibility of finding, connecting and interacting with people outside your immediate physical and social circles.

Friction in access to information and access to broad connectivity meant that there was significant friction in finding a voice in government and policy making. It took extraordinary effort to impact government policies, where that was possible at all, and a tiny percent of human society even attempted to do so. For the vast majority of citizens and subjects, government was the domain of a select few individuals. The rest of us could only acquiesce and grumble about its ineffectiveness at best, if dissatisfied.

For much of human history it has simply not been possible to have access to universal information or universal connectivity with everyone else. Absent the ability to get informed or connect broadly, human beings have, in essence, been confined to local silos or homesteads, making it nearly impossible for most to break through the natural information, communication and growth barriers that exist in society. In this environment, it is very challenging to become a national or global success, and the odds are extremely stacked against most individuals. There are only a few television channels, radio stations, magazines and newspapers in the world, and they can only talk about so many things. There are only a few countries with a few leaders, only a few companies with a few executives, only a few teams with a few super stars. Human societies have had very limited shelf-space at the top in their entire histories. The path to the top is exceedingly narrow for the teeming masses of humanity. Our champions and leaders have to thread the needle on their ascent to break through to worldwide attention and prominence. And for the rest of us, this is near impossible to do.

The fascinating question is what would happen to the world and human civilization if this were not the case. What would happen if the frictions to accessing information, to connecting, to congregating, to transacting were dramatically reduced? What would happen if there was unlimited shelf-space at the top of the various pyramids in human societies? What would happen if anyone and everyone of us could get there at any time?

This picture has an incredible parallel to one of the ground-breaking revolutions from our past—nuclear explosions. The foundation of the most fearsome nuclear force that we have ever witnessed—nuclear fusion—is the characteristic of a vast amount of energy being released when two atoms are fused together.

Now consider the effect of you connecting and interacting with your favourite friend or family member. That interaction and coming together releases a great deal of emotional, mental and physiological energy for both of you. You both leave the interaction enriched, emboldened and energized.

Now consider a third equally close friend or family member joining your interaction, and coming together with you. That creates a non-linear increase in the energy released from the critical mass of interaction between three close humans. Add a fourth, and a fifth close friend or family member to the party, and the interactions and energy released ratchets up exponentially.

Extend this dynamic to groups, such as a team, an organization and a platoon, and the impact of collective interaction and energy released multiplies even more exponentially. The greater the number of people congregating for any shared cause or purpose or emotion, the exponentially greater the collective energy released looking for an outlet.

To put this in nuclear terms, each of the 7.7 billion individuals on the earth is like an atom. Each one of us has an enormous amount of latent energy and the potential to move mountains. Each of us has the incendiary ability to light a flame in someone else—to inspire, to motivate, to trigger someone else's energy. This ability to catalyse energy and action in others is transitive, multiplicative and hence compounding in nature. We see evidence of this in group dynamics and crowd mentality. We see mob psychology at work in many instances, where a mob takes an energy of its own, and can rattle all it its path to their core.

In the systemic makeup of human society through history, all the natural barriers to communication, connection and congregation at scale have served as metaphoric cadmium control rods. These rods have been dampening our atomic energy, keeping wraps on the nuclear levels of energy release from our interactions and keeping at bay the possibility of setting off nuclear chain reactions. These control rods have been put in place sometimes by design by the controlling authorities, and sometimes by purely natural evolution, but their net effect has been to keep nuclear reactions of human energy from erupting.

For the vast majority of us humans, there has been no medium to inform, communicate, connect, amplify, resonate and scale voices on a global scale. There has been no way to be seen or be heard, outside of our own immediate circles of friends and family. The scale of compounding of human energy has been very limited thus far—a group of 5 people only has 25 circuits of interaction and energy generation, where as a group of 100 has 10,000 such circuits of energy generation, an exponential increase. The inability of most humans to band together at scale has thus fundamentally limited their collective energies and force. Since the beginning of time, mass consumers have not had a real voice at the global stages of human society.

Until now.

This Changes Everything!

For the first time in human history, we now have the critical mass of tools and techniques, and infrastructure necessary for mass consumers to do just that. We now have the tools to look up any information on anything we want in an instant. We have the tools to look up any friend or family member or contact and communicate with them in a second. We have the tools to look up new like-minded individuals we never knew about and strike new friendships. We have the tools to voice our opinion, shed light on an issue, provide a tip or a suggestion, enjoy the entertainment we like and shop the market for the best buys. The confluence of the personal computer, the mobile phone, the cloud, the Internet, the web and social media has created a perfect storm for consumers. This is tantamount to extracting the cadmium control rods from the cauldron of nuclear atoms. This is, in effect, a rapid melting away of the friction that has been holding back mass levels of human energy flow since the dawn of civilization.

How significant a development is this? Cataclysmic. This changes everything. This unleashes the bridled energy of 7.7 billion humans into the world. This empowers people everywhere like never before to connect, to inform, to share, to band together, to cross-check, to enjoy and to transact. And to trigger and enable others to unleash their innate energies as well. There are sparks starting to go off in every corner of the world. There are fires being lit around the globe.

And these are not just individual sparks. They are connecting with each other, feeding off each other and compounding at a startling pace and scale. They are sharing, setting each other off, banding about, surging and catalyzing movements in incredibly powerful ways. They are coming together and setting off chain reactions similar to hydrogen atoms coming together to set off a nuclear fusion explosion.

This powerfully-informed connectivity is the spark plug that is setting off cataclysmic fusion reactions, releasing vast amounts of energy into the world. This energy is then itself triggering other reactions, releasing yet more explosive social energy, creating a feeding frenzy of unmatched proportions.

The world has never before seen this scale of human energy being set free, and this scale of human compounding brought to life. The same building-block dynamic that applies to software is now taking hold with all human resources and endeavours. This is creating powerful network effects, where the network is getting exponentially powerful by drawing from all its constituents inter-linked through it. People are able to reuse and build on what others have done in every walk of life, creating a ferocious compounding effect on human development.

We are at nothing short of a singularity in human development—the shape of the world to come will be dramatically different from the world of the past. We are in the early stages of the greatest generation of power and creativity that our planet has ever seen. The collective horsepower, intellect, drive and ingenuity of our entire race brought together in one giant nuclear reaction is nothing short of astounding. The consumer network is now forming before our very eyes, and its network effects are poised to reshape the entire status quo of the world.

This nuclear reaction of micro human energies setting off chain reactions is shaping up to be so massive that it will dwarf the sum total of what today's macro leaders are able to produce. Merchants, manufacturers, publishers, advertisers, stars, educators, even government officials are going to feel their world change in more and more fundamental ways as the consumer network gets humming. We are in the early stages of witnessing the greatest transfer of power known to humanity—the transfer of power from leaders and stars and producers to a network of everyday consumers. A power shift that can upend the very pillars of society and commerce, re-write the rules of human engagement, and create entirely new power structures and power engines in the world.

WELCOME TO THE CONSUMER REVOLUTION!

The consumer revolution is setting in motion a tectonic shift, with you at the centre of it. Long-established axes of power are beginning to dissolve. Centuries of societal rules are starting to show cracks. Deep-rooted hegemonies established by the Industrial Revolution are starting to crumble. There is a new sheriff in town, starting to call the shots, starting to take names and starting to hold erstwhile power brokers accountable. The consumer revolution is here, and it is going to make everyone stop and take notice.

Like any true large-scale metamorphosis, the consumer revolution will not wash over the world overnight. Even the mightiest of cosmic phenomena take time to play out relative to our human clocks. Consumers don't yet realize the full scope of the power that has gotten bestowed upon them. But they are beginning to get inklings. Wheels are spinning, minds are churning and a fearsome force is starting to gather around the world.

For centuries, true power has been controlled and wielded by the select few to govern and dictate to the many. This dates all the way back to Neanderthals and Homo sapiens in the prehistoric era. The powerful few set the rules that the masses lived by. Adhering to the rules brought success and prosperity. Violating them brought death, destruction or discipline. This structure was essential to the effective functioning of society. More structured societies were able to overtake and subjugate less structured ones.

As clans and nomadic gatherings developed into kingdoms and more formalized societal structures, this rule by the powerful few was further reinforced. As communities and kingdoms grew in size, this concentration of power got even more accentuated as one leader could hold sway over a larger and larger populace. As a general rule, an individual or small group of individuals was able to govern an entire population with the aid of a mere 1–5 per cent of the populace in the military or law enforcement. Those in power were able to dictate how the masses lived and behaved. They were able to lay down the law and enforce it to ensure compliance. This all added up to a traditional pyramid hierarchy in most governing bodies. With time, most pyramids got steeper and steeper, concentrating ever more power and wealth in the hands of ever fewer individuals.

This trend continued and even accelerated with the onset of the Industrial Revolution. Large, established companies and corporations were able to wield extraordinary power over smaller, weaker ones, and of course, consumers. These companies became so big that they began to extend past political borders. The bases of their power pyramids began to expand across national boundaries, and they became multi-national power structures. Companies did not have to be saddled with all of the governance responsibilities, of course. They did not have to expend energies and resources providing military, law enforcement, tax collection, public health or general education services. They could pick and choose the products and services they made available to their constituencies that reinforced their power and profits.

Large companies and corporations did not even have to deal with the customary feedback loops, checks and balances that existed with political governing bodies. They were not accountable to consumers for anything and given free rein to meet their own profit objectives. In fact, they were able to systematically squash consumer choice, if necessary, to further their own business goals, and consumers had no choice but to go along. In many ways, large corporate leaders have historically wielded extraordinary power over the lives of consumers that far surpasses what monarchies and government systems ever did. In the process, phenomenal wealth has been created, primarily for owners and leaders of these giant corporations, ironically enough funded by consumers. This has produced inequities that are hard to calibrate and justify. For instance, it is hard to argue that one member of the human race should be worth a million times another member of the same race. Said another way, the life of one individual is worth that of a million others.

Now consumers did benefit from these large producers, of course, both as customers and sometimes as shareholders. But the value equilibrium became entirely off scale. Producers amassed untold wealth and power on the backs of the consumers patronizing and supporting them. And yet consumers held minimal sway over corporate decision-making in their capacities as minority shareholders; the lion's share of global power sat with management and governance bodies of large corporations. This propagated and accentuated the status quo of a massive concentration of power and wealth among corporate leaders.

All of this is now about to change.

Armed with the tools now available to them, consumers are just beginning to get a heady taste of their empowerment. They are beginning to see evidences of what authority they are capable of. They are beginning to scratch the surface of their own empowerment. They are setting wheels in motion that will forever change the fabric of our society.

Consumers are now starting to arm themselves with unprecedented information. They are not beholden to monarchs, pundits, professors or pitchmen for information. And they are certainly not beholden to brands for information about their products and services. The value of a brand describing the merits of its newest car diminishes dramatically when consumers can research objective reviews and feedbacks for themselves. The impact of a hotel portraying the wonders of its newest property in an exotic location gets minimized when consumers can see pictures and videos from impartial sources for themselves. And the objectivity of a news outlet takes a tumble when consumers can so easily corroborate and triangulate news from multiple sources themselves.

As the volume of information on the Internet grows exponentially, the power and influence of an individual content source diminishes rapidly. Tools such as Google, Bing, Baidu and Yandex become increasingly and exponentially important as they make it possible for consumers to find any information they want in an instant. A dramatic power shift is underway from producers to consumers in the realm of information, and the writing is well writ on the wall for producers of information.

Consumers are also now armed with unprecedented connectivity. They are no longer at the whims of a few power players to determine when, how and who they can communicate with. The value of proprietary telecommunication infrastructures is plummeting when consumers have so many platforms and forums to connect with and communicate with each other. Charges and fees for phone services, cable services and satellite services are starting to go down as more and more efficient forms of communication emerge, and consumers begin to forge new paths for connectivity with near and dear ones. Tools such as email, SMS, Facebook, LinkedIn, Instagram, WhatsApp, Twitter, WeChat and Snapchat are giving consumers ever-increasing choices for connecting and communicating with whoever they choose in whichever formats they desire. Consumers are beginning to dictate how they want to connect and communicate, and providers are scrambling to respond. The power shift from providers of communication services to consumers is now starting to gather steam.

Anchored by this universal access to information and connectivity, consumers are also now armed with unprecedented political power. Political candidates no longer have exclusive stewardship of their messaging and positioning. There is wide-scale access to their track records that consumers can review, discuss and formulate opinions on. The value of campaigning is declining, and the value of actual delivery and execution is rising. Independent, unbiased sources of analysis and assessment are emerging, and the feasibility of bouncing off perceptions and opinions amongst family and friends and just like-minded fellow citizens is increasing exponentially. Never before has this much political interpretation been available to consumers unmediated by the vested parties themselves, and this is ushering in a sea change in the political and social process.

Not only are consumers starting to hold political candidates and systems more accountable, they are also now armed with expansive powers over setting the political and social agenda. In other words, lead rather than follow. In region after region, from Europe to Asia to the Middle East, consumers are banding together for protests or political positions in ways unthinkable until recent times. In the United States, movements such as #MeToo are becoming a tour de force that are completely restructuring power structures well before any politician or power broker even realizes what is afoot. The governed are beginning to take charge of governance.

Another dimension that consumers are now armed in is unprecedented choice and control over entertainment. Consumers are beginning to migrate to the entertainment of their choice, when they want it, where they want it and how they want it. The value of a television network establishing a prime time viewing line up is all but lost when consumers can pick and choose shows and watch them piecemeal whenever they want. The value of a premier magazine composing an issue is lost when consumers can pick and choose the articles or video they like at will. And the value of a top 40 countdown is severely diminished when consumers can make up their own minds, create their own playlists, and listen to it at will. Tools such as Netflix, YouTube, iTunes, Hulu, Spotify, Xfinity and Amazon Prime are giving consumers unimaginable control over their entertainment viewing and listening habits. To add to that, consumers are now beginning to become producers of entertainment as well—the lines between the two are beginning to blur. This is all adding up to a massive power shift underway from producers to consumers in the realm of entertainment.

Finally, consumers are now armed with the power to transact like never before. Physical store fronts are beginning to be less and less relevant as consumers rush to the conveniences and efficiencies of online shopping. Store hours are becoming a relic of the past. In-store inventory and selection? Passé. Price umbrellas and protection? Vanishing, with nowhere to hide.

Consumers are starting to shop for choices in the market more and more effectively. They are shifting their shopping behaviour from offline to online in droves. They are hopping from store to store in seconds. They are criss-crossing the Internet using shortcuts to find deals and bargains. They are rewarding merchants who serve them with real value, and punishing those that don't, or even worse try to put lipstick on the pig. Consumers are starting to hold producers accountable for delivering true value.

An interesting offshoot of this power restructuring is the state of advertising in the world. For centuries, advertising was controlled by advertisers and publishers, at the expense of consumers. For centuries, no one definitively knew if advertising worked or didn't, best embodied in John Wanamaker's epic quote 'Half the money I spend on advertising is wasted; the trouble is I don't know which half'. Underlying this sentiment was the fundamental flaw that for centuries, the real impact of advertising was difficult to measure. The true economic value of that first advertisement published in *La Presse*, or a television commercial, or billboard on the freeway, is near impossible to quantify. Until the invention of the Internet and the onset of digital advertising. Now, it is possible to measure everything. If John were alive today, he would find the answer to his quandary—and be dismayed. Neither half is working particularly well!

For the first time since its advent, consumers are starting to realize the power they wield over advertising. Unlike magazines, newspapers, television or radio, on their digital screens they are realizing that it is they who have the control. They have the power to use their screen for what they want and carve out what they don't. To dictate what is presented to them when they want it and block out anything else. When they are consuming information, advertisement is just a nuisance on the page to be ignored. When they are connecting and communicating with near and dear ones, advertising is just a bother to skip around. When they are trying to watch a video, advertising is just an irritant to 'X out' at the first possible opportunity. And when they do want to buy something, they can search and compare, review and transact on their own terms, no help needed from advertising, thank you very much.

The numbers are there in plain sight. The average advertisement now clicks through at 0.06 per cent. To put that in perspective, that is lower than the odds of getting into the top university in the world or surviving a plane crash! In other words, abysmal consumer engagement and interaction. Consumers are simply tuning advertisements out, now that they can. And that is when they view them at all.

As many as 600 million consumers around the world now use ad blocking software.

That makes it the single biggest protest movement known to humanity. It is unclear how much that number would go up if the remaining 3.6 billion Internet users even knew they could block ads! The elephant in the room when it comes to advertising is the consumer. And the elephant is starting to stir.

All of this is tantamount to a cataclysmic transfer of power in the making. For centuries, there has been a parent–child relationship between those in power and those subject to it. That is now starting to change. The engine to unleash the true power of humanity is starting to whir into life. Consumers are beginning to sense it. They are beginning to assert the power they are now uncovering. More and more relationships between the powerful few and the powerless many are starting to switch from parent–child to adult–adult relationships. Consumers are starting to demand respect, and earning it. They are starting to require real value, and finding it. They are developing a real voice, and being heard.

This is not all a smooth and cohesive transition of course. After all, consumers aren't one uniform array of clones all driven by the same priorities and preferences and speaking with one uniform voice. They come in all shapes and sizes, from all walks of life, with unique perspectives and prejudices, with their own hopes and dreams. This means there won't be one uniform agenda and manifestation of the consumer's power. It will manifest itself in countless shapes and flavours, dance to countless beats and rhythms, and take on countless lives of its own.

Consumer power will be fragmented. It will be diverse and multi-faceted. It will not always be pretty, fair or just. Many adverse and perverse behaviours will be emboldened and enabled, along with the noble, productive and altruistic ones. Lives will be lost just as lives will be saved or made. The lows will co-mingle with the highs. Beauty and ugliness will co-exist in greater measure than ever before. But knowledge will reign. A light will be shined in every corner of humanity. Consumers will have the information to make informed decisions. And they will have the muscle to flex their might in entirely new ways.

Of paramount importance as the consumer revolution gathers steam will be the core tools and technologies that form the infrastructure for the revolution itself. In a world where information resides in the cloud, it is imperative that the sanctity of that information be maintained in pristine quality. It is profoundly important that valid information be preserved and protected, and invalid information be weeded out. It is of paramount importance that consumers searching for information are presented the most objective, unbiased and accurate information from the cloud, without compromising its integrity in any shape or form.

These core functions are so profoundly important that they cannot be left unfettered to the profit-making objectives of private enterprises. For instance, the consumer revolution relies on accurate access to correct information for all. This core function cannot be left to search engines such as Google and Bing that have a core (and justifiable) objective of generating profits. Information search engines generate profits by maximizing advertising dollars made when they place ads alongside the search results they surface. This creates an intrinsic conflict of interest that makes them unqualified to serve as arteries of the consumer revolution. It taints the blood flow of the consumer revolution with parasites that compromise the purity of the information for the purposes of feeding the profit-making machine.

When there is a choice between presenting the best matching answer to a consumer's query and one that monetizes the best, a profit-making enterprise is absolutely entitled to the latter.

But the consumer revolution demands ironclad adherence to the former. Free enterprise is a fabulous thing, of course, but there is a line that needs to be drawn where the benefits of free enterprise and profits pale in comparison to compromising the integrity of the consumers' pursuit of knowledge. Leaving a core societal function like universal information access in the hands of profit-making enterprises has the ethical dilemma of select corporations profiteering from the knowledge creation and consumption of the entire world. If there is indeed profit to be made from organizing and surfacing information for consumers around the world, it can easily be argued that it should be for the benefit of society at large rather than a few large corporations.

Similarly, it is critically important that consumers be able to connect with each other without compromising their relationships, integrity or privacy. This purity of connection and sharing is far too core an element of the consumer revolution to be entrusted to a profit-making enterprise such as Facebook, Twitter or Snapchat. The business model of eavesdropping on consumer conversations or activity for the purposes of maximizing advertising revenues is riddled with conflicts of interest. The connectivity pipes of the consumer revolution can afford to have no purpose other than connecting its constituents in an utterly unfettered and uncompromised way, without any ulterior motive lurking in the background.

This advertising business model further compromises consumers when you factor in malicious or look the other way kinds of misuses such those conducted by Cambridge Analytica over Facebook's network. While the full extent of the damages inflicted by Cambridge Analytica and Facebook might never be known, the mere spectre of a subversion of the political process at the premier democracy in the world is a frightening reminder of what can go wrong in the consumer revolution at scale. The conflicts of interest and operational vulnerabilities need to be carefully resolved and protected to ensure the integrity of consumer communications, and this responsibility can only be entrusted to legitimate representatives of the consumers' interests—the government—and enforced with actual laws that are in the best interests of consumers.

In a similar manner, it is of utmost importance to provide free and unbiased access to products and services from around the world to every consumer. While profit-making enterprises such as Amazon and Alibaba don't yet have the market share of a Google or a Facebook in their respective spaces, the danger is that they will prioritize profits over purity of product selection, as they have a right to do in their capacities as profit-making enterprises. In the process however, they will compromise the integrity of the consumer revolution, creating the need for an impartial network or conduit between buyers and sellers. This is again too fundamental a societal need to be entrusted in the hands of a few large corporations. They must be supervised and overseen by officials and laws representing mass consumers.

Universal and unbiased access to information, connectivity and commerce are thus of profound importance to the state of human society from this point onwards, and merit the deepest analysis and involvement of consumer representatives. These capabilities are becoming as integral to the functioning of human society as law enforcement, taxation, roadways or the military, requiring the same level of oversight and protection afforded to them.

Furthermore, the greatest integrity provisions for the consumer revolution are needed in the realm of politics and governance itself. The consumer revolution will get more and more powerful, and take more and more charge of political agendas and processes. In this dynamic, it is existentially important for societies to craft digital rules of engagement for the political process. There needs to be a cloud constitution established that lays out the rules and laws of the land that apply to the consumer revolution. Today's laws and governance rules will become more and more arcane as the consumer revolution takes hold. Fundamental government mechanisms such as elected representatives, legislative bills and parliamentary procedures will decline in relevance, as newer models of cloud-based governance emerge. It is extraordinarily important for today's governments to get ahead of the curve when it comes to regulating and enabling lawful operation of the consumer revolution. The prospect of an unregulated wild west on a global scale with all the collective energies and mob psychologies of the consumer revolution in play, vulnerable to exploitation and abuse is nothing short of terrifying. Governments need to realize that if unregulated and unenforced, this is a ticking nuclear time bomb that can have catastrophic consequences for societies.

Not only do the new rules of engagement need to get defined but also it is critical that the sanctity of the political process itself be preserved. Societies simply cannot afford to have the political process of the consumer revolution be compromised or tampered with in any way. They cannot afford to have profit-making conflicts of interest in the political process—think of malicious advertising from lobbying firms beaming incessantly at consumers as they make their way to digital polling stations. Leaving this security hole wide open for abusive forces is nothing short of subversion of the state itself. The integrity of the digital political process and political movements needs to be guarded as zealously as we guard polling booths and the constitution today.

Who should be in charge of these new rules of engagement that provide the infrastructure and basis for the consumer revolution? Today's government officials. They are best suited to act in the best interests of their mass consumers. They are the freest of conflicts of interest to do right by their populaces. This endeavour cannot be left to profit-making enterprises because of the visceral conflicts of interest that abound.

To do this effectively, government officials need to educate themselves on the technologies and business models that power the consumer revolution. They need to develop a vision for its orderly evolution. They need to come up with a robust set of laws, policies and procedures to ensure that the consumer revolution runs on the purest of rails. Doing so will ensure the greatest possible benefits to all of society from the power of this revolution. Failing to do so will have catastrophic and sinister implications because of the sheer energy and force being let loose. It would be the equivalent of setting off a nuclear explosion rather than a nuclear reactor. The consequences would be frightful.

As with the dawning of any new era, there will be a vast amount of transformation accompanying the consumer revolution. There will be severe disruption in the status quo. There will be massive winners and massing losers created over the next few decades. There will be a vast amount of energy unleashed, needing to be channelled in the right ways. There will be a massive transfer of power from producers to consumers, needing to be moderated to ensure peace and prosperity for the world. There will be untold turmoil and triumph and tribulation over this transformation.

This is nothing short of a new world order being born. The world in 50 years will look nothing like it does today. And nothing like it has looked for the past million years. The consumer revolution will accelerate in velocity at a rate of change far greater than ever before in human history. It will demand innovation and productivity in every field of life at a pace that is unimaginable today.

The consumer revolution will bring phenomenal empowerment to every human being in the world. Every individual—this means you and me—will have a platform, no less than the mightiest and the loftiest of leaders and stars. Because unlike all the other revolutions preceding this one, this is our revolution, this is the people's revolution. If you look back at the great revolutions of the past—fire, the wheel, explosives, the Industrial Revolution, the computer revolutions—they were all technology- or producer-driven revolutions. This one, on the other hand, is a people-driven revolution.

WE ARE THE REVOLUTION!

WE are making the revolution happen. We are the core building blocks on which the revolution is being founded. We are shaping it with every thought and feeling, click and tap, and expression of our will. We are powering it with every dash of energy we feel towards any topic, issue, idea or person. We are integral to the unleashing of the greatest energy and the greatest force ever seen in the world. We are powering the force that is beginning to reshape centuries of traditions and practices, and power structures in the world. We are transforming the institutions of the world to serve our means and purposes as they were meant to do.

Those that grasp the full extent of this transformation, of the centrality of our role and have a vision for negotiating it will thrive in unprecedented ways. Those that don't will be left behind feeling like dinosaurs in the Cretaceous-Tertiary extinction era wondering what happened to their world.

It's easy to decide which side you want to be on!

3

INFORMATION IGNITION

The advent of the Internet has led to a veritable explosion in information, or content, available to consumers. Not only is the volume of information exploding, but the diversity, variety, formats, mediums, durations, currency, objectives, effects and derivative effects of information are growing just as explosively.

To put this in perspective, consider this. An average book contains approximately 50,000 to 100,000 words. The *Encyclopaedia Britannica* has 44 million words, spread across 32 volumes. The English Wikipedia by itself has 3.4 billion words. And the Internet as a whole? 300 trillion words and counting! A monumental eruption of content and information available to consumers is underway around the world. This is a vast treasure chest of knowledge arming consumers with whichever nugget of information they like, far deeper and faster that any traditional book, library, university or training programme in the world could accomplish.

Layering onto this already formidable base of content is the volume and velocity of new content generation on the Internet which points to even more startling statistics.

Ninety per cent of the content in the world today was created in the past two years alone.

Every day, about 2.5 quintillion bytes of data are generated around the world. That is 70 times larger than the entire US Library of Congress. Every day!

The amount of information available on the Internet is simply mind-boggling. Consumers have access to staggering levels of content on the topics of their interest, whatever they may be. This is making it impossible for traditional producers and power brokers to control information any longer. The digital tools of today are making it impossible to obfuscate or regulate knowledge. Everything is increasingly available, accessible and in plain sight. The boundaries between information haves and have-nots are collapsing at an astonishing rate. Playing fields are getting levelled out. Information is becoming weaponized, and consumers have access to the same armaments as those in power. In an increasingly knowledge-based society, the primary resource is now becoming universally accessible to all.

Along similar lines, the number of websites on the Internet has also grown at astronomical rates. In 1994, there were fewer than 3,000 websites on the Internet. The web was dominated by destination content sites. These included sites such as netscape. com, yahoo.com, telegrah.co.uk and msn.com among others. Consumers got accustomed to visiting known destination sites to retrieve information in predictable, organized and repeatable ways. Sites such as yahoo.com then developed directories to categorize websites and content across the Internet. The directory structure had worked well historically for categorizing and organizing static or pseudo-static information such as contact lists, store directories and employee names in the physical world. The early days of the Internet world had similar characteristics as the offline world, so a Yahoo-like directory structure worked just fine. Consumers started to use these directories to find information, akin to using white pages, yellow pages or library indexing systems to find desired material.

Clearly, neither content producers nor consumers at the time could envision the explosive effect that the consumer revolution would have on the information world. The category and directory model were following the old-world library model of organizing and searching for information. This had worked well when the volume of content was manageable and growing at a modest pace as it had done for centuries in the past. But as the subsequent years were to demonstrate, this model would become woefully inadequate for dealing with the size, scope and volume of content production triggered by the consumer revolution.

Because from there the Internet just grew. And grew. And grew. The number of sites on the Internet began to proliferate and multiply at dizzying rates. Today, there are a staggering 1.3 billion websites on the Internet! And counting! The plummeting costs of content production and distribution are bringing in whole new classes of content producers into the fold. The Internet has started to give voice to more and more content creators from all walks of life, for whatever reasons they find compelling, whatever subject they want to express themselves in and whatever purpose they want to accomplish. And they are finding ready accomplices in the consumers of their content, asserting their new-found power, requesting and patronizing, and demanding better and better content for whatever they find compelling.

The complexity and cost of content production continue to decline exponentially, to the point where content production takes scarcely more effort and resources than content consumption. The lines between content producers and consumers are blurring, giving rise to trends such as user-generated content, blogs, chats and forums. There is now a direct path between content producer and content consumer, whether channelled through broad general interest areas, or narrow niches of special interests that are as plentiful as consumers themselves.

This democratization of information is now transforming the established pillars of media and publishing utterly and completely. When there is a single book, a single institution, a single publication, a single channel that is the fountain of knowledge, it garners all the stature and reverence consumers can accord it. When there are a million, or a billion, there is no more definitive source, definitive spokesperson, definitive narrative, or definitive agenda. There is no more pedestal, platform, pulpit and sermon. As more and more information sources have flourished, the marginal utility of any one individual source has started to decline precipitously for consumers. They have started to become the real arbiters of what they find useful and valuable in a sea of content, and they are starting to take more and more charge of the information they choose to consume.

This is tantamount of a dramatic transfer of power from information producers to information consumers. Never before in the history of humankind has there been this much parity between the two. The respect, the regard, even the reverence that the spoken to had for the speaker is on the wane. Looking ahead, information and content will continue to fragment at increasing rates. Legendary publications such as the *New York Times*, the *Washington Post*, the *Wall Street Journal*, the *Economist, Le Monde, Xinhua Reference News* and *Times of India* will see their stranglehold on content and their sway on their audiences chip away. Famed television networks such as NBC, CBS, ABC, BBC, TF1, China Central Television (CCTV), NHK, ZDF and Zee TV will no longer be the exclusive custodians of content and information. Content production will reorganize around what consumers want to consume, rather than what is efficient or self-serving for producers to produce.

Over the course of the next few decades, the value of traditional publishing brands, both corporate and individual, will decline steadily from their heady highs. Historical reputations, track records and past laurels will have lesser and lesser value in the minds of consumers. They will instead reward accuracy of information, genuineness of reporting, timeliness of news and the tailoring of knowledge to their specific needs. Famed news anchors and reporters will garner scarcely more respect and credibility than a well-informed neighbour, as long as the neighbour provides accurate, timely information.

Consumers will start dictating what information is presented to them, in the mediums, formats, languages, frequencies and flavours they desire. And since consumers come in all shapes and sizes, information will come in all shapes and sizes to serve their needs. 'Professional' and 'official' content will begin to look like user-generated content, rather than the other way around— such is the gravitational force of the consumer revolution. Established and elite publishers will start using colloquial language to better relate and connect with consumers, and further bring down the costs of authorship and content production. Information dissemination will begin to adopt communications styles and patterns reflecting today's chat styles and user-generated content slangs, because that is the style consumers increasingly prefer to consume and relate to.

One might argue that this will lower the quality of content and the standards of writing in the world. That the finer qualities of well-written content will be overrun by low quality content marauders. But that is simply ignoring the point and the might of the consumer revolution. It is the consumer who is dictating what is correct and what is desirable. It is the consumer who drives what content gets produced and distributed, and how. It is the consumer who is the final arbiter of its value. The consumer is placing greater value on information accuracy, speed and customization rather than on the literary quality the producer historically valued.

Traditionally eloquent literary styles might become as obsolete in the world to come as neat handwriting and spelling skills are becoming in today's world.

Not that you can argue that consumers are wrong either. Shorn of all the flourishes and garnishes, the core purpose of information is to inform. To impart the right knowledge at the right time with the right context to the right person. That is what is valuable to consumers, and they are beginning to demand value as such from producers. And they are beginning to strip out any fat in the system as perceived in their eyes. They are beginning to remake content on the Internet in their own image.

This is a dramatic change from the state of information and knowledge in the world up to this point. The consumer revolution is generating the creative energy to fuel dramatically expanding volumes of content. The consumer revolution is driving exponentially increasing fragmentation of content. And the consumer revolution is driving the style of content to mirror that of the day-to-day interactions of its constituents.

The consumer revolution in information has also led to other major side effects. As content began to proliferate at a furious pace in the 1990s, a whole new need arose on the Internet—to efficiently and effectively search for information. After all, all of the riches on the Internet could only be of value if they could be found and harvested when and how they were needed. Otherwise they would simply be morasses of bytes sitting on deserted islands, serving no purpose for anyone except the accidental passer-by.

Enter search engines. As the volume and velocity of content on the Internet exploded, consumers found the traditional directory-based search model less and less effective. Because, as it turned out, there were as many ways to organize content on the Internet as consumers themselves. And, as it turned out, there were as many ways to organize content on the Internet as moments in the day each individual consumer wanted to access any information. Content organization became a real-time, on demand and personalized requirement, not a one-time, static and universal content organization exercise. There was no way for one directory to serve as the central organizational system for the entire Internet for all consumers at all points of time. That model worked fine when the producer defined the content world into a few neatly organized segments, but not when the consumer defined it in endless and ever-fluid categories and segments. Search engines became the consumer-driven organizational tools of the Internet, just as directories were producer-driven organizational tools.

The fundamental shift here, missed by the biggest publishers and content producers at the time, was that the consumer revolution was going to drive a torrent of content over the Internet, and traditional organizational and management tools were no longer going to suffice. Incumbent content powerhouses did not pick up on the fundamental difference in medium and dynamic— that in the digital world, it was the consumer who would be in charge, it would be the consumer who would call the shots. Traditional print, radio and television-based publishing was and is inherently about producer-driven broadcasting. The tools and economics of the trade required a broadcast model, where the same content was made available to all consumers uniformly, in a format and schedule determined by producers, and packaged and presented by producers.

The radical difference with all digital environments in the consumer revolution era is that they are consumer-driven, narrowcast environments. As a matter of fact, they are narrowcast to the extreme, where each individual consumer can consume any desired piece of content at any point of time, and to serve that consumer, a content producer must tailor content to that one individual consumer. The Internet is about making everything on demand and consumer-driven. It flips the entire model of publishing from a mass-broadcast game plan of the producer to the individual narrowcast need of the consumer.

This transition led to the next major disruption in status quo— the rise of the content search engine.

In 1990, Alan Emtage, a student at McGill University in Montreal created the first ever search engine named Archie.

This was followed by other early solutions such as VLib, Veronica, Jughead, Wandex and JumpStation. In 1994 Infoseek, Yahoo, WebCrawler and Lycos were born, followed by LookSmart, Excite and AltaVista in 1995. In 1996, Larry Page and Sergey Brin at Stanford University started BackRub, which grew into Google in 1998. Perhaps not apparent to many at the time, Google would subsequently grow into a powerhouse in the corporate firmament by virtue of spotting and getting on the right side of the consumer revolution with the right solution.

At a time when incumbent content producers, directories and early search engines were coming at the problem with conventional producer optics, Google came at it with the most compelling consumer optics of the time. The Internet is developing into the information backbone of the world? Check. Costs to produce and consume content are plummeting on the Internet? Check. Volume and velocity of content production and consumption are skyrocketing on the Internet? Check. Value of finding relevant knowledge in the sea of content exploding? Check. Consumer-oriented tool to find knowledge on the Internet? Bingo.

When there is so much content available on the Internet, an even more valuable function is finding the *right* content on the Internet. What would consumers deem to be right?

There were many ways to assess this at the time, but Google was able to come up with the magic formula—relevance and implicit trust. The company was able to spider and index content on the Internet along text strings or keywords for efficient retrieval. It was able to come up with a way to score implicit trust based on referral links back to websites from other sites, factoring in their trust scores. In other words, Google came up with the most elegant solution for using the consumer revolution itself to serve its needs. The exploding volume of websites themselves provided markers to Google for what was relevant and trustworthy, and Google was simply able to weave this information into a lightning fast search experience to deliver Internet magic. This led to the greatest relevance and trust for retrieving content on the Internet relative to all other search engines at the time. The most appropriate tool to put in the hands of consumers searching for their exact information requirements. A lightsabre with which consumers would seize control over producers in their revolution.

Google then went on to innovate with several other conveniences for consumers, such as ultrafast search speed and auto suggestions to make consumers' tasks even simpler and more productive. It all added up to a seismic shift in what consumers were enabled to do over the Internet.

The search market developed and played out worldwide, and Google, Bing, Baidu and Yandex emerged as market leaders. These search engines have now gotten increasingly sophisticated at finding desired information in this sea of content in the blink of an eye. This has the effect of unlocking the power of all the information on the Internet, and making it usable as knowledge.

How useful did consumers find this tool that was on their side in their revolution? In 1998, there were 10,000 search queries per day on Google. Today, there are about 5 billion on Google alone and about 7 billion queries on search engines overall! An astronomical increase in use and utility fuelled by the consumer revolution.

Another major side effect of the consumer revolution in information was the rise of cloud computing. In the early days of the Internet, most websites were hosted on their own individual web servers and connected to the Internet via gateways. This consumed a lot of time and resources from content producers performing server administration tasks that were not part of their core competencies. In 2006, then CEO of Google, Eric Schmidt, introduced the term 'cloud computing' at an industry conference, ushering in the notion that most common Internet hosting, serving and management capabilities could be outsourced to 'the cloud'. In effect, specialized technology companies could manage standard

Internet hosting and serving functions at a much better price-performance point than the sites themselves.

The trend quickly caught on because of its clear economic and operational advantages. Cloud computing took off like a rocket, with companies such as Amazon, Microsoft and Google providing services, and companies like Salesforce becoming leading proponents of the efficiencies possible with a cloud-based solution. It is expected that in the next three years, an astonishing 92 per cent of the workload of the Internet will be handled by cloud-based data centres, and only 8 per cent by traditional self-managed server farms.

Cloud computing is demonstrably lowering economic and operational costs to setting up websites and publishing content, leading to an even greater proliferation in sites and content. It has thus become a core enabler to the consumer revolution and a key component in its empowerment. This has also allowed it to ride the wave as a result of this affiliation. Like all other technologies that are enabling the consumer revolution as opposed to fighting it, cloud computing and its core providers such as Amazon, Microsoft and Google are finding heady successes in its wake.

As consumers are increasingly asserting their power over producers of content, demanding more and more tailored content to serve their myriad needs, and producers are able to produce content at exponentially declining costs, there is a natural fragmentation of content on the Internet as can be expected. Information on the Internet is splintering almost as fast as it is proliferating, making it harder and harder for content producers to build and retain value. The value in content is migrating out of any individual site, and into the content amalgamation residing in the cloud, and into the content search engines and the cloud computing platforms that are arming the revolution. It is becoming impossible for an individual publisher or institution to keep pace with the network effects of the consumer revolution, and the content proliferation that comes along with it.

One fascinating aspect to this dynamic is its current and projected impact on the world of education. For generations, schools and universities have been the purveyors of knowledge and learning in the world. They continue to be among the world's most admired and revered institutions, the temples of pure knowledge, the hallowed grounds on which we learn how to think, how to relate, how to collaborate and how to grow up to be productive members of society. They are held in such high esteem that there is a crush of applicants every year to get admitted at these institutions, and their stamp of approval can stand graduates in good stead for their entire lives. Educational institutions by their very nature have a very formal approach to education. They impart knowledge and learning to students worldwide in very structured, heavily-researched, substantiated and formally accredited ways. Up until this point, formal education has not been overly impacted by the consumer revolution. But there are some intriguing developments on the horizon.

Colleges and universities have begun to offer students increasing flexibility on when and where to take their classes. In particular, they are beginning to offer online courses that do not require physical presence on campuses. There is a thriving online education industry that has now developed to serve the educational needs of consumers in a more flexible setting that fits in better with their lives. Institutions such as University of Phoenix, American Public University System, Symbiosis and Liberty University have emerged as leaders in this space, and are thriving in the opportunity created by the consumer revolution to learn on its terms.

These online universities often offer shorter, more specialized programmes and degrees in keeping with the needs and requirements of everyday consumers, along the lines of ITT Tech and DeVry University. Following along, colleges are beginning to offer certificates and micro-credentials that are often more useful for consumers, and do not require going through a full four-year or two-year general-purpose programme in order to get to the specific learning desired. Pioneers like Udacity have taken this trend even further with small, specialized 'nanodegrees' that teach very specific skills and learnings to students at a fraction of the time and cost of formal degrees. The unbundling and fragmentation of education appears to have taken hold, along the lines of the rest of worldwide content democratization, under the sway of the consumer revolution.

Even at formal educational programmes at formal schools and universities, the impact of the consumer revolution is starting to show. Many of the learning resources for traditional education are now starting to be found online, in the thick of the consumer revolution-driven content explosion. Students working on research projects or class projects increasingly refer to online resources for nuggets of information, to the point where they have to be cautioned on authorized and unauthorized sources, and the principle of avoiding plagiarism. The consumer revolution is growing its knowledge base at an exponential rate.

Educational and research institutions also understand the value of network effects well—that is why so many institutes and professors collaborate with each other in major research areas. What the consumer revolution is beginning to demonstrate is that it is going to be increasingly difficult for a private network including a brilliant but small group of college professors to keep pace with a giant public knowledge network including the rest of humanity. And that the fragmentation and flexibility of education will continue to accelerate, same as it is with the rest of content and information on the Internet. Educational services that help consumers harvest, analyse and apply the knowledge riches of the Internet to their individual needs at the required moments of time will find increasing success, and educational programmes that are mired in traditional rigid and structured educational content will find their appeal dwindling. Education will begin to transition increasingly from producer- or educator-driven orientation to consumer- or student-driven orientation. Centuries of teaching paradigms and models are beginning to change within a generation right before our eyes. The effect on schools, colleges and universities is shaping up to be profound.

Unsurprisingly, technology and solution providers that are on the right side of the consumer revolution—content search engines, cloud computing providers, and content creation and management tools—are seeing phenomenal growth. New generations of solution providers are being born in the market that are understanding the shape of things to come and channelling their offerings to what consumers and producers need in the new world order. They are recognizing that the state of affairs is changing dramatically with the consumer revolution now underway, and they are coming up with the right technologies and solutions for the post-revolution world. From there, the sheer force of the revolution is carrying them over to their promised lands.

One dynamic that is intriguing about this development is that while there is increasing fragmentation and democratization of information and content on the Internet, when it comes to tools, there is actually increasing concentration of solution providers. This is because tools by and large have the same functionality, and there is no market need for large numbers of tools. There are only so many search engines needed, and only so many cloud computing platforms required. Google and Amazon are incredibly successful companies that do many things exceptionally well. But their fundamental market power and economic surplus stems from being the market leader in content search and cloud computing, respectively. And in each instance, the market leader has a substantial lead over other solution providers in the market.

The information provider world is thus bifurcating into products on the one hand, and platforms and tools on the other. Or the gold in the 1849 California Gold Rush, versus the picks and the shovels. As the story goes, the prospectors and miners in the gold rush ended up with slim pickings, while entrepreneurs that sold prospectors essential supplies and materials such as Levi

Strauss, Samuel Brennan, Thomas Larkin and Faxon Dean Atherton became legendary business successes. The Internet is proving to be no different.

Information and content providers are essentially creating 'products' for information, or flecks of gold on the Internet. The more the consumer revolution revs up, the more the demands for volume, variety and velocity of content. And the more the time and costs to develop content plummet, the greater the supply of content in the world. These two torrents combine to produce a dramatic and irreversible decline in value for any individual piece of content, and any individual content producer. The evidence is all around us, where famed publications such as the *Washington Post*, the *Los Angeles Times*, *Time magazine* and the *Boston Globe* are being sold at distressed prices.

Content creation, hosting and search platforms on the other hand are seeing their values soar as the consumer revolution drives an insatiable appetite for their tools and services. The same gale force that is inexorably driving value down for individual content providers is driving value up for successful enabling platforms even more inexorably. One is becoming the backbone, the other is becoming fodder for the consumer revolution.

For technology vendors and solution providers that are able to become enabling platforms in the new world order, the rewards are astronomical. Being on the right side of the consumer revolution is leading to untold riches and power in the commercial world. So much so that the trend is leading to very profound and fundamental questions about the scope and influence of these enabling platforms, and whether they ultimately work in the public good or counter to it. Whether they ultimate serve the consumer revolution or exploit it. The consumer revolution itself will be the final arbiter of this question, and will enforce corrective action at a time and place that it deems fit.

As we review the global landscape today, the fascinating question is where will the consumer revolution in information go next? What can we expect from consumers, producers and technology providers over the course of the next year, the next decade, the next century?

You can get an inkling of the future by extrapolating the developments of the past. In many aspects of the consumer revolution in information, the writing is on the wall.

First, the volume of content on the Internet will, of course, continue to grow exponentially. But also, the formats of content will grow in multiple dimensions. The volume of images on the Internet is already exploding and will continue to accelerate. Similarly, the volume of video content and of audio content will continue to explode. Any form of expression that can be reduced to digital form will be. And the closer the format gets to visceral consumer expression and comprehension, the more fulfilment and enjoyment it delivers to consumers, the faster it will accelerate. This is because the more intrinsic and instantly consumable a format is, the less biological energy it takes for consumers to produce and consume while delivering even more sensory signal value. The greater the signal value of a content format, and the lesser the friction to comprehend it, the more that format of content will proliferate.

A picture is worth a thousand words. A video might well be worth a thousand pictures. So increasing volumes of content on the Internet will develop in these formats.

As content formats proliferate, tools such as content search engines and cloud computing platforms will have to keep up. They will need to extend their franchises into these new content formats, not just into the soaring volumes of text content in the world. For some, like cloud computing providers, this will be simpler, just entailing more digital bytes required by audio and video content to securely host and serve and manage at a faster speed. For others, like content search engines, this will be a bit more challenging—finding the right video content in video clips is a different technology than finding the right keyword in a keyword query. Content search providers who are able to provide this solution will see their advantages extend and even increase as new forms of content proliferate. This presents a major disruption opportunity for a new entrant to shuffle the balance of power in the content search world.

Second, the input and output formats for publishing and searching for information will proliferate. In the 1990s, the primary device for producing and consuming content was the personal computer, and the primary format was text. Smartphones showed up in the world as a well-recognized category in 1995 with IBM Simon Personal Communicator, but then really came into their own with the launch of Apple's iPhone in 2007. What followed was a breathtaking rise in the use of smartphones around the world, fuelled by countries leap-frogging the entire landline phone network generation on the backs of cellular smartphone technology. Smartphone adoption spread like wildfire among consumers worldwide, actually overtaking personal computer shipments by 2011. Consumers found the utility and price point of smartphones more attractive relative to computers, and from there the consumer revolution took over.

This of course forced content producers to go through a complete refresh cycle to package up their content for the smartphones and subsequently tablet form factors. The output format for digital content had to change because that's where the consumer revolution was taking it.

Another nuance in the smartphone world was the mobile app revolution. Rather than consuming content via web browsers, consumers found it more useful to consume content via mobile apps. As a result, more and more content is now being delivered via mobile apps, requiring further content publishing and tool changes.

With more and more consumers looking for information on smartphone mobile apps, and more and more content producers making their content available there, content search engines also had to extend their offerings to smartphone mobile apps. This has created an opportunity for new entrants to establish sizeable market presence by delivering a fundamentally superior content search experience than what is possible by using traditional web-based content search technologies. This is required because the technology to index and search within apps is different from the technology to do so on the web.

Other input and output formats for publishing, consuming and searching for content are starting to take hold and will only accelerate. Input and output based on images has already begun. Consumers don't just live with text, they also live with images. So, it is only natural that they will want to search with images, and get results back as images. Beats typing in and reading back 1,000 words!

Extrapolating these trends, another dimension of expanding input and output formats is video. Consumers live in a live-video world. There are moving visuals around them every waking hour. They comprehend and express things via live visuals. They find much more context and flavour and nuance in videos than can be described through text. So it is only natural that they will want to input and out information via videos.

Similarly, input and output based in voice has already begun, and will only accelerate. Consumers live in a voice-based world in their day-to-day 'real world' life. Consumers grow up with voice, they communicate with voice, they express with voice and they learn with voice. It is only natural that they want to search for information with voice, and get back results as voice.

The advent of smartphones has only accelerated consumer demand for voice-based information input and output. As the number of smartphones and their associated apps continues to grow, the need for voice-based content input and output will continue to accelerate.

The common thread here is again, consumer power. Consumers live in a sensory world, taking advantage of their five sensory facilities. It is most fulfilling and easiest for them to input and output information directly in these sensory formats. Producers will hence have to cater to every preference that consumers express when it comes to input and output. The consumer revolution is ensuring that producers move in the direction of what consumers want, rather than consumers accepting what producers made available to them, as in the past.

Extending content, input and output to images, voice and videos requires differing levels of expertise for technology providers. For cloud computing providers, the requirements are incrementally more demanding, although not overly so, thanks to Moore's law. Images, voice and videos require more bytes than text. So there will be heavier requirements for storage and serving bandwidth. There will be a requirement for more pervasive content delivery networks to ensure consumers get acceptable screen response times wherever they are. There will be a bit more heavy lifting, but in the grand scheme of things, not a structural change that challenges the leading incumbents.

The impact of extending content, input and output formats will be more on content search engines. Indexing and retrieving image, voice and video content are not exactly the same as indexing and retrieving text. A text-based franchise can be extended to provide a partial solution by tagging the image, voice and video content with text tags. But a better mapping technology would be the one that operates on the core elements of the original content itself. In other words, a content search engine that can decompose an image, a voice or a video clip into its atomic components, and then can match those atomic components with those in the ocean of the available content on the Internet, will have a fundamental advantage over today's traditional text-based content search engines.

Similarly, the notion of hyperlinking in the text format will evolve in the image, voice and video formats. Content producers will need to come up with newer and more effective ways to hyperlink various sites and apps natively in these formats. And content search engines will need to come up with newer ways to factor these links in their trust scoring algorithms for these new content formats. This is going to create opportunities for new content search engines that are innovative and specialize in the best search experiences for these newer content formats. This will create phenomenal opportunities by creating value and by being on the right side of the consumer revolution.

Information formats, and input and output formats will of course take a giant leap forward with the Internet of Things (IoT). The power of billions of standardized networked devices being governed by software central nervous systems is too profound to be denied. IoT devices come in countless different form factors, shapes and sizes. Their utility and popularity are ratcheting up rapidly, leading to a staggering 8.4 billion IoT devices out in the world today. The number of IoT units shipped is now outstripping even smartphones, and we have only just begun.

By 2020, there will be 20.4 billion IoT devices in more and more form factors, ranging from small 'wearables' to IoT-enabled refrigerators and automobiles, creating a giant new wave of content on the Internet, and giant new needs to harness and act on it.

IoT will stretch the capabilities of cloud computing providers, but again not drastically. The impact on content search engines however will be greater as there will be an astronomical new volume of content to index and make searchable, with much of it getting created continually, much of it in real time and much of it with very specialized use cases and applications. These are outside the standard use cases for a standard content search engine, so will require new technologies to solve them at scale. This area will also be ripe for new entrants in the market as there is a window of opportunity every time an existing technology franchise does not extend to a new use case such as this one.

The consumer revolution in information won't just stop here though. The next thrilling frontier for the consumer revolution in information will be enabling digital knowledge and wisdom. With the current advancement in artificial intelligence and machine learning, a vast amount of information will be processed into highly customized nuggets of knowledge, which will be imparted to individual consumers. Furthermore, these higher-order insights will be spoon fed to consumers at the right time, in line with their day-to-day tasks, so that they can benefit from the best insights the world has to offer without breaking their stride or interrupting their process.

By contrast, today's search paradigms will seem primitive and archaic to consumers in time. In today's state of affairs, when consumers need to find information over the Internet, they first need to interrupt whatever processes they are in the midst of, formulate the raw query for the missing piece of information they need from the Internet, scan and research through the results of the query, determine if they have the information they need, or reformulate until they have the right query that provides them the right information and integrate that information back into the processes they were on. The process is very tedious; it requires an awful lot of querying and scanning to find information, requires excessive context for consumers to keep while they are searching for information and doesn't always yield information in formats that consumers can easily integrate into their work processes.

Now imagine a world where consumers have questions in the midst of their processes, or perhaps don't even know they will have particular questions down the road. A content *and context* search engine, armed with truly sophisticated artificial intelligence technology, will be able to keep track of consumers' context, anticipate their information needs, fire off searches on the Internet, scan and categorize and evaluate results, select the best one, and make it available to consumers at the right times and in the right formats that is the most seamless with their processes.

For instance, imagine going to pick out your clothes for the day in your closet. And your smart closet has already looked up the weather for the day, your schedule of meetings for the day and your evening plans in making the right recommendation for what to wear. Very similar to the actual decision-making you might go through in your own mind, or a concierge might go through in making a wise decision for you.

Or imagine driving home from work, and having your smart car search what shows are playing in the evening, compute your drive time home, and buy theatre tickets for your significant other and you if the timing and traffic lines up and if you haven't gone out in a couple of weeks. The searching again is holistic, integrated and higher-order rather than piecemeal, task-by-task information searching. More what an intelligent personal assistant with context about your life would do, rather than you carrying out each individual task yourself. The difference between asking someone how you can help versus just helping out.

This level of higher-order searching will unleash even greater utility for consumers, empower their revolution even further and create incredible economic value for technology providers mastering this functionality. As this capability matures, consumers will be able to find the best advice in the world for every situation in their lives instantaneously! Imagine the implications for human society when the most trusted source of advice and wisdom is equally accessible to everyone. The impact on social structures and interpersonal dynamics will be profound.

While consumers will enjoy phenomenal benefits from having 'wisdom at their fingertips', serving the consumer revolution in this way will again pay off handsome dividends to technology providers enabling and supporting it. With more and more power transferring into the hands of consumers, they will demand greater and greater support, ease and value in the pursuit of their activities. Providers enabling this will see phenomenal growth and value.

This transformation in the consumption of content will also create opportunities for new entrants in the market as the technology required for higher-order searching is fundamentally different from basic query-based searching. If a new technology provider comes up with a fundamentally superior technology to conduct this, they will garner substantial success as they will be even more on the right side of the consumer revolution than today's leading content search engines.

An even more futuristic scenario for information publishing and consumption is where input and output formats directly transmit from and into consumer minds. This might be accomplished via electronic sensors or implants in the brain that can detect content, anticipate needs, formulate explicit or implicit questions, conduct higher-order information search and feed the best results directly into consumer brains via a bio-integration technology. With the advances in artificial intelligence now underway, capabilities such as these are getting closer and closer to reality.

The net behaviour would be one where the entire Internet becomes an extension of your mind—an incredibly powerful and ever-growing brain that can become your augmented intelligence engine—a simultaneously thrilling and terrifying prospect!

With this much information and wisdom at stake for consumers, it is imperative that the integrity of the information and its access be preserved and protected. One of the most critical emerging needs when it comes to information on the Internet is trust. When there is so much information available to all, and it is growing at such a rapid rate, how should consumers identify the sources and information that they can trust? After all it is just as easy to say that the sky is red on the Internet as it is to say that the sky is blue. And with the great democratization of information on the Internet, it is not only possible but probable that producers of content will take entirely opposing points of view in expressing themselves. This can include subjective expressions as well as objective expressions. Think of the most radical theories and beliefs—the Earth is flat, aliens live amongst us, our planet is the centre of the universe—and sure enough you can find reams of content on the Internet supporting the cause.

And this is when you look at the sincere, well-meaning differences in opinions and views between people. Layer on to this the fraudulent and malicious dissemination of misinformation, also colloquially referred to as 'fake news', and you have a recipe for catastrophic consequences. Information, or misinformation depending on your point of view, is being weaponized with the greatest of ease. It is agonizingly simple to lead entire cohorts of digital consumers down wild-goose chases triggered by spurious information. Altered articles? Check. Digitally-altered images? Check. Edited and post-processed videos? Check. If content can be altered so effortlessly, and spread around the Internet like, well, a virus, how menacing is that?

Imagine this modern-day lightsabre in the hands of malicious individuals. They can scythe through huge swaths of the Internet with their misinformation agenda, and not run into any rule of law to curtail their activity. And this is the damage that a mere individual can do. Now envision this power in the hands of a malicious group or state. Misinformation campaigns can be coordinated with the greatest of ease to unleash a nuclear explosion of malicious information on consumers at large. When this much knowledge is wired into the bloodstream of human society, this presents a catastrophic social, political and economic hazard that can be promulgated at will today.

Clearly this gaping hole in the legitimacy of information cannot be left unplugged. The consumer revolution will not stand for it. It will demand that this shocking vulnerability be addressed by a credible solution.

The primary line of defence against this systemic vulnerability is regulatory oversight. It is imperative that regulatory authorities around the world examine and understand the trajectory and implications of entrusting the knowledge base of the consumer revolution in the hands of a handful of profit-making enterprises. This laissez faire mindset about cloud solution providers, and especially content search engines, is fraught with fatal flaws. If the central nervous system of the world is compromised to the slightest degree in the interest of profit maximization, the implications for the consumer revolution can be catastrophic. Regulators must, hence, seize the initiative and get ahead of this tsunami racing ashore. They must define laws in the interest of the general good and directly regulate solution providers at the core of the information revolution. Doing so will ensure that the information flow powering the consumer revolution is unadulterated, untampered and unexploited in any way, shape or form.

This is also an area that is ripe for major innovation and new entrants. Existing content trust models, which are largely centralized, vested-interest trust models, will start to fail. The consumer revolution will demand solution providers who validate and authenticate trust in content, but also deliver impartial objectivity in presenting search results. The revolution will not tolerate providers profiting from their trust requirements, but rather enable it in the interest of the general good. This orientation makes the consumer revolution amenable to a decentralized and democratized trust model, fashioned in the shape of consumers themselves.

One of the most promising technologies to usher in this kind of distributed trust in the Internet age is blockchain. Blockchain technology is a distributed ledger and scoring system where no one company or government determines trust; the network itself houses this information in a democratized way. The network itself builds up trust in sources deemed trustable by participants in the network over time, and brings it down where sources are not trustable. Blockchain technology has mostly made waves so far in enabling crypto currencies such as Bitcoin and Ethereum, but the much larger development on the horizon is a universal, democratized model for trust. The consumer revolution will drive such a distributed trust model, to be harnessed by search engines and not compromised by advertising-based profit motives.

The blockchain revolution has only just begun. Blockchain-based content trust and search systems might be expected in the near future, driven by the demands of the consumer revolution. Solution providers innovating in this area and bringing consumers an effective solution to earn their trust for the information they access are going to become major winners on the Internet. This is because once again they are on the right side of the consumer revolution. They can see the proliferation of content, the democratization of information, the yawning trust vacuum in the Internet firmament, as side effects of consumers asserting their power. And by addressing such a fundamental need, they stand to benefit tremendously from the consumer revolution.

The consumer revolution in information is thus flipping the world from producer-led broadcast information streams with uniform content bases for all, to consumer-led, individually tailored information streams for each consumer at each moment of time with each content and process the consumer is engaged in at that moment of time. This is a dramatic shift in the world of information, content and knowledge that will impact publishers, content producers, newspapers, magazines, schools, colleges, libraries and all other sources of information in the world. Content and technology providers that enable and support this consumer empowerment with trustable information will find phenomenal success, and providers who are on the wrong side of this transformation, however large today, will find themselves on the path to obsolescence.

4

THE COMMUNICATION
CRESCENDO

Just as with information, the Internet has also brought about a complete transformation in the world of communication. To understand how profound this is, it is illustrative to roll back the clock and peer in the past.

In the early era of human development, any form of communication required the use of the five human senses, and could only be conveyed as far as the signals generated by these five senses could traverse.

There are indications that humans began to have organized ways to communicate with each other as far back as a million years ago. Even though all forms of social animals were able to communicate with each other, humans were able to do so in a much more elaborate and refined manner. They were in fact biologically enabled to do so, having a speech centre in their brains that was uniquely developed to rationally interpreting and articulating sounds and meaning. This genetic advantage took a major step forward with humans developing speech, approximately 500,000 years ago. Speech became very effective at communicating between humans and developed into the predominant communication format thereafter. In the early days, it was primarily just sounds through which humans were able to communicate with others. Over time, this gave rise to languages as a common lingua franca for humans to structure their sounds into cogent words that could be universally understood in their communities.

Another widely used form of communication developed around 30000 BC when humans developed symbols. Symbols ushered in the critical dimensions of transportability and persistence by introducing the element of recording information for the first time. The earliest symbols were carved or inscribed on rock surfaces and caves, such as at the Chauvet-Pont-d'Arc Cave in Southern France. As symbols began to get more sophisticated, humans could use them to preserve more information and knowledge, such as calendars that made their appearance around 15000 BC.

Symbols continued to get progressively more refined, leading to pictograms or pictorial representations of objects, activities, events or even concepts. As human brains developed, they were able to graphically depict even abstract ideas, leading to the development of ideograms.

Pictograms and ideograms continued to develop and get refined over the next few centuries, leading to the invention of the first writing systems around 4000 BC. Some of the earliest writing and hieroglyphic systems in the world are believed to have been invented in Sumeria, Egypt, Indus Valley, Mesopotamia, China and Mayan Americas, almost all developed independently.

The utility and versatility of language took a major step forward with the development of the alphabet, around 2000 BC. This enabled humans to componentize language, enabling far richer and nuanced vocabularies, concepts and ideas that could be effectively communicated.

The invention of written languages was a powerful enabler of the ability of humans to communicate with one another over space and time. It enabled the ability to communicate over great distances, as humans could take to physical travel to send the message from sender to recipient. The speed with which information could travel was limited of course by how fast humans and pets could walk, or at best run. But it was a great start to communicating over great distances, except of course for the limitations imposed by physical travel.

In this era and style of communication, to say anything to anyone, a person needed to set off on foot from the sender's location to the recipient's. This brought with it all the expected travel time delays, but it also introduced a significant risk in the message delivery process in case the messenger ran into a physical hazard that resulted in injury, disability or even death.

There were other message delivery risks in the process—for instance if the recipient was traveling or otherwise unavailable. The messenger would need to use their wherewithal to track down the recipient and deliver the message—no easy feat in that era.

After the message had been delivered to the recipient came the entire workflow of sending a reply back. This would entail a similar time, expense and risk profile as sending the original message out.

The cycle time for a message and reply could extend to hours or days, with no assurance and rampant risks in either of the communication flows getting disrupted. This kind of communication risk and barrier imposed significant costs on human society, forcing it to live largely in local silos, and very limited in its ability to collaborate and benefit over far-flung communities. If one single message and reply took this long, imagine trying to have a conversation with someone in a different location. Distance was a near insurmountable barrier to communication.

One charming addition to the lore of early human communication was the ability of consumers to harness trained pets to facilitate and speed up the communication process. Humans had begun domesticating and employing animals as pets since approximately 15000 BC, but the ability to use them to deliver messages added yet another utility to their purpose. Horses were able to transport messengers faster from sender to recipient. Delivery dogs, camels and reindeers were routinely used to transport messages and supplies across great distances. The legendary homing pigeon was used extensively to transport messages at, what was then considered, rapid speed, as recently as the First and Second World Wars, even receiving medals of honour for saving countless human lives by its valour!

Human communication became a lot more advanced with the invention of the wheel. As faster and more efficient forms of transportation developed, communication became proportionately more efficient as well. Horse-drawn carts and carriages, and thereafter motorized transportation sped up message and package delivery services. The benefits of collaborating across a larger cross-section of fellow consumers began to materialize, and human society prospered tremendously from the cross-pollination. This provided early glimpses of the gains in productivity possible when humans were able to collaborate across larger and larger groups. In other words, of network effects.

Another form of communication signal that developed over time was the use of sight. Humans were able to express themselves to each other using eye sight and eye expressions. Over time, they developed increasingly sophisticated visual cues and signals, such as flags, smoke signals, light mirrors and flares. These enabled humans to communicate with each other over greater distances. The earliest known use of smoke signals was around 200 BC to send signals along the Great Wall of China. In 150 BC, the Greeks devised a system to represent the alphabet via smoke signals.

Some civilizations then mastered systems to communicate through sound and light signals. Tribes and settlements in the Amazon rain forest got exceptional at communicating across sprawling distances with sounds. They established an effective vocabulary that obviated the need for physical travel to convey messages. They even established a repeater system through which messages could be repeated at interim points to transmit them even further than an individual sound signal could carry.

Further to the north, Native American tribes and civilizations got very good at communicating via light and smoke signals. They were also able to come up with a vocabulary to communicate important messages to one another via these signals, without requiring inefficient and risk-prone physical transportation between sender and recipient.

Signals such as these were the baby steps that mankind developed to go beyond delivering physical messages—to encode a message into energy signals, then to transmit these signals efficiently at greater distances, and finally to decode the signals at the receiving end into raw messages consumable for interpretation.

Communication across distances took a giant leap forward with the invention of the telegraph, and subsequently, the telephone. It was a monumental innovation to go from a cycle time of hours and days to minutes and seconds when it came to sending a message and getting back a reply. It unleashed a profound degree of collaboration and energy in human society, dramatically speeding up the pace of innovation and productivity in the world.

While the technology of telecommunication achieved breakthrough results and benefits for consumers, the range of service benefits were still quite narrow. Early telecommunications providers, such as the Bell Telephone Company, founded in 1877, controlled the formats, equipment and price points for telecommunication services. An entire communication revolution ensued, but driven entirely by producers and providers, very much an extension to the Industrial Revolution.

Telecommunication service operators and solution providers defined fundamental operating parameters for consumers, such as addressability by phone numbers, design and manufacture of instruments that could be used for making and receiving calls, sound quality, calling programmes and pricing rates, and specialty services, such as stored and forwarded messages and conference calls.

Consumers at large had to live within these rules, function within these parameters, and be subject to the prices and policies determined for them by these service providers. This asymmetry was exacerbated by the essentially monopolistic position of tele-communication service providers, given the capital and regulatory investments required to operate a telecommunication service. In fact, many sovereign governments regarded telecommunication so strategic and central to the functioning of society that they decided to own and operate their telecommunications services as a public sector, nationalized enterprise.

The invention of video technology in 1951 lead to another major development in the area of distance communication. At the New York World's Fair in 1964, the first transcontinental video call was demonstrated, ushering in the era of video telephony. Being able to see the other person in a conversation, in addition to being able to hear them, was a tremendous step forward in raising the value and impact of long-distance communication. Consumer benefits were again very distinct and compelling. However, the service and price points for video telephony were yet again determined by service providers to serve their own purposes and self-interests. Providers were able to extract premium value and pricing for the service, limiting its adoption and usage by consumers. Consumers had little say in features and costs, and had to live within the parameters defined for them by the producers of communication services.

You've Got Mail!

With the onset of the computer revolution, the next major breakthrough in long-distance communication was electronic mail, invented by Ray Tomlinson in 1972. This changed the rules of the game in several meaningful ways.

For the first time, email made it possible to send either tiny or vast amounts of information from the sender to the recipient in a matter of seconds, without requiring the recipient to receive or even acknowledge the message at the same time. The technology made for very efficient information communication, while decoupling the precise time the recipient paid attention to it from the time the sender sent it. Email also provided substantial control over size, shape, formats, contents and delivery service to consumers. It quickly began to show its utility and range in its usage. Consumers started generating as wide a variety of emails as consumers themselves. There were short, to the point emails. There were long, elaborate, verbose emails. There were formal announcements. There were informal, conversational emails. There were dry, plain-text emails. There were email works of art, enabling consumers to express themselves in colourful ways. They began to get a taste of how much richer and more expressive telecommunication could be. They began to get a taste of how much control email gave them—to determine who to communicate with and when, who and when to reply to, automatically save and retrieve communication at will, contact people or ignore people at will, forward information to others with ease, and alter audiences for each of their messages with ease.

Email provided consumers the bare beginnings of greater control, and they took to it in droves. By 2015, consumers were sending out 205 billion emails per day, or a staggering 74 trillion emails per year! Some call it the killer app of the Internet.

But the relentless forces of the consumer revolution wouldn't just stop there. The desire to connect more expansively, and to communicate with more instant gratification lead to the advent of other communication tool variations such as social networks and instant messaging.

The website Six Degrees is credited with having ushered in social media in 1997. The site enabled consumers to create profiles and connect with other consumers, setting off a fire storm of consumer activity unleashed by this new empowerment. The barriers to creating and publishing content on the Internet came crashing down even further, leading to the wide-scale proliferation of blogging or consumer publishing in 1999. The proliferation grew into an explosion, as the consumer revolution in communication truly took hold.

Websites such as Myspace and LinkedIn appeared on the Internet firmament in the early 2000s, followed by sites such as Flickr, Tumblr and Photobucket.

In 2004, two Harvard students, Mark Zuckerberg and Eduardo Saverin started Facebook out of their Harvard dorm. Facebook was similar to other social networking sites of the time, but entailed true identity friending, and was limited to Harvard students at its inception. These seemingly benign decisions started the network off on the right foot, and were fundamental to turning Facebook into the dominant social network over time compared to other similar social networks that did not quite get started with the right characteristics.

Facebook's membership base was then opened up to other Boston colleges, other Ivy League universities and soon universities around the country and world. The site unleashed the force of the consumer revolution to unprecedented proportions. Consumers around the world charged on board, connecting with friends and family, rediscovering long-lost friends and acquaintances, sharing and expressing their life events or just casual banter, essentially creating a private Internet of their own. Consumers expressed themselves via words, but especially, through pictures. In the safe confines of their social networks, they could have a virtual party, a virtual biography, a virtual conversation and virtual voyeurism any time they desired. Hello consumer revolution!

Facebook took off on a meteoric rise over the next decade. Young adults leapt on to the platform, followed to their dismay by their parents and soon grandparents. From a college social network, the site quickly grew into a worldwide network inclusive of all social, international, political and economic demographics.

By 2018, 1.4 billion people were logging on to Facebook every day—a stunning 19 per cent of all humanity.

Facebook became the de facto enabler of the consumer revolution when it came to communication and sharing, and became one of the most valuable and important companies in the world.

In 2005, three former PayPal executives, Chad Hurley, Steve Chen and Jawed Karim founded YouTube, which would soon revolutionize the world of video. YouTube enabled consumers to quickly and easily upload and share their videos with other consumers, setting off a frenzy of video publishing on the Internet. The consumer revolution seized this new tool and empowerment, and raced ahead with it. Coupled with plummeting costs of video creation and production, thanks to the proliferation of inexpensive video cameras, this efficient platform for video publishing and sharing unleashed a torrent of consumer expression in its richest, most visual form to date. YouTube was acquired by Google in 2006, and its growth and usage continued to soar. In 2018, the site reached an estimated 1.3 billion consumers. Almost 5 billion videos are watched on YouTube every day, and 300 hours of video are uploaded on the site every minute.

In 2006, Jack Dorsey, Noah Glass, Biz Stone and Evan Williams created Twitter. Twitter was different from other social networks, primarily in having a limited number of characters, 140, to convey an abbreviated message to connected consumers. This format found a sweet spot with consumers interested in the efficiency of communication. While Facebook and YouTube brought the barriers to publishing dramatically down for text, images and videos, they were still non-trivial barriers of effort.

Twitter brought the barrier and energy required to publish content substantially down by going in the reverse direction from rich media—a simple, short, text format. In recognition of the power of the consumer revolution, Twitter enabled the most effortless form of content creation and sharing. Usage took off, and by 2017, there were 330 million active users on Twitter. What this success demonstrated was that by enabling the scale of the consumer revolution, even in a specific niche, a service provider could build massive scale and value in a short amount of time.

THE NEW AGE APPLE FOR ADAM AND EVE

The social media tsunami took a major leap forward with the rollout of the iPhone in 2007. The combination of social networking and smartphones turned out to be a potent mix. The barriers to connecting and communicating, to publishing and consuming all forms of content, be it text, images or videos, came barrelling down. This unleashed yet another torrent of activity from consumers emboldened and empowered by the ease and comfort within which they could now express themselves. The universal need to communicate was now being enabled in the most powerful yet simplest ways to date.

In parallel with these breathtaking adoption rates for social networking service providers, another form of consumer communication was gathering even greater steam. Short message service, or SMS for short, was invented by Neil Papworth in the United Kingdom in 1992. This was an adaptation of radio telegraphy used in pagers, and provided a simple way for consumers to communicate with each other through short text messages. This simple utility took off like wildfire, reaching 3.5 billion active users by 2010 by enabling a simple but powerful need among consumers—to communicate efficiently. In the year 2010, users worldwide sent 6.1 trillion SMS messages, or 193,000 SMS messages per second!

The juxtaposition of text messaging and smartphones gave rise to a whole new breed of Internet capabilities and apps around the world. In the United States, two former Yahoo executives, Brian Acton and Jan Koum founded WhatsApp. The app quickly became a massive Internet hit by enabling a basic consumer need to communicate using their mobile phones in a simple, efficient manner. Rather than adding bells and whistles, and complexity to the product, WhatsApp won based on its pure simplicity, ease and ecosystem fit. Its popularity and consumer adoption caught the attention of Facebook, leading to the social media giant acquiring the company in 2014. Its adoption continued unabated, reaching an amazing 1.5 billion signups, and 300 million daily active users.

Facebook released its own Messenger in 2011. The service also took off in popularity, surpassing 1.3 billion active users by 2018, or more than one in ten humans on the planet. At the same time, 17 billion pictures were sent via Messenger, and fully 50 per cent of US teens used Messenger daily.

At around the same time, Apple introduced iMessage in the United States, Kik and Snapchat were launched in the United States, Line was launched in Japan, Skype was launched in Scandinavia, and WeChat was launched in China, each of those services surpassing 200 million in active users in short spans of time. These services started to add several rich features to serve consumers better, ranging from ease of finding and connecting with contacts, to communication formats ranging from the quick and efficient text message, to high-definition images and videos, giving consumers avenues to communicate and express themselves in myriad ways.

The development and proliferation of such a wide range of communication services tell a story. One of the consumer revolution in full flight. The telecommunication behemoths of yesteryear are now reduced to a fraction of their erstwhile market power and influence. Their rules and parameters defining how consumers could communicate with each other have significantly waned in relevance. Trying to launch a staid plain old telephone service in today's world would be sheer lunacy. That is because the consumer revolution has tasted blood. It has sampled the range of services on offer to whet its appetite for effective communication, and it isn't looking back. It is beginning to demand a wide range of conveniences and features, and technology providers are scrambling to deliver it to them. It is finding a place for the formal, as well as the playful styles of communication, all as appropriate, all as needed. The consumer revolution is demanding tools for every flavour and format of communication it desires, and providers are charging in to deliver it to them.

A fundamental consumer need is to connect with families, friends and acquaintances effortlessly, yet with maximum control. A whole host of social networking services, most notably Facebook, Twitter and LinkedIn are set up to enable true identity friending in effortless ways. Compare this with the old-world model of keeping track of numeric phone numbers, and searching reams of directory listings to find desired contacts, and there is no contest. Today's social networks win hands down. This is because they operate in the realm of the consumer. They operate in the domain that the consumer lives in. They fit in the lives of the consumer rather than the other way around. In contrast, phone companies operate in the domain of the producer—themselves. They require a translation from consumers to come over to their domain—by maintaining a map between people names and phone numbers for instance. They force a higher level of energy expended by consumers, when there is a lower-energy solution available via social networking. Prior to the Internet, consumers had to tax their brains keeping track of phone numbers—in diaries, or simply in their memory banks. This became an expertise in itself. The contemporary social networks obviate the need to do so. The utility of retaining otherwise meaningless numbers in our heads is rapidly going down. Just try recalling the phone numbers of your ten closest family or friends, and you will see how far we have come already.

Similarly, searching for contacts that consumers want to connect and communicate with has also been dramatically affected by the consumer revolution. Prior to its onset, consumers were required to recall someone's complete name, and then pore through pages of fine-print directory listings to track down the required contact information. This required non-trivial effort, leading to a limit on how extensively consumers would research out to find anyone but essential contacts. This friction in finding and communicating with potential beneficial contacts had a chilling effect on the levels of collaborations consumers were able to achieve.

Contemporary social networks have made it far more efficient to find and connect with contacts, even with limited or erroneous recall. It is extremely easy to search on the Internet for contacts even with limited information, and when found, to connect with them. The consumer revolution has demanded better service and convenience, refusing to put up with old school directory services and barriers to making contact. And service providers have been scrambling to adapt, and get on the right side of it. Those that have are winning handsomely in the market. Those that haven't, powerful as they might have been in their prime, are on an inexorable slide towards oblivion.

Another dimension of communication that the consumer revolution has disrupted status quo in is the formats of communication. In the old world order, consumers could send a written letter in a matter of days or weeks. They could make a phone call at a price set by the service provider, using handsets provided by the service provider. If you had a problem with either, you were plain out of luck.

Or consumers could also choose to send a very limited amount of written communication at very expensive prices, using specialized telegraphy equipment at the sending and receiving locations, managed and controlled by service providers.

The consumer revolution was not satisfied with those stringent service provider limitations. It demanded the ability to communicate with anyone, from anywhere, at any time consumers desired. Unable to meet these evolving requirements, the infrastructure and framework established for consumers by old school service providers started to crumble.

The consumer revolution demanded a greater range of communication options. It demanded quick, easy, efficient communication via text messages. Along came SMS, WeChat, Skype and other chat services to address that need. Text chat fills a unique void in the communication spectrum, between phone calls and email. Consumers were not satisfied with those two extremes in their spectrum of needs, and wedged a chat solution in between to meet their exact needs.

The consumer revolution demanded a richer set of expressions than what written text or voice calls could provide. Along came Instagram, Snapchat and YouTube to give them many more forms of expression. Try forcing consumers today to limit communication to written text and voice calls only, and you will see the kind of reaction that will produce! The consumer revolution is marching, and it will not retreat.

The consumer revolution also demanded more control over who to communicate what to. In the old world order, consumers could write and speak with others, one person at a time. Or they could write and speak with others en masse. The parameters were firmly established by service providers, and there were no interim parameters and variations permitted.

Then along came Facebook and LinkedIn, and enabled consumers to pick and choose exactly what they wanted to communicate and to whom. They could communicate efficiently with one person, as cryptically and as elaborately as they preferred. Or they could communicate with a group as broad or narrow as they desired and permitted. Or they could communicate with the world at large. The consumer revolution expressed its will, and service providers emerged to become corporate behemoths by addressing their new found needs.

#THECOMMUNICATIONREVOLUTION

One important development in the arena of enabling consumers to congregate and rally around a cause was the hashtag, or #. The origins of the hashtag lay in computer programing languages of the 1970s and 1980s, where it was used to connote special meaning or special treatment for the keyword that followed. In 1988, Internet relay chats began to use hashtags to label topics. This inspired Chris Messina to propose the use of the hashtag to indicate any group, cause or purpose in 2007.

Since then, the hashtag has developed into a major organizing and rallying force of the consumer revolution. It empowers any consumer to anoint and enable a cause with the greatest of ease, and other consumers to band together on the cause just as easily. The hashtag has brought the barriers to congregation dramatically down, and has become a critical enabler of the consumer revolution. You only need to look as has as #MeToo, #BlackLivesMatter and #NeverAgain to see how powerful a force this has become.

The enthralling question now is where will the consumer revolution in communication go next?

To extrapolate, it is illustrative to look at the past trajectory and extrapolate forward. The consumer revolution is gathering momentum and seizing more power relentlessly. It will next demand better connection capabilities. How can service providers raise their capabilities when it comes to enabling consumers to connect better? By enabling better people search engines, for one. Today, the primary index for connecting with people is searching by their names. That indexing mechanism is still too service provider-driven. Consumers see the name as just one attribute associated with a person. That same person has countless other attributes that should also be searchable. For instance, people searching with queries like 'the guy I used to play tennis with on weekends at Santa Barbara' or 'that girl I used to have lunch with at high school'. Consumers are going to expect higher value-add people searches catering to their unique, contextual associations, the same way they do it in their regular lives in the physical world. The same way people refer to others by name, association, context, or other indexes, they will expect to do so as the consumer revolution gathers further momentum. Limiting people searches to by name is going to become as archaic as keeping track of people's phone numbers.

A variation of higher value-add connecting is going to become consumers connecting with others they don't even know, but should. Think of a delightful party, where you met five new people you had never met before, but found remarkably engaging and engrossing. Why? Because the hostess introduced you to the right five people she knew you would get along with.

Now amplify this a billionfold. We are just scratching the surface of social networking. The next big frontier will be finding you friends you didn't even know existed. Specialty sites and apps such as Match.com, eharmony and Tinder are making progress doing this in small use cases, but there is a massive appetite in consumers for befriending new fellow humans, not merely for the purposes of dating. Entire new generations of machine learning algorithms will be deployed to find new friends for consumers, and service providers for developing and delivering this service will become astronomical winners in the corporate landscape.

One giant requirement in this realm that the consumer revolution will demand is, again, trust. How can consumers be assured that the person they think they are connecting with is in fact the person of interest. This is true when consumers use social networks to connect with others known to them in advance. It is even more critical when consumers use technology service providers as the 'party hostess' to find them matching consumers of interest. With communication and interaction across far-flung corners of the world, it is incredibly important to have trust in communication—that you are in fact communicating with the person you think you are communicating with.

As with information, one of the most promising technologies developing to validate trust in communication is blockchain. Connectivity across trustable consumers is too critical a function to leave to a centralized, profit-making enterprises. The only entity trustable with the authenticity of connections in the consumer revolution is the revolution itself. This is likely to give rise to blockchain-based solutions that guarantee trust as determined by the network itself, likely bolstered and secured by state governments further buttressing the legitimacy of connectivity across the network. Ensuring the integrity of connection and communication across consumers is going to become one of the most important responsibilities of governments around the world.

As with access to information, access to communication between people is a critical and essential artery of humankind. Regulatory authorities around the world need to take a very close look at how the early days of the consumer revolution are playing out when it comes to communication. This is a core utility that the consumer revolution is built on, and any attempt to mediate, manipulate or monetize such a fundamental link between consumers has disastrous implications. Instead of the cursory review and analysis of these dynamics, government officials chartered with ensuring the public good need to go through a rigorous analysis of the status quo and trend line, and get ahead of it by instituting strong controls and policies to protect consumers from rabid exploitation and deception.

There are other trust elements associated with securing communication across the digital landscape up to the standards that will be demanded by the consumer revolution. An example of this is how secure is the line of communication between the parties in conversation. There is a long history of wiretapping and hijacking conversations on the Internet. Some of it is lawful, such as governments listening in on conversations in lawful, authorized manners, and others are unlawful and often fraudulent and malicious.

The consumer revolution will absolutely insist on secure and private communication between conversing parties. It will reward trusted, secure communication channels handsomely, creating a wide open market opportunity for service providers in this arena.

There will be some tussles ahead over communication security between consumers, their governments and security apparatus, service providers looking to monetize their connectivity services and malicious forces trying to abuse the system for their personal gains. Consumers will demand secure and private communication to fully harness the power of the Internet for communication. Security organizations and the state itself will have legitimate requirements to listen in on conversations to track down illegal activity and subterfuge. Service providers will juggle a difficult balance between enabling the consumer revolution with better and better tools, and also monetizing them in bigger and bigger ways. And adversary states and criminal organizations will try to abuse the system wherever they can for their personal gains. A battle royale is getting underway between these formidable forces, and it is imperative for government officials to step in with laws that ensure the right balance between them all.

Service providers that align with the consumer revolution and enable this desire amongst consumers to protect their interactions and communications from others will proliferate rapidly. The meteoric rise of Snapchat, with its ability to convey information and then vanish, provided a window into this consumer need. However, other business limitations have since slowed down this rise, as the consumer revolution is very quick to pass judgment in either direction.

These advances aside, the biggest advances in telecommunication will come from enriching it to the point of lifelike human communication.

Let's take audio—simple voice-based communication. The gold standard here is you talking to your friend in person—in the same room or immediate vicinity. There is an effortlessness to the conversation. You don't have to strain to catch a word. You don't have to strain to catch an intonation. You have all the non-verbal cues to assist in your comprehension. This is the highest fidelity communication you can have. This is also what you have gotten accustomed to in your daily life, after centuries of conditioning and evolution. This is communication in its most natural and efficient state.

Now take traditional, landline phone-based communication. Over the past hundred years, many billions of dollars have been spent enhancing the technology and services for phone lines. The technology itself is fascinating. It began with voice communication transmitted over copper wires. It then evolved to a superior technology for transmitting voice communication—fibre optics cables. Fibre optic cables were invented all the way back in the 1790s, by the Chappe brothers in France. Fibre optics technology was used to transmit light signals in its original incarnation. In wasn't until the late 1970s and early 1980s that telecommunication giants began to use fibre optics to transmit voice communication more precisely and economically across great distances. In the mid-1980s, Sprint launched its network entirely based on a digital fibre optics-based technology.

Despite all the telecommunication advances to date, the quality of phone communication does not yet mirror in-person communication. The consumer revolution will demand that be addressed in time.

The quality of voice communication degraded further with the proliferation of cellular phone-based communication, and even further with Internet-based telephony. In 2016, for the first time, cell phone service accounted for 50.8 per cent of US homes, whereas landline phone service fell to 45.9 per cent. The mobility and flexibility of cell phone-based communication are unmatched of course, and the voice quality is acceptable to most consumers. For now.

Internet telephony as a technology began as early as 1973, but did not get commercialized as a service until 1995 when VocalTec launched the first Internet-based phone service. The technology advanced in leaps and bounds, seeing the emergence of large, successful service providers such as Vonage, RingCentral and Skype as major winners in the market. They have enabled easy and inexpensive telecommunication across the world, especially for international communication which has been typically under-served by landline and cellular phone service providers.

While Internet telephony has made baseline levels of communication possible for consumers, the quality of communication leaves much to be desired. Despite all the technology and bandwidth enhancements, the sound quality is still quite subpar, sound glitches still happen because of lost data packets, and time lags still happen leading to communication by turns rather than the free-flowing natural communication we are all used to in our daily lives.

The consumer revolution will not accept these limitations. It will force service providers to keep raising call quality to the level of a face-to-face live conversation so that there is truly no difference from talking to someone in person versus via telecommunication.

The next sensory dimension to consider in consumer communication is visual. Sight is invaluable in effective human communication. Beyond the words we speak, the sounds we make, we send out an enormous amount of signal value in our non-verbal gestures. We have all been through experiences when a simple 'yes' can carry widely varying messages based on the expression on a person's face when they said it, their body language, their cadence, their hand signals and other non-verbal cues. And once you add more complexity to the words being spoken, the non-verbal cues multiply in significance and value.

Service providers recognized this need for the visual element of communication in inventing video telephony. In the 1920s, John Logie Baird in conjunction with AT&T's Bell Labs invented the first video telephonic communication. By today's standards, the video was of poor quality—both grainy and choppy—but it enabled consumers to look at each other during a conversation for the first time. The costs of video telephony in its infancy were prohibitive, and the overall process required special end-point equipment to conduct a conversation, which lead to the technology being mostly used in business settings.

The advent of the Internet brought about the next generation of video telecommunications. Video transmittal over the Internet, or TCP/IP, brought about a skyrocketing use of video telephony.

The democratization of the technology brought about a proliferation of usage amongst consumers—to see family and friends, and colleagues they were conversing with, rather than being limited to just voice. Coupled with the broadening standardization and deployments of video cameras, this produced a tremendous explosion in the usage of video amongst consumers. Around the world, grandmas were thrilled to see their precious grandchildren during a conversation. Friends were delighted to connect visually while talking. Singles were able to have unprecedented ability to see each other during conversation, leading to the rapid expansion of Internet dating. Mobile applications such as WhatsApp and FaceTime have grown dramatically by addressing these consumer needs to communicate more visually, yet with great ease and economy.

In business settings, video telephony led to a dramatic increase in business done over the Internet. The ability to see colleagues you were having a business discussion with while conducting business made a material difference to the need to travel for business meetings. Interviewing candidates across distances became far easier, obviating a need for interview travel. Services such as Skype and GoTo Conference flourished by addressing these evolving consumer needs.

One consumer need that progressed in leaps and bounds was distance education. The untethering of teacher and pupil ushered in by video-based education lead to a massive increase in online colleges and distance learning. This dramatically expanded the reach of teachers, and served a vast need in consumers to learn and receive a better education, further unleashed by the time-delayed nature of recorded video training sessions. Online education providers such as University of Phoenix and Capella University have thrived by serving this new requirement being demanded by the consumer revolution, and major mainstream universities have followed suit to service this clearly apparent consumer need in the market.

An adjacent technology to video telephony was screen sharing. The ability for two or more people to look at the same shared screen at the same time enabled a powerful advancement in distance communication, by further simulating the environment of having a conversation with others in the same room. Google Hangouts, Join.me and others have productized this capability in very effective ways, leading to commendable success in the market.

The consumer revolution, thus is demanding more and more service in more and more use cases enabled by video telecommunication. A generation of technology and service providers have prospered by serving the demands of consumers.

The consumer revolution however is far from done. It has an insatiable appetite for better quality and service in video telephony. It will demand a relentless increase in service quality until it reaches that of physical human communication. Glitches and lags will be tolerated less and less. Picture quality will be required to reach the fidelity of in-person visual detail. In fact, the consumer revolution will force picture quality to surpass in-person visual quality. It will demand video quality enhancement even if either conversationalist is in a darkened or dimly lit room. It will demand ambient noise reduction so you can see and hear your colleague in even greater fidelity than if you were together in person in a noisy room or arena.

The consumer revolution is not going to care where the shortcomings come from, it is just going to demand that they are driven entirely away. If the video camera has limitations, or the Internet bandwidth is limited, the consumer revolution will demand service providers to identify, diagnose and fix the impending problem even before it happens. This will create a host of opportunities for today's service providers, or a whole new generation of technologies to meet the escalating needs of consumers.

The consumer revolution will also demand value-added video telephony. For instance, it will seek augmented video, where additional context about conversationalists, such as their authorized professional details, biographies and public statements are presented seamlessly with the video during live conversation, enhancing each participant's gestalt signal quality from the conversation. This will present massive new opportunities to entirely new generations of technology and service providers. This might be today's video telecommunication providers, or it might be today's augmented reality providers, or a fusion of the two, but anticipating and serving this insatiable appetite of the consumer revolution to be better served in video communication will bring handsome rewards to solution providers delivering it.

Another variation of this desire in consumers to connect and communicate will be through virtual reality and holograms. The consumer revolution will demand more and more realistic, three-dimensional (3D) communication across its constituents. Consumers will want to see each other in a 3D visual format, as in real life, and not a two-dimensional flat screen representation of it. Service providers enabling this capability will profit tremendously from enabling it.

One aspect of a real-life conversation found wanting in the digital world is security and privacy—both malicious as well as accidental. Consumers have seen the adverse consequences of communication hijacked or otherwise reaching unintended audience's, either in real time, or after time delays. Imagine the plight of the thrilled high schooler being admitted to Harvard University, only to have the offer later rescinded upon discovery of their offensive Facebook posts. Or an excited new hire at a company immediately terminated upon unintended discovery of their Instagram posts. The consumer revolution will demand better security and privacy safeguards in these regards. It will reward service providers who deliver as secure communication as real-life conversations can get. In particular, it will reward service providers who ensure that video communication is ephemeral. The sanctity of a real-life conversation is compromised if the video conversation is saved on servers and retrievable at a later time by skilled hackers. Consumers will hence reward service providers handsomely for making their video communication disappear permanently after they are done, if that is their preference.

As with everything else, the shape of things to come is being fashioned by consumers, not producers. Consumers have a taste of the power they wield, and are asserting it now with gay abandon. Service providers who address their burgeoning desires stand to gain tremendously from it.

The consumer revolution's appetite for distance communication will not stop merely at perfecting today's sensory dimensions. It will require that entirely new dimensions of human interaction be served by technology producers and service providers.

Take the sense of touch. It is one of the fundamental senses and mediums of communication in a live human setting. In fact, the most primal and the most original. We have all experienced the communication power of a hug. Or of a kiss. Or a high five. Or a slap!

Tracing back human roots, touch might even have been the first form of communication between humans. And yet, we have barely scratched the surface when it comes to touch-based communication over the Internet. The producer ecosystem is in its infancy when it comes to communicating physical contact. The consumer revolution will demand that this change. It will demand that its expectations to have human communication be of the calibre of an in-person meeting be met.

This means that there will need to be a whole new generation of input and output devices for touch. Beyond a point, consumers will no longer accept being limited to either a keyboard, a mouse, a microphone or a video camera for inputting and outputting information. They will demand a proliferation of devices that can input and output sensory contact. You will literally be able to reach out and touch someone who has authorized you for this. And they will be able to touch you back if you have permitted them to do so. You will just be sensing and expressing through devices.

Entire new forms of input and out devices will be born. Your device might take the form of a pillow. It might take the form of a massage chair. It might take the form of a brush. Or it might even take the form of a simulated person!

A major derivative of this consumer desire will be artificial intelligence coupled with these sensory devices or simulated humans. Artificial intelligence is already enabling human-like conversation and mobility skills. It is only natural that once technology and service providers can create sensory input and output devices, they can be used for human-triggered responses, as well as human-like machine triggered responses. The implications of this innovation and the capabilities this can deliver are, of course, mind-boggling. So much so that this will require careful government scrutiny and regulation that the products and services on offer are working in the interest of the general public good, and heading off unlawful or unethical practices well before they begin to take shape.

The societal impact of sensory devices are difficult to understate. The ability of consumers to give each other hugs, kisses or smacks, further compounded by machine learning sensory devices will have a profound impact on consumers. The area is fraught with challenges, not the least of which are ethical in nature. But the consumer revolution will stop at nothing less. If it can demand every form of written content and communication, audio content and communication, video content and communication, it will not stop at anything less for sensory content and communication.

As with other expressions of consumer will, this one will create massive new opportunities for technology and service providers to service their needs for sensory expression. Billions of wearable and other sensory devices will need to be created, and consumers will have an insatiable appetite for them. Producers addressing this demand will stand to gain handsomely for their efforts.

Other far-flung applications of lifelike communication might develop out of the consumers' relentless drive for better experiences. For instance, another of our core senses is smell. It is conceivable that the consumer revolution might require providers to invent devices that release fragrances on demand. Imagine sending a picture of bouquet of roses to someone special, and as they open it to view, there is the fragrance of roses released to make the experience even more lifelike for the recipient. Or fragrances released on cue from the sending of a digital birthday cake or someone's favourite perfume whenever they come on video for a live conversation. After all, scent is one of the most powerful associations humans are capable of—it makes perfectly logical sense to layer that on to human communication.

The other primary sense consumers are endowed with is taste. It is conceivable that consumers might desire the ability to send culinary experiences to each other. Think of 3D printing capabilities coupled with kitchen racks, ovens, ingredients and condiments. It seems far-fetched, but consumers could potentially prepare exceptional dishes for others operating their recipes and supplies remotely. The fulfilment and gratification from grandma being able to bake cookies or your favourite desert from her remote location would be priceless!

The consumer revolution in communication is thus demanding more and more real and lifelike communications and interactions between humans. It will, in fact, start demanding better than life-like interaction, communication fidelity and fulfilment. Technology providers that can service this need will benefit massively from it. Providers that don't will be left with relentlessly diminishing profits and proceeds.

The consumer revolution is taking distance communication to entirely different levels, each more far-fetched than the other. In time, you can envision a conversation with a family member around the world where they sound as clear as if in the same room, look as clear as if in the same room and give you a handshake or a hug as if in the same room! The consumer revolution will settle for nothing less.

The next frontier for the consumer revolution in communication could well be at the intersection of individual identity and artificial intelligence. It is quite conceivable that consumers will begin to harness augmented intelligence afforded them by the consumer revolution in information to develop augmented identity! In other words, consumers will be able to leverage the connectivity power of the Internet and artificial intelligence to augment aspects of their identity that they wish to augment. For instance, they could grant themselves exceptional empathy, or exceptional emotional intelligence as a way to better connect and energize others in their digital circles. This is so their identities become tailored and augmented to achieve the connections they desire.

Taken a step further, the consumer revolution in communication could next go to scenarios where the digital person you are connecting with isn't a person at all, but purely an artificial identity spawned off or created by someone for some purpose in mind. With sufficient information and sufficient connectivity links, artificial intelligence will be able to create digital identities and personas that are indistinguishable from actual human beings. And you will get all the fulfilment and gratification in interacting with these artificial identities as you do from interacting with a genuine, true human being!

And when you couple the power of an in-person like one-on-one interaction with anyone else in the world—actual or synthetic—with the mass connectivity of the consumer revolution, you have the ingredients for the most powerful nuclear explosion of human energy. The potential for each human interaction to trigger energy in both, multiply to many others, feed on itself and create a veritable explosion of energy and action. At any point of time, any event or phenomena in any corner of the world has the potential to become a tidal wave of human energy that can move mountains and part oceans. Understanding and enabling this fear-some force in the right ways, to serve the intended consequences, is of paramount importance to human societies and their govern-ment representatives. Doing so will usher in a glorious new era of human energy and creativity around the world.

5

REWIRING
RELATIONSHIPS

Few things touch us as deeply and intensely over the course
of our lives as our own personal relationships. They define us,
they shape us and they anchor us. They are the bridges that the
English author John Donne meant when he famously said 'No
man is an island'. We live most of our lives surrounded by our most
important personal relationships. We spend the bulk of our time,
our emotions and our energy dedicated to them, and we draw the
deepest of our joys and fulfilment from them.

Think of the most important relationships in your life. Your
parents, your siblings, your significant other, your children,
your friends. Beyond that your team mates, your co-workers, your
neighbours, your community friends. You draw so much from
your personal relationships in your micro, day-to-day lives. You
give so much of yourself back into your personal relationships.
They constitute the single biggest influence in your life.

Interpersonal relationships have been the foundation of human
society since its inception. Our ancestors picked up where the
primates left off when it came to relationships. The earliest relationships were biological in nature of course—consisting of mates

for procreating, and mother–child for nurturing and sustenance. These relationships were essential for survival and the propagation of the species. They were also primal, pristine and unambiguous in nature. That made them a class apart from the various other forms of relationships that emerged in human society over time.

These biological and mating relationships developed and evolved in many ways from their primate roots. True, life-long monogamy is a very rare occurrence in the animal kingdom overall, as it turns out. What is a bit more commonplace is social monogamy, where mates come together for a breeding season or longer to procreate and raise offspring. Even social monogamy is limited to only 3 to 5 per cent of the 5,000 or so species of mammals in the world—a clear minority of the various species inhabiting the earth. So creatures, as a rule, don't do relationships much!

There are various theories and hypotheses regarding when and why human beings turned predominantly monogamous, but there isn't a great deal of consensus on the subject. One theory that has been put forth is that human offspring needed a longer period of child-rearing and protection for the greater mental development associated with the human brain. This in turn created a genetic instinct among fathers to protect and provide for their offspring, for sharing responsibilities with mothers, and hence staying monogamous.

Other theories have also been put forth to explain this curious development in the human race. Some attribute it to a defence mechanism against the rampant spread of diseases proliferated by polygamy. Others characterize it as a mechanism to manage and allocate wealth and resources, such as ensuring that the wealth of two families was preserved through marriage and monogamy.

Regardless of the precise reasons for this phenomenon, humans have developed into deeply interconnected, relationship-oriented social creatures. Around their core biological relationships, humans have built myriad other relationship structures, each with an end purpose at its core. The core mother–child and mating relationships naturally expanded into sibling and extended family relationships over time. Human social and emotional development made sure that expanding families didn't lose contact with each other as they grew, maintaining and building on relationships over time, even as sub-units began to venture away from each other in search of livelihoods and opportunities.

Human relationships took a quantum leap forward as humans progressed from being nomadic hunters to becoming agrarian settlers. The effect was a dramatic deepening of relationships within neighbourhoods and communities, as human beings came in frequent and recurring contact with others in the communities. Humans became increasingly social creatures, and substantial relationships with friends, neighbours and community members emerged.

With further societal development came other affiliations and organizations. As farms grew bigger, owners began to employ farm help, leading to employment relationships formed between people who worked for employers or with each other. As schools and colleges developed, academic relationships were formed between students and teachers, and amongst students themselves. In fact, as every facet of human society developed, interpersonal relationships of one kind or another formed its foundation.

In the entire course of human history up to this point, however, relationships were predominantly defined by physical proximity. Family members, neighbours, friends, community members were all people we came in frequent personal contact with. Whether we formed relationships for fun, entertainment, work or any other common cause, we inevitably bandied together physically and frequently to deepen and leverage our relationships. Physical proximity was thus a major determinant of who we formed interpersonal relationships with, with very few exceptions.

Another unique characteristic of human relationships up until this point was that they were heavily shaped by a predefined natural order. While people did form new relationships with others that they came in contact with, many of their deepest relationships were mandated or even preordained in a way. Take a traditional parent–child relationship. While there were many different flavours and tenors around the world, the fundamental nature of this relationship was still one of the nurturer and the nurtured, the protector and the protected, the provider and the provided, the teacher and the pupil. There was a natural order of authority flowing from the parent to the child, until the child reached adulthood and was able to strike out independently.

This natural order was reinforced in many ways. Since as far back as a child could recall, the parent was almost always stronger, larger, wiser, better informed, better resourced and better equipped. All through their growing years, children were socialized to the authority and care of their parents. This became a deep-seated value—more pronounced in certain parts of the world such as Asia and South America than others, but always there. This relationship had a profound impact on the shape of human lives.

Many other interpersonal relationships had similar preordained patterns. Siblings were expected to be close together, especially in their early years, the perennial sibling rivalries and quarrels notwithstanding. Except the older sibling automatically assumed a position of authority, simply by virtue of their age and the natural strength in intellect and physique that came with it. Age, as it turned out, was one of the biggest determinants of authority and influence in interpersonal relationships.

Similarly, in communities and villages, the village elder auto-matically assumed a position of authority and power. Others in the community defined their role in society, and their interpersonal relationships in reference to societal leaders and chiefs and elders. Age, again, was one of the most salient determinants of interper-sonal authority and structure. But also, the relationship was defined by where people lived, what their pre-existing social structure was and what the established leadership norms were. Order was maintained and propagated in keeping with tradition.

Another flavour of interpersonal relationships that had a natural order to it was one between teachers and pupils. Once students entered an educational institution, such as a school or college, that essentially defined a whole set of interpersonal relationships for them. This included relationships with faculty members as well as peer relationships with other students. In all these instances, people had to operate within the parameters of such a predefined relationship, and had limited flexibility to venture outside of those pre-established norms.

As a matter of fact, all organizations that humans belonged to had their own parameters, norms and guidelines within which its constituents were required to operate and relate to one another. These norms provided stability and structure within their organizations—be they educational, commercial or militaristic in nature. Among other things, these norms dictated fairly precise interpersonal dynamics and relationships, and members of these organizations were typically bound by them.

Another fundamental characteristic that has defined interpersonal relationships through the course of human history is their relative longevity. Human beings are social creatures that have historically persisted with their relationships for extended periods of time, typically years or even entire lifetimes. Human relationships have been defined by purpose and meaning, if not actual mandates, and that has led to a nurturing and development of deep interpersonal relationships over time. This has resulted in an innate stability and sustenance of structure in human societies, providing a stable reference frame by which humans have defined themselves for eons. Not only is no man an island, but every man is rather well connected and linked with other human beings in well-defined and predictable patterns that stay stable across extended periods of time!

Put together, these characteristics of human relationships have thus meant a gestalt perspective on relationships, where you related to your family and friends across most of their dimensions and personality traits, over extended periods of time. You structured and sustained your relationships with your significant others, your parents, your siblings, your neighbours, your teachers, your bosses, your friends, holistically. You accepted them as a whole person— with all their plusses and minuses—and adapted yourself to their quirks and characteristics in order to make the best of the relationships you have. You might even have put up with undesirable traits in your relations simply because they were there, they were your core network, and they weren't going to be going away. You acquiesced at every turn when you needed to in order to accommodate the important relationships in your life.

At the same time, you invested your time, energy and emotion heavily in making each relationship be the best it could be for you. You worked at it. You adapted yourself to fit each relationship and each situation. You sacrificed for the common cause and the common good. You gave a bit of yourself to ensure that the greater bond was preserved and nurtured as much as possible.

Think of all the times you listened to your parents or teachers and obeyed, even when it wasn't remotely pleasant or desirable. Think of all the times you changed your behaviours and patterns to accommodate a boss, a superior or an elder that you came in contact with. Think of all the times you sacrificed your personal optimum to ensure that your significant other or your family member was well taken care of. Collectively, human society invested enormous amounts of emotion and energy cultivating and growing interpersonal relationships. It just became a cost of doing business in the societies and structures we lived in, and we all got accustomed to making these pragmatic investments.

All that is now beginning to change. Profoundly.

THE TIMES THEY ARE A-CHANGIN'

The consumer revolution is beginning to take centuries of norms on human relationships in its throes, and churn them into something radically different!

Take the centrality of physical proximity in interpersonal relationships. Unlike ever before in human history, the consumer revolution is putting people in digital proximity with billions of others around the globe. That means billions of potential relationships to be struck at a moment's notice. That means infinite choice in who you want to befriend at any point of time, for any reason whatsoever. That means a dramatic expansion in the number of potential relationships you have access to at any time. It is as if you just went from a room with a few dozen of your close relationships to a colosseum with billions of potential ones!

Imagine the impact this will have on your traditional relationships. As consumers get more and more drawn into their revolution, the significance of physical proximity in establishing relationships is bound to fade. Digital relationships are now beginning to form, and grow stronger and more meaningful in rapid progression. What began as brief and insipid information-sharing touchpoints between people digitally during the early days of the Internet are now beginning to develop into meaningful mental and even emotional bonds—across the room or across the planet. As technology matures, the natural connectivity needs of human beings continues to shape its direction in ways that serve their needs. As a result, the desire for human contact and interpersonal engagement is beginning to increasingly be met over the pipes of the consumer revolution.

The natural corollary to this is that the consumer revolution is starting to alter the landscape of our traditional in-person relationships, and in fact might even begin to supplant some of them over time. Physical proximity is starting to become less and less pertinent, and consumers are instead starting to be closely connected with others they have mental and emotional proximity with over the Internet. The writing is already on the wall. Parents around the world are starting to complain about children 'stuck to their phones' all their waking hours, even while on trips or sightseeing forays. Memes are being sent around with couples having dinners while glued to their respective phones across the table from each other.

Physical, in-person conversation is dwindling as the consumer revolution draws its constituents into its digital folds. Physical relationships are weakening as digital ones strengthen. The battle for consumers' mind share and heart share is on, and digital relationships are surging in the wake of the consumer revolution. Relationships in the immediate physical vicinity are diminishing in purpose and value, and an entirely new mosaic of digital relationships is emerging in its place. Human relationships are undergoing a protracted metamorphosis and hurtling towards an entirely new equilibrium.

The intriguing question is why are digital relationships on the rise and physical relationships on the decline? What is it about their nature that is appealing to consumers in greater and greater degrees? Choice, as it turns out; massive amounts of choice, all accessible in an instant. In the digital realm consumers can actually choose their relationships with others they like. Once you take the physical proximity constraint away, the choices for potential relationships expand dramatically. Instead of being limited to a few dozen preordained relationships, consumers now have the choice to connect to any one from billions. The result of this expanded selection is much greater ability to find the right relationships, and benefit from them. The consumer revolution is serving up interpersonal relationships that are far more on the side of the consumer than traditional in-person relationships, and consumers are gobbling it up! As in every other way, any offering that enables and empowers consumers more than the status quo overtakes it in no time, and interpersonal relationships are no different. This is producing quite a sea change in our relationship dynamics.

Another characteristic that is enabling this massive expansion in choice for digital relationships is the fact that they do not need to be preordained or mandated. Unlike in the physical world, in the digital world there are no predefined relationships to cater to. Every relationship can be a fresh new beginning, if that's the consumers' desire. There are no obligations and responsibilities to live up to, there need be no accountability, and no relationships that consumers have to enter into by mandate or by fiat. It is all utterly by choice. It is all about who they want to connect with, and for what reasons they want to connect.

For the first time in human history, consumers are able to forge relationships with anyone they like anywhere in the world for any reason they choose.

This is emerging to be a profound difference in the nature of human relationships, and its impact on traditional, physical world human relationships. Unshackling consumers from preordained relationships is facilitating a radical departure from the fabric of human society today.

Digital relationships are also fundamentally different from in-person relationships in another significant way. Physical world relationships tend to be longer in term, most often lasting months, years or even a lifetime. This is because they are borne out of our core biological and physical existence, our day-to-day living, our livelihoods, and those relationships are inherently longer-term. They require the commitment, the dedication, the energy, the nurturing and the compromises that are required to make long-term relationships sustain and flourish. They require effort, in fact they demand effort, in order to get the purpose, value and benefits they are intended for.

Digital relationships, on the other hand, can be positively fleeting by comparison. They do not require biological or social antecedents to come together, and they do not have the same barriers and consequences when they come apart. Consumers can connect with others for the briefest of interactions, about the briefest of interests, and then move on to other interests and relationships. Digital relationships thus require far less effort and commitment to nurture and sustain over time, while still serving a very direct purpose at a given moment in time. Instant gratification without the effort and commitment. The fast food of human relationships. And consumers are signing up en masse!

Empowering consumers to form on demand relationships only when they are of interest or relevance to them, and then being able to abandon them whenever they like has a profound effect on their behaviour. It introduces freedom, spontaneity, pursuit of passions, liberation and instant gratification. It stokes the fires of the consumer revolution. It unleashes extraordinary levels of human energy as their interests, desires and impulses take flight in the moment. It facilitates whole new levels of relationship building on impulse, convenience, expediency and chemistry. The compounding effect of this energy release is profound and akin to nuclear fusion. And it is forging an entirely new chapter in the structure of human society.

INSTANT GRATIFICATION AND VALIDATION

The surge towards digital relationships is also however beginning to rattle traditional social and in-person relationship norms in major ways. When central, lasting, anchoring relationships in human lives are replaced by transient, transactional, interest-based ones, the core fabric of human society as we know it begins to get frayed. Interpersonal relationships are hence starting to become increasingly short-lived and issues-based. Social structure is on the beginning stages of becoming increasingly fluid, dynamic and thematic.

This is a radical departure from interpersonal relationships as we know them. Think about what this all means. Think of the core relationships in your life. Significant others, parents, children, siblings, neighbours, friends, bosses, colleagues, employees, teachers and students. All of these close relationships have the potential to weaken over time as the consumer revolution begins to take hold. As the revolution grows bigger and bigger, its siren call on consumer relationships will continue to grow exponentially too, increasing the proportion of human relationships that are formed online, at the expense of relationships that were once formed in person.

The consumer revolution will thus redefine the very nature of interpersonal relationships. The very foundation of human society can, in effect, change in the course of this transformation. So much so that in sufficient time the consumer revolution might even begin to supplant these long-standing, staple human relationships with dynamic, new, fleeting, virtual ones. There will be a loss of stability that humans are accustomed to, for sure. But in its place will appear a new equilibrium, where humans get accustomed to thousands of short-lived relationships instead of a few deep, long-lasting ones.

There are many far-reaching consequences of this transition. Traditional anchor relationships serve as major structural stabilizers in people's lives. They often provide the first checkpoints for people on views, opinions, reactions and emotions. They become effective sounding boards and affective counsel for most people. As part of this, they also serve to dampen overreactions and extreme emotional swings by injecting a heavy dose of pragmatic realism in most situations. In effect, they tend to draw you to the mainstream—a regression to the mean of sorts.

A change in the fundamental nature of human relationships thus can have a fundamental impact on views and beliefs in society. In particular, the consumer revolution also has the potential to make human attitudes more extreme and radicalized. This is because no matter what your individual point of view, you can find someone else in the digital world with the same exact point of view. If you hold a belief that progressive, liberal policies are the best for your country, you can easily find others with the same beliefs. If on the other hand you hold a belief that conservative policies are the best for your country, you can find plenty of others with that belief set too. If you hold the belief that climate change will wreck the planet then you can find validation for that. If you want to believe that Ronaldo is better than Messi, you can find validation for that too. If you want to believe that the Earth is flat and Martians have landed, you can find validation for that too!

Without the dampening effect of close interpersonal relationships, it will become far easier for consumers to lock in on their view and opinions, however radical or extreme. The consumer revolution makes it convenient and lightning fast to find others who agree with you, thereby multiplying both people's convictions. It will thus make it far easier to dig in on beliefs, get entrenched in mindsets and locked down on convictions.

In contrast with traditional relationships, digital relationships in the consumer revolution will prompt increasing radicalization, polarization and hence conflict.

Compounding the entrenchment in people's positions ensuing from one-on-one digital interactions, the new relationship structure is also very prone to groupthink. It is easy to congregate in rapidly growing groups of people with similar beliefs, reinforcing the convictions of the entire group. It is also easy to cut out any dissenting voice in the group and to not even engage in meaningful debate on any of the issues. It is far more gratifying to find an endorsing voice than to debate an opposing one. This is leading to an increasing polarization in society, unlike any seen before.

In many different countries around the world, and in many different situations and scenarios, there are increasing instances of polarization and radicalization to be found. In the United States, as an example, the political landscape and discourse is becoming increasingly polarized, vitriolic and uncompromising. Both sides of the political spectrum—liberal as well as conservative—are getting increasingly polarized and entrenched in their views. Even at an issues level, beyond the political parties, society is getting increasingly polarized about central issues such as race, equality, government involvement, gun control, LGBTQ, immigration, open borders, trade sanctions, government integrity, foreign intervention, data privacy and a host of other topics.

Similarly, in Europe, positions are getting increasingly hardened and entrenched across countries in ways unimaginable a mere decade ago. On central issues like immigration there are widely divergent points of view established, each with its own vigorous and vocal base. On the one hand, countries like Germany have let in over one million immigrants. Most countries in Western Europe, ranging from Sweden and Denmark to France and the United Kingdom have had large influxes of immigrant populations. At the same time, the same trend has given rise to nationalist, conservative parties and movements such as Alternative for Germany (AfD), Five Star Movement in Italy and National Rally in France. Each side of the argument is equally and progressively more entrenched in its position, and there is no trace of compromise or reconciliation in sight.

In the United Kingdom, the raging Brexit debate is another stark example of this growing trend in society. Britons who seek to leave the European Union and those who seek to stay in its folds are equally fervent in their established points of view. The consumer revolution makes it so easy to connect and congregate with other like-minded people that there is no perceived need to compromise and collaborate across divergent points of view. As is apparent with Brexit, elected officials are simply unable to come to consensus on how to act on such a strategic step in unison. Their disparate entrenched positions are on full display as parliament vote after vote fails, and the government lurches from one failed attempt at consensus to another.

ONLINE RADICALIZATION

At an individual level this same dynamic can be held responsible for some horrific tragedies and acts of terror. Many of the recruits for global terror organizations are radicalized online, in powerful fringe networks tucked away from the gaze of mainstream society and sane voices. Many of the most tragic acts of mass violence are the product of radicalization and extremism online, as individuals get and retrench in more and more extreme positions, egged on by others holding similar beliefs. There are even heart-breaking episodes of friends and significant others spiralling deeper and deeper into suicidal thoughts and suicide pacts, with no safety net to bank on or rescue them from their fatal slide. The new era of relationships is letting people connect with others and go as extreme or far out in their views as they want to go, with no course correction in place.

The consequences from this unfettered radicalization and groupthink ushered in by the new era of interpersonal relationships can be quite catastrophic. We are just seeing the early days of what havoc it can wreak. There is thus an absolute and utter need for mediation in these digital relationships. One of the big priorities for the consumer revolution is to determine how best to modulate the utter freedom ushered in by the revolution in the interest of the common good. Societal leaders will need to tackle this wave head-on, constructing the right mix of human and technology elements to monitor, mediate and resolve threatening issues before they escalate.

This will call for a judicious blend of policy making and advanced technologies to find the right balance between privacy and protection. Either extreme will be unacceptable to the society. Government agencies and policy makers will need to get ahead of this wave, and define laws and policies that better protect their citizenry. They will also need to tap into sophisticated artificial intelligence technology that can track troublesome conversations and relationships without interfering and violating privacy laws and standards. So great is the potential for extreme and radical relationships that the time is now for government agencies to respond to the emerging threat and get ahead of it.

Add to this simmering situation the possibility of malicious misinformation from bad actors, and you have a truly explosive powder keg. It is eminently possible for either a rogue individual, group or even regime to conduct coordinated misinformation campaigns, and lead small or large groups of consumers astray by leveraging the dynamics of digital relationships. This could have catastrophic consequences for human society, and needs to be nipped in the bud by responsible government agencies.

As with other areas of the consumer revolution, the adverse consequences of laissez faire administration are too dire to leave responsibilities such as these in the hands of profit-driven private enterprises. It is imperative that governing bodies take this matter in their own hands, and implement policies and solutions that will safeguard the public interest. As with other aspects of the consumer revolution, the energy release is too great to be left in the hands of private enterprises to manage and modulate. The consumer revolution in interpersonal relationships demands the best of our civic and societal governance to negotiate its course, and the time to engage in this for societies is now.

6

POLITICAL POWER
IN PLAY

Not only is the consumer revolution beginning to impact our lives at individual levels, and within small groups, it is beginning to impact entire societies, nations and our entire global village. From its humble, sputtering beginnings, it is beginning to impact trends, norms, political discourses, and now even laws and governments at a national and international level. The size, scale and velocity of change in policies and government ushered in by the consumer revolution is simply staggering in the context of the history of political changes in human development. The revolution is arming and empowering the governed to take charge of their own governance in stunning ways, unimaginable a mere decade ago.

At the same time, the people's revolution is drawing political leaders and politicians at large into its folds—they are people too after all. They are beginning to pay attention and listen to their constituents as their voices get louder and louder, and harder to ignore. They are beginning to take their constituents' lead on issue after issue, in substance no doubt, but also in style. The consumer revolution is starting to look like a policy making body at times, even as political leaders begin to look like a mob at others. The lines between the governed and the governing are starting to blur, with no end in sight. It is now conceivable that the consumer revolution becomes THE policy making and governing body of human societies, and the current government apparatus becomes simply an implementation arm of it. The impact of this change in the making is monumental. The implications and safeguards needed to negotiate this true transfer of power are even more monumental.

To understand how enormous this shift is, it is illustrative to look back at the history of politics and governance to put it all in context.

Politics and governments date back to the beginnings of human history itself. Ever since a human being came in contact with another, one likely took the lead and other agreed to be led!

It is most likely that the earliest political order was determined based on physical power alone. The more powerful human likely took charge, and the less powerful agreed to go along with it. The human in charge defined basic norms and rules for the other to conform to. A benevolent leader developed fair and healthy norms, a malevolent one unfair and oppressive ones, but norms established a micro-social order that the two lived under.

Layer on to this the addition of a third and a fourth human being as the group expanded, and the dynamic extended to include new members of the group as well. There likely developed a hierarchy amongst the members of the group, with one member inevitably taking on the mantle of overarching leadership.

Over the next thousands of years, humans coalesced into bigger groups, roaming the landscape as nomads in increasing numbers. This happened because humans uncovered that there was strength in numbers, and there was value in critical mass. They found greater safety, ability to protect themselves, ability to hunt and procure food, ability to take care of and tend to one another in times of need, and ability to procreate.

As the groups grew in size, the rules and norms of governance also had to grow. Larger group sizes required more sophisticated rules, and more specialized role definitions and responsibilities. These lead to a natural stratification within groups, and a natural order defining the modus operandi of the groups. The hierarchy was almost always power-based, calibrated by physical power, or mental, or both.

Groups with strong, competent leaders and effective rules thrived better than groups without. They served the leaders well, but they also served the group members well, leading to a healthy symbiotic relationship between the two that benefitted all or most members of the groups. More competent leaders developed rules that benefitted their constituent groups better, increasing the health and attractiveness of their groups, thus acquiring more group members, which in turn increased the resources and capabilities of the group, thereby increasing the power and influence of their leaders. There was thus a natural virtuous cycle reinforcing competent leadership, governance and groups.

As nomadic groups roamed and came into contact with other groups, they had a range of outcomes, ranging from conflict to indifference to assimilation. The stronger, more thriving groups conquered or assimilated weaker ones, leading to greater scale and benefits for the leadership and the membership of the acquiring groups. This called for further sophistication and implementation of group norms and rules, further reinforcing their health and prosperity.

As nomadic human groups got stronger and more prosperous, they began to uncover the notions of space and territory. If a particular stretch of land had the best game for hunting, or the best fruits and berries, the strongest groups began to stake out their claim for it. This demanded further sophistication in their rules and norms, which further reinforced their strength and sustainability, enabling them to fend off weaker groups from encroachment.

Around 12000 BC, an ancient hunter-gatherer society called the Natufians is believed to have ushered in the era of farming and agriculture. Hailing from a region of the Middle East called the Levant, the Natufians first transitioned to a farm-based society, and first domesticated animals. Ironically enough, the best evidence substantiating the dawn of the agricultural era comes from analysing teeth patterns in everyday mice. They show a marked transition during this era from predatory canines to sedentary molars, reflecting a shift in feeding patterns tied to agrarian societies.

Agriculture enabled humans to essentially create their own food, an utterly novel invention for its time. Humans uncovered the merits of growing their own food to supplement their sustenance needs, thereby greatly reducing their reliance on finding the right game or the right berry tree at the right time when desperately needed.

While this progression from hunting and gathering to farming was monumental in and of itself, it also ushered in the notion of dwellings, habitats and lands. Entire new rules and norms had to be developed around staking claims to lands and protecting those claims against all malicious groups. This introduced a new level of laws, requiring stricter compliance and enforcement to ensure the sanctity of land ownerships and harvest assets. This in turn required a greater level of competency and calibre from group leaders, with the strongest ones being able to expand their sway and power. This further amplified the virtuous cycle between competent leaders, well-run groups and thriving memberships, reinforcing the powers and benefits of each.

As agricultural societies and settlements became bigger, they developed into kingdoms. The earliest kingdoms are believed to have been in Sumer (modern-day Iraq) and Egypt, around 3000 BC. The Sumerians and Egyptians developed more sophisticated versions of laws and several societal advancements to further their quality of life. This included languages to facilitate communication within the kingdoms, construction projects like canals to aid in their agricultural efforts, trade with adjacent kingdoms to bring mutual prosperity and wars to protect their precious assets.

Kingdoms were of course called as such because they were led almost always by male leaders who evolved into kings. Kings took charge and responsibility for their kingdoms and accumulated as much power as they could to govern. Kings came up with even more sophisticated rules and norms for their kingdoms to govern effectively. There were rules for law and order. There were rules for protecting their respective kingdoms. There were rules for farming and producing other forms of output. There were rules for taxation. There were rules for social interactions and for procreating. There were rules for births and deaths. There were rules for celebrations and tragedies.

Kings exercised their powers to define their preferred forms of government. Some chose to be autocratic and govern by excessive force. Others chose to delegate governance to their chosen ministers and administrators. Kings protected and provided for their subjects. In return, they enforced taxes and tolls from their subjects to fund their resource needs. The more competent a king's governance, the more his subjects thrived and produced, and the more the resources the king had at his disposal.

The king almost always laid down the law of the land. He then announced or otherwise disseminated his rules using his desired communication channels. He enforced his rules with the military force he had at his disposal. He had absolute authority. Absolute power. Absolute control over his subjects.

There were benevolent kings. There were oppressive ones. There were wise and progressive kings. There were savage and ruthless ones. But they were always the law. They were the power. They wielded considerable influence over their subjects. They accumulated considerable power. They were the ultimate authority in their kingdoms.

One expression of royal authority was kings anointing their own children as successors. Other societal norms developed, such as the oldest male child automatically being anointed king after the current one died. The king took on the mantle of ruler, and in many instances even that of a parent, or that of a god. There was a marked distinction between the ruling class, and the ruled.

As you would expect, kingdoms grew, and expanded their foot prints. Expansion meant access to greater resources for the king and the kingdom, and lowered risk from undesirable conflicts or loss. Kingdoms expanded by encroaching and conquering other, weaker kingdoms. They also effectively expanded by creating matrimonial alliances between friendly kingdoms. The legend of Helen of Troy is a classic illustration of re-inforcing alliances through a state marriage.

As kingdoms grew, they developed into empires. Empires required yet more sophisticated laws and rules of governance. Kings grew into emperors, and put yet more sophisticated systems of governance in place to administer and enforce their laws. They amassed substantial resources and power to assert their will on their subjects, as well as other adjacent kingdoms and empires. They assimilated their acquired kingdoms and territories into their own set of rules and norms, all designed to reinforce their strategic advantages.

The earliest empire is widely regarded to be the Akkadian empire in Sumer in 2300 BC. Over the next few thousand years, the world saw dozens of empires. Some, such as the British Empire, the Mongol Empire and the Russian Empire became massive. The British Empire famously boasted that the sun never set on its sway, implying its truly worldwide reach.

Empires required further sophistication in rules and laws, and further refinement in government apparatus to administer their laws. Imagine trying to come up with laws in London, to be administered in far-flung destinations such as Delhi and Cape Town and Sydney, all before the invention of the telephone or airplanes or the Internet.

Empires also required complex assimilation efforts between the acquiring and the acquired. Norms had to be established, cultures had to be assimilated, and subjects had to be trained to fall in line. Empires that could conquer thrived of course, but empires that could effectively govern and assimilate thrived even more. They were able to extract resources from their acquired territories to further enhance their lives.

As kingdoms and empires expanded and accumulated power, they also introduced a profound imbalance between the rulers and their subjects. Many kings and emperors grew autocratic and unfair. They asserted their authority in arbitrary ways, changed the rules on their whims, eradicated their oppositions with savagery and took advantage of their subjects at will. The power imbalance between rulers and subjects grew increasingly asymmetrical.

In response to these malfunctioning autocratic governing systems, an alternate form of government emerged around 500 BC —democracy. Many city-states emerged in ancient Greece founded on the principles of power sharing amongst all members of the state. Democracies came up with many different variations of governing models, but the common theme was always the principle of representative government and equal power among members to elect their governing members, and consequently laws.

Democracies were not perfect by any means, and had their own sets of challenges and shortcomings. But democracies did address some of the foundational flaws of kingdoms and empires. They rectified the power imbalance and inequity prevalent in kingdoms. They self-corrected flawed leaders and laws. They dismantled the lines of succession from kings to their children. And they ushered in the notion of meritocracy in governance.

More than anything else, democracies raised and addressed a very fundamental question in human societal structure—who is really in charge? Who ought to have power over whom? Where did power flow from, and where did it flow to? Who was supposed to serve whom? Democracies raised these questions for human societies, and did not always yield the most comfortable or convenient answers. But the flag on the hill was planted, and nations everywhere started to experiment with democracy.

The democracy movement took a massive step forward with the voyage of a group of disillusioned British subjects in 1607 across the Atlantic to find a new home in America. The began to settle in the Eastern seaboard of America to form an alternative society, fashioned after the democratic models of ancient Greek democracies, and far removed from the oppressiveness of the British monarchy.

As word spread of the merits of this burgeoning democracy, other disillusioned Europeans from France, Spain, Portugal and the Netherlands began to migrate and settle in the new continent, drawn by the same principles of democracy that the earliest settlers espoused. As settlers moved more inland, power struggles and conflicts emerged between settlers and indigenous residents of America, and between the settlers themselves, but the democratic core of America only continued to get stronger and more entrenched over time. The settlements and colonies gradually became beacons of democracy and the power of the people to the entire world.

Those in power obviously did not relish the notion of democracy. Their interests were heavily vested in preserving their power and privilege. Those without power were greatly energized by democratic principles. But they did not have the resources or tools to express their will. Therein lay the roots of a tectonic power struggle, simmering in places, explosive in others, but ever present.

Rulers used a wide variety of strategies and ploys to project their power and keep their subjects under their thumbs. They controlled information. The ancient Mayans used their knowledge of astronomy and eclipses to demonstrate their might over uninformed subjects who would believe that evil forces were devouring the Moon or the Sun because they were not serving their rulers right. Rulers controlled resources and money. The Sumerian city-state of Lagash enforced taxes as early as 6000 BC. And they controlled lives. As far back as 1800 BC, the Code of King Hammurabi of Babylon outlined the law for capital punishment, and since then rulers executed contentious subjects at will.

Subjects of kingdoms, though much greater in numbers, were no match for the power of rulers at an individual, isolated level. Neither did they have the means to band together to exercise their collective will at any meaningful scale. So, for centuries, dissent was destroyed, contention was crushed, power imbalance was propagated and subjects suffered in silence.

PEOPLE POWER

There were moments in history when the power imbalance became unbearable enough to cause societal explosions. These were times when rulers became so oppressive, and the state of suffering for subjects so overwhelming, that they bandied together despite their powerlessness, and lack of tools and techniques to force catastrophic change. In other words, revolutions.

In 1763, on the heels of a British victory over the French and Native Indian forces in Eastern America, Britain issued a Royal Proclamation prescribing various rules for its purported subjects who had settled in America. Simply sailing away to America evidently didn't absolve them from the responsibilities and governing rules of King George III of Great Britain!

The Proclamation brought to a head simmering contention and conflict between the British settlers in America and their apparent ruler. This gave rise to the American Revolution, triggered by settlers in the 13 Colonies rising in revolt against the British Empire in 1765. Eight years of conflict ensued, with the Americans supported by the French who were earlier vanquished by the British.

In the course of this revolution, America declared independence from Great Britain in 1776, giving birth to the United States of America. By 1783, the newly formed nation had completed its victory over the British Empire, and began its journey as an independent nation free to govern itself at will. The American Revolution became the first major blow from a people-powered democracy defeating a monarch-ruled empire in the world.

Right on the heels of this major upheaval, the second major revolution in the world got underway in France. The autocratic monarchy that had ruled France for hundreds of years reached a point of asymmetrical privileges and oppression of the masses that became simply unbearable to them.

In 1789, the French subjects convened the Estates General as an assertion of independence from the hegemony of the monarchy. What followed was three years of intense social and political upheaval. A multitude of democratic forces and principles began sweeping the land, butting heads and overpowering the elements of the conservative monarchy, edifice by shattered edifice. Centuries of pent-up reaction came exploding out, leading to unprecedented death and destruction. This culminated in the proclamation of a republic in 1792. The coup de grace was the execution of the monarch, King Louis XVI in 1793. The world just witnessed the second major blow delivered to a conventional monarchy by democracy.

Other revolutions followed as the idea of self-government and democracy took hold, some voluntary and some involuntary. In 1822 Dom Pedro declared Brazil's independence from Portugal and won it in 1825. In 1917 the Bolsheviks led the Great Socialist Revolution in Russia. And in 1947 the British saw the writing on the wall and granted India and Pakistan their independence.

After thousands of years of monarchies, a powerful new idea had taken hold—people power. Democracies began to take shape around the world, in many different forms and sizes, each an expression of the will of its people. When millions of people began to understand and assert their collective power, it became more and more difficult for a tiny number of rulers to govern and overpower them, state apparatus notwithstanding.

Such is the draw of this people power, and so compelling the evidence of greater peace and prosperity that comes with people-driven democracies, that now 123 out of 192 countries in the world are democracies. With each passing decade, that number continues to grow.

Democracies around the world operate in a wide variety of ways. They have their own laws of governance and structure. There are direct democracies and indirect democracies. There are presidential democracies and there are parliamentary democracies. There are unicameral democracies and bicameral democracies. There are democracies with term limits and others without. There are simple majority democracies and others requiring special majorities. But at their core, they each represent the will of their people, and their preference for self-government.

A common thread across all democracies is the practice of the voting public electing its government representatives at periodic intervals, with equal distribution of voting authority for all. Elected representatives then organize and govern their constituents to the best of their abilities, knowing they have to go back to the constituents for reaffirmation at each election cycle.

Most democracies have some combination of a legislative branch, an executive branch and a judicial branch. This introduces a healthy system of checks and balances, which is core to the democratic principle and ideals. But this also introduces some innate contention when it comes to interpreting the power and scope of each. The boundaries between each of the three branches of government are not crisply and universally defined or interpreted, sometimes leading to confusion and contention between the three.

In the United States, this can lead to accusations of 'overreach of executive authority', or 'government by executive order', or 'legislating from the (judicial) bench', or 'legislative paralysis' by one branch of government targeting the other. The process often gets in the way of the principle. The little picture often gets in the way of the big picture.

Over time, democracies have developed other forms of dysfunction, though far less traumatic than the alternatives, leading to the famous quote attributed to Winston Churchill: 'Democracy is the worst form of government except all the others that have been tried'.

Democracies have elaborate election systems and processes that consume huge amounts of national time, energy and money. And after it all, many times they produce inconclusive results, a reflection of the myriad preferences and desires of their voting constituents. Around the world, nations get paralyzed by hung parliaments and ineffective coalition governments, sometimes for months and years. This produces a significant interruption in the advancement of their constituents, under the potential premise that inaction is preferable to incorrect action. Democracies have thus becoming slow-moving and laborious. It takes them a vast amount of time and energy to pick who should govern, a vast amount of time and energy to decide how they should govern, a vast amount of time and energy to make decisions, a vast amount of time and energy to execute on decisions and vast amount of time and energy to evaluate governments before the cycle repeats itself.

The process takes its toll on officials who serve in government and political office. But it takes an even bigger toll on citizens, or in other words, consumers. It can be very draining for everyday consumers, everyday constituents to wait for action, wait for resolution, wait for relief while the democratic process lumbers and churns through its motions. This process can be very inefficient for the populace it is meant to represent and serve.

PORK BARREL POLITICS AND GERRYMANDERING

Democracies also have an intrinsic dynamic of polarizing their populace, sowing the seeds for further discord and discontent in societies. In vibrant, thriving democracies two or more political parties have a real, credible sway and influence, and real stints at governing their nations. In less-developed democracies there is often extreme asymmetry of power between competing political parties, rendering democracy all but a farce, but even there the siren call of people power is so strong and undeniable that nations go through the motions of democratic processes just to project democratic form, if not function.

In the United States the democratic process gave rise to two major political parties, the Republican Party and the Democratic Party. In the United Kingdom the Labour Party and the Conservative Party emerged as the major political parties. In India the Congress and the BJP developed into the major political forces of the nation.

Political parties and political processes, by their very nature, resulted in 'bundled' policies and governance. If all the societal, economic, political and law enforcement issues, and alternatives, beliefs and values of the land had to be synthesized into either two, five or twenty political mandates or representatives, by definition you would end up with a composite set of beliefs and policies you could choose between, rather than individual issue by individual issue.

In the United States, if you choose to support the Republican bundle of values, you largely choose a bundle that includes conservative beliefs, minimal government, fiscal conservatism, military and law enforcement strength, lower taxes, private enterprise, traditional values, limits on abortion and freedoms on the rights to bear arms. If you choose the Democratic bundle of values, you largely choose a bundle that includes liberal beliefs, an expanded role for government, fiscal liberalism, social safety nets and programmes, higher taxes to fund social programmes, public services, progressive values, freedom on abortion and limits on the right to bear arms. If you agree on some values of either political party, but not others, you are plain out of luck!

This rigidity of choice carries down to the individual candidate level also. As a candidate from any major political party, you are largely defined by the value system of your party. You might deviate from your political party on a policy here and there, but you are largely restricted to your party's positions. If you are a constituent of either a city, district or state, your choices are again limited to bundled groups of policies, rather than individual policies you might care about. You can choose to get three policies that are important to you, but you have to accept two that you don't care about, or even outright disagree with.

This bundling dynamic is also evident when it comes to legislative bills. Bills are often arcane and complex to begin with, making it near impossible for most consumers to understand and follow. Whereas their sole purpose is to serve mass constituencies and consumers, they in effect become complex negotiations of legal language between competing lawyers, and produce a work product that is difficult to understand for the average consumer.

Where this becomes particularly egregious is in the practice of pork barrel politics. The practice has been alive in the US Congress since the 1800s. In an effort to gain support or favour with elected officials for a particular piece of legislation, their favourite local policies would often be bundled in the overall bill. This could entail clear and direct favours to award business contracts to supporting politicians and their interests, dating as far back as the American Civil War, to funding ill-conceived appropriations like the Alaskan 'bridge to nowhere' infrastructure project in 2005. The intent in such earmarked provisions is clearly to escape extensive scrutiny by the voting constituents, and ride on the coattails of larger, core legislation. This is expedient and clever, but clearly a violation of the spirit of government, and a mechanism to sub-optimize the voting populace.

The interplay between money and politics is even more pronounced in the election process itself. Political campaigns in today's democratic processes require vast amounts of funds to run. In the United States a presidential election cycle can run over $2 billion in total expenses. In the United Kingdom campaigns can run over $100 million in spending. In India campaign contributions can exceed $2 billion in an election cycle. A significant portion of these funds come from private and corporate donors to support their candidates. Clearly, those donations come with strings attached, and earmarking and pork barrel programmes often end up being the quid pro quo for such support. The net effect of this is limitations to the core doctrine of democracy—equal vote and representation for all—by in effect rewarding the individuals and corporations with the most resources already with even more resources as appreciation for their efforts by elected representatives. In other words, a corporate or special interest would only support legislation that provides a return on its investment. The conflict is that this return comes at the expense of the voting populace at large.

Another vexing artefact of democracy that strikes at the core of its values is the practice of gerrymandering. Through perfectly legal ways, legislatures can redefine district boundaries to game the democratic system and reinforce their power positions. Like many checks and balances in democracies, this process goes through legally sanctioned processes as well, but the outcome is clearly not consistent with the true spirit of democracy. So once again the true purpose of democracy is subverted by a perfectly legal artefact of it. In countries around the world democratic governance has been in large part an exercise in gaming the system, rather than in serving the populace.

The democratic process has other adverse consequences and side effects (even though it is still a better form of government than all others!). Most elected officials hold office for a predetermined period of time. This can be a 4-year or 5-year term, with limits on how many times you can stand for office, or not. This leads to scenarios where elected representatives stay in power far beyond their most productive years, and even set the stage for their progeny to take their place when it is time to retire—shades of a reversion back to monarchy dynamics. In other words, democracies often keep regressing back to preserving the interests of the governing rather than the governed, and need to be rescued from this slide.

THEATRICAL POLITICS

Another side effect of representational politics is that politicians are expected and empowered to make decisions for their constituencies on all matters. They clearly cannot be the domain experts in all matters they are making decisions on. In particular, many elected representatives are not up to date with contemporary technology solutions and strategies, which is a critical shortcoming in this day and age. This inadequacy was on painful display during the April 2018 testimonies held for Mark Zuckerberg, the CEO of Facebook by the US Congress. Depending on ill-informed political representatives to make policy decisions in domains they have limited expertise on is a major risk faced by democracies.

This mismatch leads to governments making policy decisions on net neutrality, fake news, foreign government intervention, crypto currencies, and cyber security without a deep understanding of the technologies and business models involved. Or governments making policy decisions on healthcare insurance, pricing of drugs and medical services, public versus private trade-offs in healthcare or vaccination policies without a deep understand of medicine. In fact, often times the core expertise of many lawmakers is in making laws themselves, leaving vast information gaps in their understanding of the core domains covered by their laws. This is almost the only major field in the world today with people making decisions on things they know very little about!

Most other careers in the world are built on domain-based core competencies and leadership. Except politics. You could argue that our laws would be better under a regime of an issue-based political system, rather than a time-based one. This seems to be common refrain from constituents and consumers—that they care more about the issues than the candidates. But such is the lack of clarity and discourse on the issues, and so much coverage and emphasis in the media on candidates and personalities, that election cycles become obsessed with that. Elections have increasingly become great theatre, with personality and charisma trumping issues and policies which in reality affect consumer lives to a far greater extent.

Ultimately, all of the inherent complexities and challenges of the democratic process come to a head at the actual legislative decision-making step of the process. Governments have elaborate decision-making processes around the world, but they all have their natural limitations.

For instance, in the United States certain decisions require absolute majority of voters, and others require super-majorities. Decisions require passage in two houses of Congress, and then by the President of the country. There are complex rules on when a bill can be voted on and when it cannot. There are rules on how long a bill can be debated, and artefacts such as a filibuster, which provide for great theatre, but unclear value beyond that. Issues are brought to a head on a grand stage, the drama and personalities take over, politicians 'take to the airwaves' to promote their views and justifications, bills take a long time to compose and then pass, and at the end nearly half the constituents are dissatisfied with the outcome.

This is why consumers vent. This is why approval ratings of many politicians are so low, regardless of party or affiliation. This is why voting populaces vote out those in power at regular intervals, despite the inherent advantages of incumbency. Politicians in and of themselves aren't vile and evil, of course. If you need convincing, just look at ex-politician interviews after they have left political office. They look and sound perfectly engaging, thoughtful, well-meaning and, in fact, actually likable!

CHALLENGING THE POLITICAL ORDER

It is the process of democracy that takes its toll on people. Expecting one individual to have domain expertise on all major subject matters that affect consumers is itself flawed. The election process in most countries is gruelling and can be personally and professionally offensive, weeding out some of the most competent leaders in the world who have no desire to go through the grind. The interaction between government members and commercial interests via lobbyists is itself prone to conflicts of interest, and compromising the interests of the many at the hands of a few. The energy it takes to get legislation through itself drives bundling, pork barrels and earmarking in legislation. The decision-making process itself grates on lawmakers, leading to embittered rivalries and polarization that flow down to constituents.

In other words, a perfect recipe for the consumer revolution to show up. Democratic systems are doing a lot of good around the world. But not enough in the minds of the consumer. Democracies are caught up in their own knitting. There are perfectly valid reasons why the current systems were put in place. There are perfectly well-meaning politicians who step in to make this a better place. There are perfectly understandable allowances that can be made to account for the human frailties and failings of politicians. But the consumer is being underserved. The state of affairs could be, and should be better for the world.

And consumers around the world are catching on. They are now armed with unprecedented information and communication. They are beginning to understand issues better, trade-offs better, reality on the street better and their own power better. Ironically, the same information and communication tools that are increasing their awareness and power, are decreasing the power advantage of their elected officials in relative terms. The underlying information that forms the basis for analysing situations and developing points of view is now available to all. The communication basis for comparing points of view and banding together with like-minded individuals is available to all. The information gap between constituents and their elected politicians is narrowing, perhaps even reversing. The congregation gap between constituents and their elected officials is narrowing, perhaps even reversing.

Consumers are beginning to question, and even challenge the political order with more and more frequency and authenticity. If a world expert on either technology, medicine, education or finance can express their views just as easily as a politician who is not an expert by any means, how does that credibility mismatch play out? If a 100,000-strong virtual town hall stakes out a position that is different from 50-elected officials in a government building, how does that scale mismatch play out?

As with information and communication, the Internet and its tools are arming consumers with the implements needed to take the concepts of democracy to the next natural step in its progression. The initial illustrations of this true people power phenomena are beginning to take shape.

On 17 December 2010, Mohammad Bouazizi tragically self-immolated himself in Sidi Bouzid, Algeria in protest of his mistreatment and abuse at the hands of local authorities and police. This came on the heels of years of exploitation and oppression of the people of the country at the hands of President Zine El Abidine Ben Ali and his government apparatus.

The self-immolation touched a raw nerve with a populace suffering from years of tyranny, leading to protests that were largely peaceful in nature. Government forces attempted to quash the protests, but the power of social media enabled a surprising base of citizens to start joining protests, upsetting the political calculus for the first time. As more news and pictures got out in the hands of the people, more joined the movement, eliciting a stronger and more violent response from police and government personnel, drawing in turn more citizens into acts of martyrdom and violence, developing into a growing circle of escalating violence. The government had gotten accustomed to keeping consumer unrest under wraps for decades. But this time it was different. The more the government suppressed, the more the people power surged, armed with the full array of social media tools, and the explosive power of congregating with other mobilized consumers. A monumental tide was turning.

On 14 January 2011, President Ben Ali dissolved the government and declared a state of emergency, announcing a timeline for fresh elections. But it was too little and too late. Seeing the writing on the wall, and the fearsome power of the people of Algeria banded together via social media, the military stepped in and took charge, restoring law and order, and prompting President Ben Ali to flee the country for Saudi Arabia and into political obsolescence. And the world got the first glimpse of what the power of people armed with technology could accomplish against a powerful and oppressive regime.

On 25 January 2011, youth groups across Egypt launched a social media-fuelled campaign to protest and counter the oppressions and brutality of President Hosni Mubarak's presidency. Empowered by the connectivity afforded by social media platforms, protesters organized a wide variety of demonstrations, strikes, marches and other forms of civil disobedience. A movement started by youths grew into a sprawling force comprising consumers and constituents across a broad cross-section of society. Millions of protesters joined the movement, confronted and clashed with the state apparatus, leading to thousands of casualties. At the heart of the protests was the visceral desire for freedom and equality, and a rejection of oppression of the many by the few in power. In the face of stiff resistance and use of force against its own citizenry, the power of the people would not be denied. The critical enabler of this consumer power surge was the technology enabling the consumer revolution.

On 11 February 2011, the state buckled. President Mubarak resigned and was relieved of power, the armed forces took over administration, suspended the constitution, dissolved parliament, and instated a fresh model for governance. The power of the people notched up a second monumental victory that would have been inconceivable only years ago without the congregating power of the consumer revolution.

The Arab Spring of 2011 brought about similar transformations in several other nations, such as Algeria, Jordan, Oman, Yemen, Libya and Morocco. Some transformations were truly revolutionary and brought about a total change in government, some were less so, and some like the Iranian protests of 2011–2012 were not even successful in bringing about real change. But the world had been put on notice. The power balance between government and their citizens had shifted, even in the most authoritarian of regimes. The Internet and social media had given the people connectivity and network externalities. For the first time, mass consumers could band together, get behind a cause, organize and assert power, and overthrow entire governments. A tiger was awakening.

On 17 September 2011, Kalle Lasn and Micah White of a Canadian publication called AdBusters launched a movement called Occupy Wall Street in Zuccotti Park, Manhattan. The movement sought to mobilize the masses to protest against social and economic inequalities, and the disproportionate influence by financial institutions and corporations over governments meant to serve the people. The movement grew in size and scope, powered by the tools of social media, and spawned off several adjacent movements, expanding demographic profiles, protest themes and expressions of unrest. The protesters were eventually driven out of Zuccotti Park on 15 November 2011, but the movement continues to simmer, rearing up at various economic events worldwide, and looking for the next opportunity to battle the economic world order. The movement has splintered into many derivative causes, leading to a more diffuse transformation goal, but the clarion call has been sounded. Consumers are not going to suffer economic inequality in silence forever. They will be heard, and the economically privileged will be well served by understanding the implications, and responding to them in order to preserve their assets and quality of life.

On 13 July 2013, George Zimmerman was acquitted by a jury in Florida of murdering Trayvon Martin. This led to three African American community organizers, Alicia Garza, Patrisse Cullors and Opal Tometi starting a hashtag called #BlackLivesMatter on social media which became a rallying point for Americans who felt wronged by alleged police excesses and brutality against African Americans. The movement gained national prominence after organizing demonstrations following two more prominent African American deaths—Eric Garner and Michael Brown— and ensuing riots in Ferguson. Armed with social media tools, the movement gave voice to the sentiment of oppression and injustice held by the African American community.

The movement has brought to light and highlighted other perceived injustices and oppression especially at the hands of police officers. In 2016, Colin Kaepernick of the NFL's San Francisco 49ers decided to protest social injustice by kneeling during the national anthem at football games, further igniting the public policy and ethics debate, and the #BlackLivesMatter movement. Social media technology then coalesced and galvanized the movement into a powerful, organic expression of people power, leading to public responses from several people in authority including none other than President Trump.

At the same time, the movement has given rise to competing movements by communities and constituencies wanting to express alternative points of view. #AllLivesMatter and #BlueLivesMatter are just two of the competing movements vying for public support, and the balance of public opinion is still up for grabs on this count. People power can be as diverse and diffuse as people themselves. If there are competing points of view, there will be competing forces of social movement. If there are diffuse goals that people have, they will be reflected in diffuse and disparate directions that the movements take. But if a large body of humans bands together around a common point of view, the Internet and social media technologies of today can produce a fearsome force never before seen in human history. Social media, in effect, becomes the life-blood, the arteries, of these movements, creating an unprecedented mass of humanity to act and react as one. For the first time in history, this creates a power greater than the sum of its parts. For the first time in history, the power corridors and brokers of the world can feel the gravity of ten thousand or ten million people moving as one. And so great is this force, that when it unites behind a cause, no one can stand in the way. No one can resist. No one can escape justice at the hands of such a movement.

A powerful demonstration of this force is the #MeToo movement. On 5 October 2017, *The New York Times* published a story detailing decades of sexual harassment allegations against movie mogul Harvey Weinstein levelled by actresses Rose McGowan, Ashley Judd and others. Enabled by social media and its unprecedented empowerment for self-expression, an increasing number of actresses and performers began to come out with their untoward experiences with Harvey Weinstein, in a way that would never have transpired a mere decade ago. This led to Harvey's ouster from his own company and his getting subjected to multiple legal proceedings.

In 2006, social activist Tarana Burke had created the phrase 'Me Too' in inclusive support of minority women who had been subjected to sexual abuse and exploitation. On 15 October 2017 actress Alyssa Milano latched on to the phrase and the #MeToo hashtag as a rallying cry for women who have been wronged to come out and express themselves. At the 2017 Women's March on Washington, Ashley Judd gave a fiery speech on the identity and rights and privileges of women and other underserved minorities, further fuelling the movement. The movement has since grown explosively in size and scope, bringing out more and more women, and even men, who have been wronged or taken advantage of, causing the ousters and downfall of top producers, actors, politicians, doctors, sports programmes, sports stars and corporate executives. After decades, even centuries of exploitation and abuse of the powerless masses by the powerful few, the consumer revolution is starting to show up. Armed with networking power of the Internet and social media tools, consumers are beginning to realize their power, and that those in power draw theirs from those of the people. When they feel wronged, they take to the digital and physical streets, express themselves, and bring even the most storied power brokers and edifices crashing down.

On 14 February 2018, Nikolas Cruz gunned down 17 people at Marjory Stoneman Douglas High School in Parkland, Florida, making it one of the most horrific mass shootings at schools in America. Following up on the heels of other tragic mass shootings, this was one tragedy too many for the consumer revolution to take. After dealing with their shock and grief at the tragedy, the students of Parkland started the #NeverAgain movement to force definitive change in gun laws in the country. The movement is still underway, ebbing and flowing as the consumer energy behind it ebbs and flows, but it has already forced a deeper re-think and stronger action on gun control than any prior government activity to date.

As with most technologies, there is immense potential in today's people power infrastructures to create movements for the common good of the populace. Even in its fledgling state, the consumer revolution is demonstrating that it will move faster and with more purpose on issues it cares about until traditional political leaders catch up.

However, as with most technologies, there is also immense potential for sabotage and subterfuge when it comes to the consumer revolution in politics and government. While there are numerous instances of cyberattacks and cybercrimes perpetrated by individuals or groups to profit from fraud, and just as many instances of countries conducting cyber espionage against one another, it is the pre-meditated meddling by foreign governments in election processes that are particularly alarming to democracies. For they illustrate how fragile the power appropriation process is in today's digital-heavy democracies, and how egregiously today's democratized election processes can be exploited to achieve perverse results.

The most prominent case of potential foreign government meddling in a country's democratic process is the one that was just completed by Special Counsel Robert Mueller, looking into the possibility that the Russian state interfered in the 2016 US Presidential Elections. While the investigation was ongoing and far-reaching, with many findings still to be reported, there was and is clearly enough doubt and suspicion that the interference led to the election of President Donald Trump to warrant a full-fledged investigation, consuming vast amounts of the country's time and energy.

In true democratic fashion, the entire investigation has led to a competing investigation on whether Democratic contender Hillary Clinton's campaign framed this suspicion of collusion to gain an edge with consumers before, during and after the election. The intense polarization and bad blood in the country will now lead to an extensive investigation into that allegation, consuming vast amounts of national political energy and mind share. Allegations will be made, challenges will be tossed around, tempers will flare, blood pressures will rise and scores will be settled. And through it all, the voting populace will wait and look for policies and programmes that actually make a difference to their lives.

While the evidence of actual collusion between the Russian state and the President Trump's campaign is still under various forms of investigation, as is the investigation into a potential framing of this suspicion, the evidence that the same social media arteries that form the foundation of a people-led movement can be used to power a people-misled movement is beyond refute.

The same digital systems that feed information to mass consumers can be used to feed misinformation to the same consumers, producing a mass movement doctored by a foreign power rather than a pure expression of self-will.

The allegations and counter-allegations about Russian state meddling in US elections will of course continue for some time, but the point has now been demonstrated that consumer movements have fearsome power that can strike at the very heart of democratic foundation itself—whether legitimate or illegitimate. Clearly the saga points to the needs for entirely new generations of tools to safeguard the integrity of the democratic process, to protect it from external or internal malicious forces, to preserve its integrity and faith. But regardless, it signals a dramatic shift brewing in the landscape for a transfer of power from the government to the consumer that were inconceivable only a decade ago. The consumer revolution has shown up in politics and governance.

The fascinating question is where the consumer revolution will go next in this realm. What #BlackLivesMatter and #MeToo and #NeverAgain demonstrate is that the consumer revolution is starting to take charge of the issues that matter to the populace. It is starting to take the initiative to seize the agenda.

This has the potential to completely redefine the relationship between constituents and their elected officials. Constituents are showing that they will now take the lead on issues that matter to them. Whether it is equality, law enforcement, immigration, healthcare, taxes, women's rights or gun control, the consumer revolution will develop a point of view, and when it does, watch out!

A BILLION MINDS BANDING TOGETHER

Now the consumer revolution is not going to operate entirely smoothly or always in concert either. Just as consumers themselves have myriad points of views, so will the consumer revolution as it is an aggregation of the collective will of consumers. There will be strong, concerted initiatives, and there will be weaker, more diffused ones. There will be initiatives built on the energy of a billion like-minded consumers, and those built on the will of ten. There will be competing initiatives just as there are competing points of view amongst consumers, with the larger, better-organized, better-mobilized initiatives winning out. But once the consumer revolution stakes out a position and mobilizes behind it, it will become increasingly difficult to stop.

The consumer revolution will increasingly express itself more and more vehemently. It will tell those in charge where it stands on the issues it cares about. It will make it increasingly obvious to power brokers and those in authority where their power and authority are derived from. And they will have no option but to follow. To fall in line.

The consumer revolution will fundamentally flip the model of leadership in the world. Political leaders might no longer function as true leaders, but become executers of the consumers' will. When consumers have the ability to band together en masse, to express themselves in unison as the voice of the people, what is the point of a leader to represent them, to guess at their points of view, to go out on a limb and stake a position? What is the point of seeking their validation after taking a stance, rather than soliciting it beforehand?

The consumer revolution will also demand that it be served when it has a need. #BlackLivesMatter and #MeToo did not wait for an election cycle to get the action they demanded. They created an intensity that demanded action when the need arose. They did not wait patiently to craft ballot propositions and to go through the next election cycle to see the actions they desired. In countless instances, the consumer revolution is not willing to be bound by the artefacts of traditional government and democratic processes. It demands and expects results how it wants them, when it wants them, where it wants them. It will push the governance model from representative government to direct government.

Extrapolated to the extreme, the consumer revolution might transform the entire democratic model itself. If you can stake out a point of view, and mobilize people power behind it, why do you need a political leader to do it for you? If you can structure a decision, and vote on it in an instant, why do you need arcane and glacially moving political processes to do so? If you can set up a vote for debt ceilings and government funding, why do you need to bundle immigration policies with it? And if you can make a collective decision on going to war or making peace with other nations, why do you need to entrust a person or a representative body to commit the lives and resources of a nation to it?

Ironically, the artefacts and institutions built to buttress and reinforce democracies might themselves be contributing to their demise. The quagmire and malaise in many government institutions and processes under-serve the very consumers they are meant for. The paralysis in government, caused by rabid polarization of elected officials and risk-averse voting systems, is producing a deep dissatisfaction amongst consumers with elected officials charged with serving them. This is leading consumers to take matters in their own hands more and more, rather than wait for a flawed political system to handle them.

Other artefacts also get in the way of consumers being served adequately by today's political systems. Laws are typically written by lawyers that are difficult for consumers to understand. The backroom negotiating and deal-making sometimes leads to deals that are optimized for a few at the expense of the many. Lobbyists and political donors wield extraordinary political influence with elected officials, leading to laws that are not always for the general good. The consumer revolution is taking note and is now armed with the tools to rectify perceived wrongs. It is starting to take charge of its own destiny and demanding that politicians fall in line.

You can imagine a world where the consumer revolution will make its own laws. It will elect officials to execute its laws and policies, and interpret its laws. But it will not tolerate inaction or paralysis in government. It will demand that its needs be met. It will demand faster decision-making and execution as a result of this direct democracy model.

This is a profound change in the power structure of the world when it comes to politics and government. But there is no denying or escaping it. The consumer revolution is on a charge, and all in its path will be brushed aside or assimilated.

This transformation also brings with it tremendous challenges and needs for safeguards. For starters, this phenomenon is striking at the very roots of power—how nations define their laws and govern themselves. The consequences are mind-boggling, and the risks of mis-execution catastrophic. This movement will hence require exemplary safeguards by state institutions to protect democratic integrity against bad actors hijacking the political process. New technologies and systems will need to emerge that authenticate true identities and consumer voices on the Internet. New safeguards will need to be developed against impostors and impersonators meddling with or hijacking legitimate movements. New tools will need to emerge that facilitate framing social and political causes, canvassing support from like-minded consumers, polling, elections and collective decision-making.

As the consumer revolution morphs the democratic process further and further away from today's indirect representative governance models, and towards direct mass movement-driven governance models, entire new generations of systems and processes will need to emerge. Rules will need to be drawn up for which decisions are to be made directly by the voting populace, versus by elected representatives. One transitional step might be a third 'House of the People' to go along with the Senate and the House of Representatives in the United States, with all three needing to approve a measure before it becomes law. Any of the three might initiate a bill or issue, empowering consumers to seize the initiative and define the agenda that matters to them.

The 'House of the People', whether formal or informal, will need its own set of rules for governance by the people. It will need rules for how a motion can be brought for the general body to vote on. This could take the form of petitions with a Wikipedia flavour—where anyone can craft a motion and put it up for consideration by the voting populace. Once the motion gets a critical mass of legitimate support—from real humans not bots—it can be put up for a vote of the general body of the populace in a national referendum.

The process might then have a time window for deliberation. Once consumers internalize the power they have given themselves, they will feel even more responsible for making the correct decisions than their representatives do today. They will want to avoid hasty decisions. They will want due consideration, and that disparate voices be heard. New processes will emerge for how debates should be conducted in the digital world with thousands or millions of participants. Thresholds will need to be set for what critical mass of consumers has the authority to affect what decisions or changes in law. Rules will need to be set for how much deliberation and how many votes need to be conducted before the populace feels comfortable and convinced it is making the right decisions.

Consumers will realize there is a mob mentality to mass movements and put in safeguards to self-correct. They will realize that there is heavy volatility in rapid collective decision-making and put in measures to dampen the oscillations. They will come up with rules for issues requiring majority votes and those requiring super-majority votes. They will define rules for critical issues that require multiple votes over an extended period of time to avoid making impulse decisions that could be wrong. In other words, they will put in similar rules to what responsible humans go through in their individual decision-making, just compounding them to account for millions of decision-makers at a time.

The consumer revolution in politics calls for nothing short of a new constitution. One that is crafted for the new realities of the day, where the will of the people can be expressed very precisely, and yet collectively, in the moment.

Entire new laws of engagement need to be defined and implemented. Entire new government apparatus needs to be created to handle the infrastructure of the consumer revolution. From taxation to intellectual property, and from vandalism to theft, a new framework for law and order needs to be defined to protect the interests of the consumer in the new, digital, interconnected, instant world. Not doing so will only create a giant vacuum that will be filled by chaotic or even worse, malicious instigators in a new wild west that will put prior ones to shame for its sheer size, scope and impact. Letting this happen will be one of the greatest abdications of responsibility and one of the greatest absences of foresight among government officials around the world. There is an alternate governance model emerging, and it behoves government officials to take note and respond.

And therein lies the crux of how the consumer revolution in politics will play out. The true power in any democracy, and any society or nation for that matter, is derived from consumers, from the people. Absent the technology to express views and to band together, people power may be held at bay by either anointed, appointed or elected officials. Absent the tools for the consumer revolution, a 10 per cent advantage in power can be translated into a 10 million percent advantage in privilege and benefits.

But once the consumer revolution is armed with the technologies and mindsets to come together and express its collective will, nothing can get in the way. Every other form of power pales in comparison. The consumer revolution will force its government to serve its purpose. It will not be denied or exploited indefinitely.

And, if you think about it, this is actually good news for governments around the world. When people can't express themselves in unison, violent and cataclysmic revolutions happen. Wars happen, coups happen, mutinies happen, riots happen. Those in power can actually benefit from enabling consumers to express themselves, rather than sitting on a pressure cooker longer and longer. Not only does that align them with their true purpose and mission, it also aligns them with the ultimate power brokers in the equation, and ensures their longevity and prosperity. It lightens the burden of them taking responsibility for consumers' well-being in a parent–child relationship, to simply aligning and executing their will in an adult–adult relationship.

The consumer revolution in politics and governance is coming. It is showing its power and speed in remarkable ways in the past decade, considering how many centuries it has withstood the forces of oppression, exploitation and abuse of power. Technology and service providers who understand its trajectory and enable it will benefit handsomely in the market. Leaders and politicians who understand its dynamic will benefit handsomely in government. And those that don't will be left behind in the dust. The consumer revolution in politics will not be denied.

7

EMANCIPATION IN ENTERTAINMENT

A s in other areas, the consumer revolution is turning the world of entertainment on its head. Unlike ever before, consumers are taking control of their entertainment experiences in myriad ways. For starters, the entire model of media producers being in charge of when and where their productions are being consumed is changing. The on-demand era is taking hold, and consumers are increasingly in the driver's seat when choosing where and when they consume entertainment. The digitization and ubiquity of entertainment is taking it further and further away from production-driven realms to consumer-driven realms.

Consumers are also taking charge of what entertainment they are consuming. Traditionally, it was the producers that were determining the genres of entertainment, packaged up into categories and formats that suited them best. The consumer revolution is now beginning to fragment and unbundle long-standing packages, consuming entertainment in ever-exploding genres and ever-expanding formats. As a result, the nature of entertainment is evolving and multiplying in more and more ways, reflecting the multi-faceted preferences of its audience. Entertainment is progressing from broadcast bundles, at best bucketed into select consumer segments, into personalized bits and bytes that are as tailored and fine-tuned as consumers themselves.

And, as a coup de grace, consumers are taking charge of production itself. The lines between the producer and the consumer are increasingly beginning to blur. Consumers are producing their own entertainment, and consuming each other's entertainment more and more. Some of the biggest entertainment stars of today are emerging from the ranks of everyday consumers themselves. And an increasing share of public attention is being absorbed by home-grown stars and entertainment.

This is a far cry from how the world of entertainment used to be since the beginning of time.

From their earliest days, human beings sought and relished entertainment in a variety of forms. People likely found a way to make each other laugh with an antic or gesture at the very dawn of the human race. Others found a way to tell stories as early as the first days of being able to communicate and describe complex ideas.

One of the earliest forms of entertainment was art. There is circumstantial evidence that as far back as 500,000 years ago, our predecessors were already engaged in some form of artistic activity. The earliest art forms actually found so far date back to 50,000 years ago, and primarily consist of cave paintings and figurines. The art forms of the era progressively developed into 3D art in the form of pottery and sculpture over the next 40,000 years.

The Bronze Age around 5000 BC ushered in the era of metals, such as bronze, copper and iron, used for the purposes of art. Metal enabled artists to craft entire new genres of art, such as menhirs in France, and cromlech in England, epitomized by the legendary Stonehenge. The era also saw the beginnings of specialized artists and artisans who could craft superior works of art compared to the general populace. Art was a form of entertainment for both artists and audience. New forms of art developed in the different regions of the world, ranging from Mesopotamia to the Mayan civilization, and from the Indus Valley to China.

Over the next two millennia a vast range of artistic expression unfurled, producing masterpieces of creativity around the world. Mesopotamian art thrived around 4000 BC and produced the architectural marvel of the Hanging Gardens of Babylon, so named because of the remarkable tiered garden terraces that showcased different variety of flora around palace structures.

Around 3000 BC, one of the first great civilizations of the world was born in Egypt. The Egyptian civilization took art and architecture to dizzying heights—figuratively and literally! The mastery of architecture, the concept of immortality and the centralized power structures combined to produce breathtaking pyramids and temples. Pyramids, such as Saqqara and Giza, underground tombs such as the Valley of the Kings and temples such as Karnak, Luxor and Abu Simbel significantly raised the bar as artistic marvels for the world to behold. Other works of art such as The Sphinx and Tutankhamun's Tomb were further expressions of human creativity, and inspired and entertained millions of people for generations.

Egyptian art inspired derivative art forms amongst Greek and Etruscan artists, and subsequently Roman artists, who adapted the look and feel of the art forms to their features and environments. Art, thus adapted to reflect the context and characteristics of each local populace.

The Los Millares culture subsequently emerged in Spain, characterized by human pictures with exaggerated big eyes. Elsewhere in Europe, Celtic, Greek, Etruscan and Scythian art emerged, focusing especially on decorative swords, shields, spears and carts. These disparate styles thrived for centuries, until the great Roman Empire brought its own style and influence across much of the continent of Europe.

From its founding by Romulus in 753 BC, the Roman Empire grew into one of the greatest empires the world has ever seen.

An empire of its size and scope of course produced extraordinary feats of architectural accomplishments. The Romans revolutionized construction with advanced forms of cement and concrete. They built exceptional roads and bridges, such as Trajan's bridge over the Danube that lasted for over a thousand years! Other remarkable architectural feats included aqueducts and dams which could transfer and store water across great distances, greatly enhancing the survivability and sustenance of people. They also constructed public baths and arenas, with its showcase accomplishment being the Roman Colosseum.

The Roman Empire also saw the production of exceptional pieces of art. Roman art was heavily influenced by Greek art and was largely commissioned by wealthy patrons for use in their own private residences, or displayed in public baths as a gift to the masses. The artists themselves were treated as labourers, thus requiring affluent sponsors to mediate the art and its appreciation between creators and consumers. Art flourished and thrived in all its myriad forms, from portraits and paintings to sculptures and mosaics.

As the Roman Empire and its influence waned in the arts, the era of medieval art began in Europe and surrounding areas. Early Christian art started approximately 100 years after Christianity itself, even though it was constrained by a lack of patronage and resources in the period immediately following the dawn of Christianity. Subsequent to that it thrived for 400 years once people were able to express themselves more expansively.

Around 550 AD, Christian art transitioned into Byzantine art, so named after the Byzantine, or Eastern Roman Empire. Byzantine art was characterized by classical aesthetics and symbolic representation, and produced incredible masterpieces such as the church of Hagia Sophia in Constantinople and St Mark's Basilica in Venice. Byzantine art was held in high regard and influenced artists far beyond the domains of the Empire itself. Craftsmen and artists from Eastern Europe, Russia, Greece, Cyprus and Turkey took their Byzantine inspirations and adapted them for their own cultural and geographic contexts.

This period was followed with other derivatives, such as Anglo-Saxon, Viking and Gothic art, each contextualizing major art forms of the time to their unique locales and interpretations. The end of the Byzantine Empire, marked by the Fall of Constantinople in 1453 at the hands of the Ottoman Turks, is credited with triggering one of the greatest artistic movements in human history—the Renaissance.

The Renaissance began in Florence, Italy, in the 14th century, triggered by a confluence of scholars and artists migrating after the Fall of Constantinople, and a powerful patronage of the arts promulgated by the Medici, the dominant family of the region. The Renaissance thereafter began to take hold in other Italian city-states as well, and found ready resonance in its core belief of humanism, or the centrality of human beings in the world. People flocked to the universal appeal of humanism and the desire for people to express and be seen and heard by other humans as human!

Humanism was reflected in the exemplary pieces of art depicting humans and the environs in very factual, direct and representative form. The period gave rise to legendary pieces of art, paintings, sculptures and monuments, and legendary artists such as Michelangelo, Leonardo da Vinci, Botticelli and Donatello. The skill and mastery these artists brought to depicting human form and nature in realistic ways continued to find great appreciation and allure for consumers seeking art that they could identify with and relate to.

Over the next 200 years, art evolved to the neoclassical and realism genres, and eventually to the art forms of the 20th century. This ushered in two main trends, reflecting the state of mind of artists and consumers themselves. First, a much wider range of artistic styles took hold—ranging from impressionism to expressionism, and from cubism to surrealism. The second was a much greater degree of global influence in art work, leading to

fusion elements that further multiplied the emerging proliferations of styles. These trends point to a greater desire amongst artists
to express themselves in myriad ways, and a greater desire amongst
consumers to appreciate and patronize art forms in myriad ways.
Freed from strong cultural or religious directives, freed from
funding constraints and with the patronage of financial sponsors,
artists were finding more and more diverse ways to express themselves, leading to a greater range of artwork than ever before.

This range of creativity of course took a major step forward
with the advent of the computer. An entire new genre of art form
emerged—digital art. The effort and costs it took to produce digital
art fell to a fraction of the effort to produce traditional art.
The tools available to artists digitally far surpassed those available
to traditional artists. And the Internet made it incredibly easy to
publish and showcase artwork to others.

Since then this has produced a remarkable transformation in
the world of art production and consumption.

The lines between artists and consumers are blurring. Every consumer
can now be an artist. Every digital sketch or diagram is a piece of art.
Every doodle, every photograph is a piece of art. And yes, every selfie
is a piece of art!

The digital art form took another significant step forward with the
invention of 3D printing in 1983 by Charles Hull in the United
States. Over the next 20 years, the ability to bring to physical life
any object that could be imagined in an artist's mind, empowered
creativity in unprecedented ways. 3D creations to date include
cameras, guns, items of clothing, toys and even edible food!

AN ARTIST IN EVERY CONSUMER

With the Internet and social media, every consumer now also has
a studio. Consumers can choose to showcase their art to private or

public audience at the click of a button. They can display it for free or charge a viewing fee for their art. Digital art production, consumption and distribution is entirely democratized and not constrained by any patrons or states or mediators any more.

The digital world has unlocked the artist in each of us. Consumers have so much of themselves to express, and now they can. Art is no longer the domain of a few artists and their patrons. It is the now the domain of all.

What this has also unlocked is the true will of consumers when it comes to art.

In 2014, consumers uploaded 657 billion photographs to share with others. Every two minutes, consumers take more pictures than what existed in total 150 years ago!

This is how the consumer revolution is now expressing its will in art. It is defining art first and foremost by relevance. The Mona Lisa is an incredible masterpiece at the Louvre in Paris. The Birth of Venus is a breathtaking painting at the Uffizi Gallery in Florence. But they pale in comparison to a mom's picture of a child taking her first step, or a grandma looking at her grandson's graduation picture. What determines the value of an art is the audience's appreciation and utility for it. The consumer revolution will require art to be relevant and valuable in an individualized, personalized context for it to be most appreciated. It is setting in motion a profound democratization in the realm of art.

THE PROLIFERATION OF MUSIC

Another fundamental form of entertainment for the human race has been music. Music also dates back to the early days of human development, and is believed to have been formally invented in Africa 55,000 years ago. Early music was likely drawn from the sounds of nature and developed with patterns and rhythms humans discovered in their natural habitats. The earliest musical instrument was the human voice itself.

The earliest musical instruments found date back to 35,000 years ago in modern-day Germany. A variety of musical instruments and singing traditions have been discovered, ranging from Australian Aboriginal to Native American music. The earliest forms of music were chants and hymns to the gods, conducted by priests and choirs that formed cultural centres for these art forms in civilizations like Sumer. The Sumerian civilization is credited with the oldest known song, replete with patterns and harmonies, approximately 3,400 years ago. Elsewhere, the Elamite Empire in ancient Iran is known to have produced music as far back as 2500 BC. The Indian civilization has records of music dating back to 1500 BC and is credited with having invented the first string instrument.

The Greek civilization is known to have developed and patronized music to an extensive degree, with traditions such as Greek theatre, and a wide range of reed-and string-based musical instruments. Typical themes were religious and spiritual, but also celebration and entertainment. The oldest surviving musical composition found to date is Seikilos epitaph in Greece, dating back to 100 AD.

Other civilizations around the world developed musical artists, talents and productions. From early Biblical regions to Persia and the Arabic civilizations, from the Indian subcontinent to China, and from Africa to Brazil and South America, music developed into a universal form of entertainment. The instruments and sounds varied greatly, but the emotion and appeal behind it were universal, drawing in increasing followings and audiences between impassioned musicians and their equally passionate audiences.

In many regions of the world, musical trends ebbed and flowed, new instruments and sounds emerged, and the best musical traditions continued and thrived for hundreds of years. Saint Gregory the Great who was Pope of the Catholic Church from 590 AD is credited with composing worship music known as the Gregorian chants that still continue till today.

Musical traditions took a significant step forward with the Renaissance, along with other art forms that flourished at the time. The root of the musical movement wasn't Italy however, but the northern European regions of France, Belgium and the Netherlands. The universal appeal of music spread from there to southern Europe and the British Isles.

The Baroque musical tradition emerged towards the end of the Renaissance and gave rise to an incredible wealth of musical masterpieces at the hands of classical composers such as Haydn, Mozart, Beethoven, Schubert and Bach. Music began to express more emotions that consumers could relate to, leading to the Romantic music era typified by the genius of Chopin, Strauss, Brahms, Tchaikovsky and Puccini. Composers drew heavily from one another when exposed to each other's work, and the musical trends and patronage from those in power and privilege began to provide them larger and larger platforms to perform. The emotional appeal to consumers started to draw in larger audiences, and the art form began to grow in popularity.

Music, however, remained regionalized, as the only way to listen to it was being physically present at a performance. The only other way to transport music was via written form, to be rendered and played at another venue by another musician. This prompted the development of very different forms of music around the world. For instance, the Indian musical tradition was very distinct from its Western counterparts. Even though the evidence of music dates back to the ancient Hindu text of Samaveda in 1000 BC, there was almost no crossover with Western styles or sounds for thousands of years. Indian classical music itself had a Carnatic tradition from the southern region of the country that preserved its purity through the years. The Hindustani tradition of Indian classical music thrived in the northern region of the country, and incorporated styles and influences of the Mughal rulers of India. Indian music had entirely different instruments, schools and traditions than what were prevalent in Europe at the time, reflective of the lack of contact and transportability of the art form.

Music always had a powerful and universal appeal, but its proliferation had to be limited to physical audience. All that changed in 1877, when Thomas Edison invented the phonograph. This had a profound effect on the spread of music around the world. For the first time, you did not need to be at the same venue as the musicians to listen to their music. Consumers were able to enjoy and appreciate and discover music from around the world— at any time and place of their choosing.

They did, however, need to possess the specialized piece of equipment called a phonograph to enjoy their music. And they did need to possess a copy of the music on a record or other device to be able to play their music. And of course, the musicians needed the equipment to record their music in the first place.

This created a tremendous opportunity for companies to create these pieces of equipment, and enable both musicians and consumers to accomplish their respective needs and desires. Huge companies such as Bang & Olufsen, Columbia Gramophone Company, Harman Kardon, Panasonic and Philips were born, and thrived by meeting the needs of the market. These manufacturers grew to positions of tremendous leverage and power over consumers and musical artists by virtue of their mediation between the two.

The ability of consumers to enjoy their favourite music changed further with the invention of the radio in 1895 by Guglielmo Marconi. Consumers no longer had to buy individual copies of all the musical pieces they wished to hear. The radio service operator would do it for them. Consumers simply needed to buy one piece of equipment—the radio—and leave the rest to the radio operator.

The value proposition of radio was powerful, and led to very wide spread adoption. Millions of consumers flocked to radios to get entertained and informed, and thousands of radio stations emerged to meet their needs. Amplitude modulated or AM radio could reach a large base of audience, albeit at somewhat lower quality, leading to radio stations with massive reach, such as BBC, Voice of America and All India Radio. Frequency modulated or FM radio could reach smaller, more targeted audience bases, at higher quality, resulting in a great variety of local programming consumers could enjoy.

Radio created another powerful class of intermediaries in the mix—radio stations. They became the purveyors of consumers' entertainment experiences, the core enablers for consumers and musicians. Large AM stations had the reach and economies of scale to begin with, but even FM stations got in the act by merging or banding together to produce behemoths such as Clear Channel and iHeartMedia that could really mediate and control consumer listening experiences.

Radio introduced another fundamental constraint for consumers—they had to listen to what the radio stations chose to broadcast, when they chose to broadcast it. This correlated by and large to what most other consumers wanted to listen to as well, and there was typically a choice of dozens of radio stations to choose from in a town to find one that largely played the right music, but it was still an experience of listening to what and when someone else wanted to play for you, rather than you picking it yourself.

For this reason, radio co-existed with recorded music for decades. Consumers could listen to a musical station or programme that by and large fit their interest profile in a fairly effortless and inexpensive manner, or for select musical pieces, they could listen at any time or place but for a cost. Both models served the consumers' needs, and they each had their pros and cons, so consumers went along with both.

That began to change, like everything else, with the advent of the personal computer and the Internet. Now, for the first time, consumers did not have to choose or compromise on their musical entertainment. The technology reached a point where it could deliver them exactly the music they wanted, when they wanted it, without needing to buy and store physical records or tapes or cassettes. Once enabled by the technology, the consumer revolution in music has taken over. It is now fundamentally resetting the power dynamic between consumers, producers and distributors of musical entertainment.

Over the Internet, consumers have seen that they can get choice and control. They are increasingly consuming their music on demand—theirs and not the radio operator's. They are increasingly compiling their playlists, in effect creating their own radio programmes and radio channels. They are deciding what their morning commute, their easy listening at work, their gym music, their drive home, their fall asleep music should sound like.

Consumers have seen that they can unbundle music. They no longer have to listen to a playlist composed by someone else. Whether it is composed by a radio station into a radio programme, or a record company into an album, there is no reason to put up with songs you don't like just to get to the to the ones you do. And consumers won't. The fundamental purpose of record companies and radio stations is disappearing. The part of the food chain with the most power and leverage is dissipating.

Consumers are also exploring new music on their own. Musical artists are exploring new audiences on their own. The process by which they find each other is fundamentally changing from one mediated by radio stations and record companies, to one enabled by search engines and bookmarking services. This is getting enabled on a worldwide scale. This is what enabled PSY's Gangnam Style to become such a global phenomenon. Before the Internet, this would never have happened.

Layer on to this the enablement power of social media, and you have a whole new dynamic emerging. It is becoming extremely inexpensive for consumers to record and distribute their own music. In other words, become musical artists themselves. For every

Taylor Swift musical hit, there are thousands of covers recorded and published. There are thousands of musical artists expressing their art and publishing it for all who care. As long as they have a passion, an emotion, they now have a voice. And as long as they strike a chord with someone else, they now have an audience. From digital formats to household karaoke, music is becoming more and more participatory. The lines between performer and audience are blurring more and more.

This is how the consumer revolution is starting to express itself in musical entertainment. It will increasingly require that music be relevant and tailored to individual consumers. It will require that music be served when and where it desires. Consumers will seek out musical artists who touch them, speak to them at a certain point of time. Professional artists will need to produce exemplary quality music to get consumers to pay for it. Otherwise they will get drowned out by the volume of musical selection available for free. And radio stations will need to produce exemplary quality programme composition, exceptional compering and storytelling to engage consumers, and exquisite community building to fill a loneliness void in consumers. Otherwise they will be side-stepped by the pure elegance of unadulterated playlists.

THE WRITTEN FORM

Another core art form in the world is literature. Arts and entertainment, and civilization itself, took a major step forward with the invention of writing around 3500 BC in Mesopotamia. From the first writing codes on clay tablets, writing developed in leaps and bounds, evolving through pictographic and ideographic elements, syllables, hieroglyphics and ultimately to the alphabet, likely first used by the Hebrew language around 1800 BC. This journey demonstrated the constant urge of humans to express themselves and convey information in more and more precise, particular, yet efficient ways. And of course, this gave rise to one of the core pillars of entertainment—literature. From this point onwards, humans would continue to express their creativity, passions, emotions, ideas, fantasies, musings and ponderings in written poetry and prose, and others would continue to find tremendous fulfilment and entertainment in reading them.

While the early days of writing focused on recording information rather than what we today classify as literature, in the 17th century BC, the Sumerian civilization produced the *Epic of Gilgamesh*—one of the first acknowledged masterpieces of actual literature. A vast amount of literature produced in this period followed the oral tradition, such as the Rigveda and other Hindu epics from India, the Hebrew Tanakh and the Chinese poems of Lao Tzu. In Europe, Homer's *Iliad* and *Odyssey* became standard bearers of early literature, from the 8th century BC.

In the 5th century BC, Sun Tzu wrote the Chinese epic *The Art of War*, which became a bible for generals and corporate readers even through today. In the 3rd century BC, Hebrew literature completed the Old Testament after decades of refinement by scholars. Greek literature brought philosophy to the world of literature via texts such as Plato's Socratic questioning, and Aristotle's *Poetics*. Greek literature also produced the New Testament in the 1st century AD, which remains deeply contextual and contemporary in today's culture and society as well. Latin literature produced Virgil's *Aeneid* and Augustine's *City of God*. Indian literature produced derivative philosophies and epics such as the Ramayana and the Mahabharata. What was fascinating about these works was that they were largely created independently, physical distances making it difficult to share and follow other examples. So the need amongst consumers to express themselves in all societies was immense and universal, and the appetite to consume and enjoy literature insatiable and equally universal.

As the Roman Empire dwindled in influence, Islamic literature rose in prominence, highlighted by the epic *Book of One Thousand and One Nights*, also called *Arabian Nights*, which was created over an astonishing 400 years, culminating in its final form in the 14th century AD. The style of storytelling, and epic characters such as Aladdin, Ali Baba and Sinbad have become global icons to this day. Subsequently, the Persian culture produced the legendary *Rubaiyat of Omar Khayyam* in the 11th century AD.

Literature took a big step forward with the Renaissance in Europe in the 15th century AD. The range of creativity and expression was testament to the continual and relentless desire by humans to be entertained and informed on more and more subjects, themes and genres.

An even greater impact to the art form was the invention of the printing press by Johann Gutenberg in 1455. This changed the rules of the game completely. Books were no longer rare and expensive, and created by hand one laborious copy after another. Reading was no longer the domain of the select and the privileged few. For the first time ever, reading and literature became exposed to consumers everywhere, and they took to it with enthusiastic abandon. The printing press democratized literature, and the world would never be the same again.

With this mass access and appeal, literature evolved from religion, spirituality and philosophy to folk tales and storytelling. William Caxton ushered in mass printing with English texts such as *Le Morte d'Arthur*, and Geoffrey Chaucer gave us *Canterbury Tales*. Other innovations in literature followed, such as Petrarch inventing poetic sonnets, Giovanni Boccaccio introducing romance in texts, Francois Rabelais popularizing satire, Michel de Montaigne inventing the essay, and Nicolaus Copernicus famously debunking the prevalent notion of the earth being the centre of the universe.

Another literary form that took flight during this era was the play. This art form was popularized by perhaps the most legendary writer the world has ever known—William Shakespeare—in the 16th century AD. The 'Bard of Avon' produced a stunning sequence of literary masterpieces, ranging from *Julius Caesar* and *Romeo and Juliet* to *Merchant of Venice* and *Hamlet*. Such was the power of

Shakespeare's work that his stories were put in theatrical production at the time and continue to make some of the most acclaimed productions to this day. Consumers were being served up literary entertainment in an ever-expanding tray of delights, in whichever format they fancied.

In 1605, one of the most dominant forms of literature was created—the novel. Miguel de Cervantes is credited with having been the first true novelist in the world with his classic *Don Quixote*. This format grew in popularity as consumers found the novel's form and storytelling style very appealing. As literary content became more relatable and entertaining rather than didactic or pedantic, it registered increasing amount of consumer interest and patronage.

The themes covered in novels and literary texts became more and more contextual and relevant, a nod to the mass appeal of the literary art form. There was interplay with current events, such as in the Elizabethan poem *The Faerie Queene* by Edmund Spenser. There was satire about the political elite and earlier literature itself in *Don Quixote*. There was metaphysical poetry such as that of John Donne and Andrew Marvel, seeking to mirror and shed light on the consumers' quest for understanding and enlightenment. And there was the epic *Paradise Lost* by John Milton, reflecting a religious point of view on the sentiments of the day. Literature was taking myriad forms to reflect the myriad perspectives of its audience.

This democratization and diverse nature of literature has continued to thrive in the modern era. There have been powerful writings of enlightenment and knowledge from Voltaire, Immanuel Kant and Adam Smith. There has been exquisite romance in the poetry of William Wadsworth and Lord Byron. There have been enchanting storytelling in the works of Hans Christian Andersen.

The volume and range of books has continued to grow as the barriers to publishing and consumption have fallen, and the interests of consumers have multiplied. By one estimate, there are now 130 million books in the world. That is one book for every 57 people in the world!

The popularity and utility of literature, of course, took a major step forward with arrival of the personal computer. Writers could now write books much more efficiently, aided by word processing and editing software, and tools such as spell checkers and thesauruses. Publishers could now publish books on electronic media, leading to even lower production costs and even greater production efficiencies than the printing press. And consumers could now read books in electronic text form, or for the first time, in audio form, greatly expanding the range of consumption for literature.

The Internet further enabled the consumer revolution in literary entertainment, ushering in even greater ease of literature production and consumption. The forms of literature began to evolve in keeping with the medium, giving rise to shorter formats and an ever-expanding array of topics and genres to keep pace with the consumers' disparate interests. In many cases, styles began evolving to the more direct, shorter, to the point, highly relevant and highly contextual communication style of the Internet.

This evolution gave rise to one of the most ubiquitous forms of literature in today's world—the blog. In 1994, Justin Hall, a student at Swarthmore College created his personal home page called Links.net which is credited with being the first blog ever produced. In 1997, Jorn Barger at Robot Wisdom coined the term 'weblog' to describe the art form of chronicling and logging the web. Eventually, Peter Merholz abbreviated the term weblog to blog in 1999.

The blog developed into the signature literary art form on the Internet. It also became a powerful expression of the consumer revolution showing up in literary entertainment. The colloquial, conversational style empowered anyone and everyone to become an author. The short and contemporary formats made it much easier to create and maintain blogs. They made it equally easy for the audiences to consume and digest their content. And of course, the Internet made it extraordinarily simple for blog authors to find audience, and for consumers to find blogs they found appealing.

The consumer revolution prompted an explosion of creativity with the blog. Blogs emerged everywhere, and on every conceivable genre and topic you could imagine. There are now blogs for spiritual beliefs and alternative medicine, there are blogs for financial analysis and entertainment industry gossip, there are blogs for cats, dogs, babies, travels, art, cuisine, guns, weaponry, science, celebrities, festivals, sports, dolls, religions, fashion, legal issues and love. In short, for everything. As of 2017, there were more than 440 million blogs in the world, and counting!

The last 20 years have produced more than three times the number of pieces of literary art as the entire history of humankind up to this point! The consumer revolution in literature has arrived.

Another phenomenon ushered in by the Internet is the ease of interaction between writers and readers. It has become just as easy for authors to write, as it is for readers to respond and write back. The lines between the two are beginning to blur. And the dynamic of shared authorship between the original writer and the original reader has taken hold. Writing reviews or other forms of what is labelled user-generated content have become as integral to literature as the original text itself. Consumers read articles, and then read reactions from other consumers oftentimes with as much interest and enthusiasm as the original article itself. Literature has entered the realm of interactive or collaborative writing. The consumer revolution is unleashing the creative energies and expressions for both readers and writers simultaneously, a compounding effect that is creating explosive literary output compared to anything human society has seen before.

Over the next several decades, the consumer revolution will drive literature to more and more variety and range, in addition to the inevitable growth in sheer volume and scale. Every conceivable topic will have been written about. There will be an author and an audience for every topic of interest that can be conceived. Blogs will enable an expression of interest and passion for every consumer and every writer. Consumers will get more passionate about their beliefs and preferences and likes. And they will get less passionate about just about everything else!

There will be increasing fragmentation in the literary world. The readership of any given book or blog will go down over time, but the passion with which it is consumed will skyrocket, and the number of books and blogs will increase astronomically. Authors and books will need to be of exceptional quality and appeal to get widespread readership and rise above the noise level, but once they do, will be fuelled and promoted by, well other books and blogs themselves!

This fragmentation and proliferation of literature is powered by consumer desire and expression, and cannot be stopped. The consumer revolution will reward authors and producers who appeal to large enough cross-sections, or to ultra-passionate and motivated audience members. And it will shun those who don't. Literature will become less about an author's self-expression and more about consumer appeal. It will become less about the author and more about the audience. The consumer revolution is shifting power from authors to audiences in unprecedented ways.

As this power shift happens, there will also be increasing transfer of value and power from authors of books or blogs on myriad topics to technology providers that enable consumers to find them. Search engines will thus play a massive role in the evolution of literature in the era to come and realize massive gains from serving this universal need. Finding the right literature piece will become as valuable if not more so than the piece itself. The consumer revolution will create a massive concentration of power in content search engines.

The literary art form will evolve in other ways too. The media format itself will evolve into formats that mirror the basic human senses. After the invention of the cassette tape in 1963, some libraries started distributing books in audio form. Today, audiobooks are seeing a rapid increase in proliferation and sales, as consumers switch to consuming literature in a sensory form that consumes less mental energy and has higher absorption efficiency—listening rather than reading. Audio will continue to rise in popularity as a more effortless and hence more enjoyable way to consume literature than reading alone.

THE ADVENT OF PERFORMING ARTS

When it comes to entertainment, one of the core art forms has been theatre, and more recently, movies, television and videos. The origins of the art form lie in the performance of rituals dating back centuries ago. From religious to social to family rituals, humans found ways to amplify and express sentiments through increasingly elaborate forms, entailing locales, dresses, movement and music. As the rituals got more sophisticated, the acts of performing them became more elaborate, leading to the earliest theatrical performances. Naturally, consumers gathered around the most compelling such performances, fuelling greater passion in performers to continually raise the quality of their performances. This in turn drew in more audience, and the cycle built on itself.

As theatre performers got more refined and sophisticated, they began using props, costumes and masks, and became adept at storytelling. This branched out theatre from the traditional ritualistic themes to other themes dealing with societal, personal and emotional themes. A more expansive version of theatre thus began to take shape.

The state of theatrical performing arts took a major step forward in Greek society in the 6th century BC. Greek theatre formed the foundation of the Western art form and covered many of the prevalent themes that affected Greek society. Greek theatre gave us the art forms of Greek tragedy, Greek comedy and Greek satyr that have survived and thrive till today. Performance arts centres and amphitheatres around the world can trace their origins to the Theatre of Epidaurus, the best preserved of the Athenian theatres dating back to the 4th century BC.

The mantle of exceptional theatre was taken over by the Romans after that period. The Romans refined and enhanced the theatre substantially through festivals, street theatre, and of course, stage performances. Roman theatre drew heavily from its Greek counterparts, and elaborate, sophisticated situation comedies and tragedies were born. With the spread of the Roman Empire, theatre spread to much of Europe, England and the Mediterranean, spurred by its powerful artistic expressions, and the enthusiasm with which it was received by the audience. By the 2nd century BC, drama was firmly established as an art form within theatre, and the first writers guild was formed in Rome.

With the decline of the Western Roman Empire, theatre along with the seat of Roman power shifted to Constantinople and the Byzantine Empire. Evidence points to the development of several variations of the theatrical art form during this period, ranging from mimes to pantomimes to dances. This was followed by a period of religious and liturgical theatre that lasted for several centuries, through Europe's Dark Ages.

Like other art and entertainment forms, there was a revival of theatre during the Renaissance with theatrical troupes known as the Commedia dell'arte. By some measures, the golden age of theatre was the period that followed in English Elizabethan theatre. Under the patronage of Queen Elizabeth I, a rich range and variety of theatre thrived on the Elizabethan stage, and in the sprawling suburbs of London. Consumers flocked to these theatres, galvanized by the mastery of the likes of William Shakespeare and Ben Jonson, and the talent of the actors on stage.

Theatre as an art form also thrived in various regions of Spain, France, Germany and Scandinavia. Evidence of theatrical events has been found dating back to 2000 BC in Egypt, and 1500 BC in China. Indian theatre developed around the 2nd century BC, and developed a rich tradition and variety reflecting its many regional cultures and styles. In Japan, one of the most recognized and beloved theatrical art forms, the Kabuki theatre, took form in the 16th century, and introduced variations such as dancing, singing and acrobatics. Persian theatre took shape in the 7th century AD and reflected the storytelling and puppetry interests of local audience.

Through the course of its history, theatre continued to evolve and diversify into themes and genres increasingly sought out by the audiences and consumers. It became one of the dominant forms of entertainment around the world. It still, however, required physical presence and proximity to be seen and heard.

That all changed with the invention of the motion picture. The roots of this innovation go back to the invention of the still camera by Nicephore Niepce in 1816. The ability to capture a photograph and be able to share it with others at a different time and place had a major impact in the world. Photographic exposure however took an hour or more until 1870 when the exposure time was brought down to one-hundredth of a second. This triggered the beginnings of the first motion picture, commissioned interestingly enough by Governor Leland Stanford of California, a name to be associated with many of the most remarkable innovations of the modern era. Governor Stanford hired a British American photographer, Eadweard Muybridge to photograph a horse multiple times in rapid succession to visually prove that all four hooves were off the ground for split seconds when the horse was at full gallop. Muybridge was able to project these images as a moving picture to prove Governor Stanford's hypothesis. And in the process, he created the world's first motion picture!

In 1887, Hannibal Goodwin came up with the idea of using celluloid for photography, and George Eastman commercialized the technology in 1889. Subsequently, William Dickson was able to combine the celluloid and rapid image capture technologies to come up with the first motion picture camera under the stewardship of Thomas Edison in 1888. The technology continued to develop in laboratories and trial shows, until the first commercial screening of the Lumiere Brothers' short films in Paris in 1895. One of the most dominant art forms of today's society had been born.

From there, motion pictures continued their proliferation at a rapid pace, as for the first time theatrical performances were unshackled from physical audiences. A dizzying array of motion pictures could be made anywhere in the world and shown anywhere else at any later time. The efficiency of entertainment went up dramatically, and consumers lapped it up. With their produce-once, show-many model, motion pictures were able to produce movies with far greater production quality, and amortize their investments with extended returns. The economics became far superior to traditional theatre. This in turn produced a dramatic expansion of the volume and categories of motion pictures produced, feeding the insatiable appetite of the audience to consume them.

The quality and richness of motion pictures continued to evolve over the next several years. In 1927, *The Jazz Singer* became the first motion picture to introduce sound mixed in with the video. The effect on the audience was electrifying, as they took in the significantly enhanced viewing experience augmented by sound. Colour was introduced into motion pictures in stages, triggered by Technicolor in Walt Disney's Silly Symphony cartoons, The Cat and the Fiddle in 1934 and Becky Sharp in 1935. Colour was immortalized in motion picture by Gone with the Wind and The Wizard of Oz in 1939. Colour brought the art form to life, and lead to a further proliferation of the art form amongst consumers. The appeal of movies, the power of their storytelling, the deep emotional connection with consumers soon made it a staple entertainment format for consumers around the world. Movie producers, actors and actresses, and movie theatres developed significant prestige and leverage from becoming the purveyors of such mass appeal amongst consumers.

THE RISE AND FALL OF TELEVISION

Even though the performances in motion pictures weren't live, consumers still had to physically go to movie theatres to consume their entertainment. This wasn't quite the barrier it was to physically attend live theatre, but still took some energy for consumers to expend. This was all set to change in 1927 with the invention of the television by Philo Taylor Farnsworth. Now, for the first time, consumers could enjoy motion pictures and other forms of audio visual entertainment from the comfort of their homes, at a fraction of the time and cost it took to see them in theatres. Televisions rapidly developed an audience that scaled to cover nearly all consumers. They started to consume more and more television entertainment by the year.

As the audience grew, a powerful new class of service provider emerged—the television network. Television networks became the bridge between motion picture and television performers and their audience, and began to wield enormous power. They accumulated the power and leverage to decide what programming they showed when, which audience they targeted with which shows and established a powerful influence on society. Television networks such as ABC, CBS, NBC, BBC, Canal+, Doordarshan, CCTV, ARD and Univision became household names, and major influence centres worldwide.

Television spread like wildfire around the world. The flames were further fanned by the arrival of live sports coverage on television. International sporting events such as the Olympics and World Cup in football/soccer became major television phenomena drawing in massive audience. The 2014 World Cup Football final between Germany and Argentina drew an audience over 1 billion people. The tournament as a whole was watched by 3 billion people! Similarly, a 2015 World Cup Cricket game between India and Pakistan drew an audience of 1 billion people.

Nation by nation and region by region, sports leagues sprung up around the world, ranging from the English Premier League for football to the NFL for American football, the Indian Premier League for cricket to the National Basketball Association for basketball. The thrill and drama, and athletic brilliance drew in live audience of course, but they also started to draw in massive television-based audience. Some sports, such as the longer formats of cricket, have become television-primary events, seeing bare stadiums and low physical attendance rates, but vast numbers of sports enthusiasts watching the games from home.

Other live events also fuelled the popularity of television amongst consumers. Entertainment industry award shows such as the Oscars and the Grammys became major television and cultural events, with consumers taking in the live drama replete with glamorous viewing parties of their own. Even political events, such as presidential debates and inauguration ceremonies, royal weddings and funerals, and global summits became major television events.

Audience flocked to television in many different forms and fashions, for many different reasons. They were drawn in by the wide array of television programming on offer. There was something on television for everyone. Some watched television in solitude—it offered company when there was none other to be found. It filled a void in people's lives when there was nothing else to fill it. It provided enthralling entertainment, poignant characters, merry laughter, myriad stories and vignettes to relate to. It brought the world into people's homes.

Others watched television in their communities. It became a prop, a rallying point for communities to come together for a shared experience. There was a community and a shared interest for more and more themes and beliefs, and values and interests. People got together for important national or community events, viewed together, celebrated together, bonded and gelled around televised events and programmes.

Television gradually became the primary source of entertainment around the world. In the United States, in 1996, an incredible 98.4 per cent of the population had one or more televisions at home. The average amount of time televisions were switched on per American household was an astonishing 7 hours 40 minutes every day! Television had incredible sway over consumers, to the point where they structured their days and habits around television programmes.

In the process, television networks, manufacturers, producers, actors, actresses, singers, dancers, athletes, coaches, cheerleaders, studios and distributors became enormously powerful and influential. They became superstars, legends and role models that consumers wanted to follow and emulate around the world. An entire paparazzi industry was born to feed the insatiable appetite for celebrity glimpses and vignettes—real or fabricated! Tabloids were born for consumers' cravings to feast on. Every celebrity stroll was recorded, every sneeze became a news feature, every dinner outing a global event. And every celebrity romantic association or separation fodder for gossip. Pure grand theatre! Consumers lapped up every minute detail of these larger-than-life stars and events.

And then the Internet happened. And social media happened. And as with everything else, the giant wheels of the consumer revolution started to turn. As with everything else, the consumer revolution set in motion a relentless trajectory that is threatening to upend the status quo.

Consumers began to seize power and control from producers of entertainment. They began to watch movies and television shows at their own time and place, rather than when broadcasters chose to broadcast them. They chose to be entertained under their rules, not under the rules mandated by television networks, such as needing to watch a programme late at night, or suffering through commercials to get to the entertainment they wanted. Entirely new companies such as TiVo, Comcast DVR, Netflix, Hulu and Amazon Prime sprung up to serve the consumer revolutionary wishes.

Now, the consumer revolution has begun to impose its will on the nature of programming it likes. Producers are branching out, even scrambling to address the themes consumers are expressing interest in, leading to extensive fragmentation and a widening range of movies and television. The mainstream is getting carved up into smaller and smaller niches as consumer power and interest trumps the economies of scale in producing entertainment.

Layer on to this the democratic appeal of social media, and you have a gale-force wind coming at the entertainment industry. The centre of gravity for what is appealing entertainment is defined by the consumer more so than the producer. And increasingly, the lines between the two are blurring. Consumers are becoming producers of entertainment, and they are able to distribute their entertainment with as much ease as professional producers. Any teenager can produce either a funny video, skit, cover song or meme with ease. Once produced, the teenager can then distribute the production to 500 of his or her closest friends and family members with complete ease.

Consumers are already empowering themselves to consume mainstream entertainment of their choice, on their own time, in a giant entertainment-on-demand paradigm. Now that choice is further expanded in real time by 'micro' entertainment produced by near and dear ones.

This friends and family generated-micro entertainment is highly relevant and appealing to consumers. Johnny's game winning goal in his local club soccer can be far more appealing to grandma than Cristiano Ronaldo's in the Champions League. Sarah's cover of an Ariana Grande song can be far more appealing to grandpa than the original itself. What is familiar, what is immediate, what is up close and personal can offer far more relevant and meaningful entertainment than what is out there. Consumers are producing more and more compelling micro entertainment that is highly relevant to their micro audience and that is providing stiff competition to mainstream professional entertainment. This is leading to a further fragmentation in the world of entertainment, and an erosion of audience for even the most prime of entertainment programmes.

For the first time since its advent, traditional television has been in slow decline in the 2010s, as on-demand services such as Netflix, Hulu and Amazon Prime ramp up to astonishing levels over the same period of time.

Netflix added nearly 9 million new paying subscribers during the final three months of 2018. The service now has 139 million subscribers globally, and its growth in international market is exceptionally strong, demonstrating it is fit for today's consumers.

Over the same period of time, another on demand service on the right side of the consumer revolution, Amazon Prime, surpassed 100 million subscribers. So while television viewership is going down, the viewership for on demand services is actually going up rapidly. Clear evidence of the consumer revolution at work!

What is particularly eye-catching in 2017 and 2018 is how even the most sacrosanct of television programming is now in decline. While there were many factors at work, television audience for the NFL fell 9.7 per cent from 2017 to 2018. Television audience for the 2018 PyeongChang Winter Olympics fell 7 per cent from the 2014 Sochi Winter Olympics. The 2018 Oscars viewership dropped a whopping 20 per cent from its 2017 incarnation. The television sacred cows are being slaughtered. What is going on? Where are all these consumers going?

Enter the consumer revolution. Not only are consumers switching to on demand entertainment, they are spending their time with much more social and personal entertainment. This also produces a significant audience loss amongst 'loneliness viewers'—the cross-section of the consumer base that turned on television not always because of scintillating entertainment, but simply to fill an emotional or personal void. Especially in nuclear societies in North American and Western Europe, television had become everyone's friend. The company of choice to keep when there was no other around. The passive, ambient noise and visuals that filled up a void for a cross-section of consumers.

That emotional void is now filled up by social media. By the 24x7 chatter of friends and family sharing updates, episodes and laughs, all of high relevance to their near and dear ones, if not to the world at large. Who needs a television rerun in the background when you can have first runs of life unfolding for your closest associations in the foreground?

This all presents a major wake-up call for the entertainment industry. Entertainment appeal and economic power is shifting from mega celebrities and sports stars to consumers. And because this has been such a heady rise for the entertainment industry, it is going to be a tough fall to swallow. Stars and celebrities who understand this power shift, and adapt to it, can benefit handsomely. Those that don't are looking at a Greek tragedy in the making.

Celebrities such as Taylor Swift, Beyonce, Katy Perry, Justin Bieber, the Kardashians and the Jenners, Steph Curry, LeBron James, Cristiano Ronaldo and Virat Kohli have built mega consumer followings by understanding the dynamic of the consumer revolution and aligning with it. They can clock Twitter followers in the millions and YouTube views in the hundreds of millions with ease.

To do this, they have had to become part of the consumer revolution. They use the same social media outlets as consumers at large—Twitter, Facebook, Instagram and Snapchat among others. This lets them join the consumer revolution, become part of it. It enables them to adapt to the new form of stardom—through over-exposure rather than under-exposure. Stars and celebrities in the traditional producer-lead era thrived on limited, carefully staged vignettes of audience exposure. You could only see a glimpse of Cary Grant or Gregory Peck in a movie, at the Cannes film festival or the Oscars. This fanned the flames of audience passion for celebrity sightings.

In the current consumer-lead era, celebrities thrive by exponentially greater volume of exposure rather than less. They promote, they express, they share, they bare far more in social media than their predecessors were able to do. They marshal their fan bases adroitly, drip-feeding their audience bases with a steady dose of news, gossip, pictures and videos. Social media has become integral to celebrities, and celebrities have become integral to social media as they ride the consumer revolution. Artists and performers increasingly buck the status quo, often choosing to make major announcements to their fan bases or social communities rather than through the incumbent media outlets and channels they had been using for decades. Celebrities have become among the greatest exponents of how to ride the consumer revolution in entertainment, becoming the envy of politicians and corporations seeing less success in their attempts to ride the same wave.

Riding the consumer revolution in entertainment, however, is a two-edged sword. In the process of assimilating and co-opting the consumer revolution, celebrities have to become and act like consumers too. If an update or a release has to be drip-fed into the fan base every day, or multiple times a day, it cannot be of the same quality as an annual presence at an awards gala. In an effort to humanize themselves, to be relatable and relevant to consumers, celebrities also have to expose their vulnerabilities and weaknesses. How they look on weekends without any makeup on. How they get out of shape during the off-season. How they have the same trials and tribulations in life as any other consumer. How they go through romances and breakups, passion and envy, births and deaths, good times and bad like anyone else.

This human element endears celebrities to their fan bases. But it also becomes the grand equalizer. It brings celebrities to the same level as mainstream consumers. The mystique and the allure of catching a glimpse of your favourite larger-than-life star starts to dwindle. The same blood stream that is driving celebrity fandom to stellar levels is also bringing it down to ground level. Once this happens, Johnny's soccer goal and Sarah's music video begin to peel off audiences that would have been otherwise glued to internationally televised events. The consumer revolution is churning relentlessly towards consumer-centric, micro-relevant entertainment, the traditional forms of entertainment are starting to see precipitous decline in appeal and economics.

Another related and powerful trend that is emerging in entertainment, as consumers impose their will on the entertainment complex, is participative entertainment rather than pure spectator entertainment. As can be expected, consumers are seizing their new-found power to craft entertainment with themselves as the centrepiece, rather than the performers. In sports, this entails the new and rapidly growing forms of entertainment such as sports betting and fantasy sports.

Sports betting is how consumers participate in a game without actually playing it. It is how they become the principal rather than the prop in a sporting event. During the annual American sports extravaganza of the Super Bowl, it is great entertainment to watch the game and the festivities around it. But it is also great entertainment to bet on game scores, quarterly scores, individual scores and other events that transpire during the course of the game.

The annual college basketball tournament, colloquially known as March Madness, is great theatre and thrills for the audience. But it is also great entertainment to create brackets, which are predictions for which teams will win which games, leading up to the tournament champion itself.

Like many things, there are legal ways to bet on games and there are illegal ways. But the consumer draw is clear and demonstrated. And the underlying reasons are in plain sight.

In 2015, the worldwide sports betting market was valued at $205 billion. In 2020, it is expected to reach $253 billion, or an annual growth rate in excess of 4 per cent, accelerating to over 8 per cent annual growth rate from 2018–2022.

When it comes to March Madness, in 2017, 23 million viewers watched the championship game. The two semi-finals were watched by 16.8 million viewers each. And the number of consumers who filled out their March Madness brackets? A staggering 90 million, or nearly 30 per cent of the US population. Nearly five times as many people filled out a bracket as watched the game itself!

Another facet of consumers taking charge of their own entertainment is fantasy sports. Consumers are spectators in sporting events. They are the audience, they are secondary to the action on the field. Sports stars are the primary players on the stage. Fantasy sports change all that.

In fantasy sports the centre of gravity shifts to the consumer. The consumer becomes the primary entity in the sport, and the actual sports stars become props. The game becomes about the consumer, not the sports stars performing on the field. This is a phenomenal transfer of power when it is put in perspective. This transfer of power can appear harsh and unfair. It is the athletes on the field who are training, exerting, battling and performing at the peaks of their abilities. They should be adequately compensated for it. And for the most part, they are. Just like they have been in the past.

Except something is changing. With the Internet and social media, the consumer revolution is stepping in. Consumers are making the sport more about them, than about the actual players on the field. They are doing this by creating fantasy leagues and teams. They are drafting players, composing teams, and tracking wins and losses for their fantasy teams. Often times, they are tracking their fantasy teams more closely than the actual physical teams on the field. They are more emotionally vested in their fantasy team performance rather than the on-field performance. If a player gets injured on the field, they are sometimes more concerned about the impact on their fantasy team than on the physical team itself.

As the consumer revolution takes charge of entertainment, fantasy sports are on the rise. In 2014, 14 per cent of the US population was playing fantasy sports. In 2015, it increased to 20 per cent, or a whopping 52 million people. Also fantasy sports are drawing in new audience. Earlier in the decade, women accounted for only 20 per cent of fantasy sports. In 2015, that number rose to 33 per cent. That's a vast demographic development. The consumer revolution is drawing in new audience that were never as much into the actual sport itself. The consumer revolution is disrupting the world of entertainment and making it more about consumers rather than about stars and athletes. That is a profound change that entertainment producers have to understand and adapt to.

GAMES PEOPLE PLAY

Another dimension where the consumer revolution is expressing itself is the growth of video games. At its highest level, a video game is simply a movie where the consumer controls the plot and the action rather than the producer. It's an active form of entertainment rather than the passive form of traditional entertainment. With advances in computing and connectivity, games are getting more and more sophisticated and high quality. The picture quality, the sound quality, the levels of storytelling and production are beginning to rival those of traditional motion pictures. Massively multi-player gaming is introducing an exciting new dynamic of live interaction with other consumers against the backdrop of a game, ushering in wide range of variations in experience, and drawing in different audience for different games.

Consumers are beginning to broach the tipping point, where they are drawing as much enjoyment from playing a video game involving the Golden State Warriors as from watching the live game itself! Or playing a game of Candy Crush rather than watching the newest rom com or the newest mystery movie.

This trend towards increasing computer gaming adoption is reflected in the numbers as well. In 2012, 58 per cent of the US population played video games. In 2016, that number increased to 64 per cent. The time spent by each consumer playing games has also increased—from 10 minutes in 2003 to 15 minutes in 2016, a 50 per cent growth. The growth rate among women playing games is even higher during this period, pointing to a broad, cross-sectional growth pattern among consumers.

The consumer revolution in the realm of entertainment has arrived. It is disrupting producer hegemony and reclaiming market power back for the people. Consumers are starting to make entertainment more about them, rather than about the producers and the stars. The consumer revolution is reaching far and wide—from television to motion pictures, and from sporting events to cultural events. The Internet and social media are becoming the grand equalizers in the world of entertainment, and consumers are showing their preferences in the entertainment they consume. The lines between traditional, passive entertainment, and social, active entertainment are starting to blur. And consumers are starting to express their will, voice their preferences, and the entire producer–star complex has to adapt or be left out in the cold.

In this new era of fragmented, consumer-driven entertainment, what might transpire over the next 50 or 100 years? For starters, the entertainment world will become more and more fragmented. Consumers will look for increasing amounts of micro-relevant entertainment, and service providers will be well served enabling and supporting this wave rather than fighting it. This means that whether it comes to art, music, literature or video, technology and service providers that provide an easy and powerful platform for publishing and distributing micro entertainment will win big over traditional mass media entertainment producers. If existing incumbents can adapt fast enough, the spoils are theirs for the taking. But if they don't adapt rapidly and effectively enough, this will spawn off huge new companies and service providers that step in to fill the void created by the consumer revolution.

Similarly, platforms and technology providers that enable sports betting, fantasy sports and video games will win handsomely as consumers co-opt entertainment to be more and more about them, rather than about traditional stars. Service providers that enable consumers to make entertainment more about them, and less about the performers and stars will win big as the centre of gravity shifts.

The consumer revolution will also drive the emergence of new generations of augmented reality and virtual reality entertainment. It is exciting to see a cricket game. It is exciting to play a video cricket game. The combination of the two can be heady—such as facing the bowling of a Shane Warne or a Dale Steyn in real time in your augmented reality environment, as the live event is unfolding on the next screen. Or inserting yourself as a Barcelona player, moving without the ball, receiving a pass from Lionel Messi in the exact same spot as in the live game, and trying to convert a goal.

The consumer revolution might drive entertainment in other breathtaking ways. Physical team composition might start to mirror fantasy team composition, with general managers factoring in preferences and recommendations of their fan bases in building their teams. Even more thrillingly, coaches might start calling in plays based on what a majority of their fan bases (securely!) called for. The lines between real sports and fantasy sports or video games might start to blur, as the consumer revolution asserts its influence, and demands better and better service and customization.

In the realm of arts, music and motion pictures, the consumer revolution might similarly demand a greater interplay between the original storyline and its individually tailored preferences.

Consumers might want to insert themselves as the lead guitarist in place of Edge in a live performance, playing alongside Bono in their own tailored rendition of the music.

Consumers might similarly want to insert themselves in their favourite movie, wanting to play Gal Gadot in the Wonder Woman and experiencing her adventures first hand.

As virtual reality advances in leaps and bounds, and new generations of audio, visual, sensory and other devices come to life, consumers will expect a completely lifelike movie immersion experience, with the power to change the storylines at will much like in today's video games.

Innovative technology and service providers that recognize the trajectory of the consumer revolution, and service the new demands emerging in the market, will benefit handsomely from these efforts. Incumbents who do not will find themselves drifting off into increasing irrelevance on the wrong side of the revolution.

As with everything else touched by the consumer revolution, a critical technology will be the search technology to find the best entertainment as and when individual customers desire. Today's incumbents, such as Google, Bing, Baidu and Yandex are well positioned to ride this transformation. But they will need to adapt, for instance to search for new formats of media—ranging from videos to audios to sensory entertainment. They will need to deliver an all-encompassing search experience that can find consumers the best entertainment on demand, from the general pool of media or a micro-targeted social pool. They will need to anticipate what individual consumers might be most interested in, so they can surface recommendations whether consumers are aware of what they are looking for or not. Artificial intelligence will play a key role in intelligent algorithms that function like a good friend, making recommendations that you don't even know about.

As with everything else, the consumer revolution in entertainment will create one or two massive powerhouses that mediate and service the consumers' interests, and match them with producers and productions. These companies will become so powerful, and wield such enormous influence on the world, that government regulators will need to take a hard look at managing their social utility and corporate citizenship. They will want to ensure that a service as powerful and universal as this operates in the interest of the general good, rather than just the profit motives of shareholders.

The consumer revolution in entertainment is coming with guns blazing. Consumers are seizing control of their entertainment experiences, and making their demands heard. The power in entertainment is transitioning from producers to consumers. The status quo has a few years to adapt before the tide washes all over. Movie producers, sports leagues, famed actors and actresses, and legendary sporting figures have a few years to make the transition to a consumer-centric world. Those that do will benefit in substantial fashion and find their stock in sharp ascendance. Those that don't will find themselves marginalized, and left behind in the dust as the consumer revolution continues its inexorable churn towards the entertainment universe of the future.

8

CUSTOMER-CENTRIC COMMERCE AND ADVERTISING

Perhaps nowhere will the full brunt of the consumer revolution be felt more than in commerce and advertising. The core money flows of human society are starting to get disrupted in fundamental ways. The greatest re-distribution of wealth in human history is now underway. The global community is in the process of transitioning from a producer-driven economy to a consumer-driven economy. This means that products, services, processes, channels, experiences are increasingly being driven by consumers rather than by producers. Economic value is draining out of standardized production, and into serving bespoke consumption. In every geography, every industry, every category, bit by relentless bit, the metamorphosis is gathering momentum.

Businesses that understand this fundamental transformation are thriving, and racing ahead. Businesses that don't are finding their fortunes draining away, no matter how hard they persevere with their tried and tested ways. The playing field itself is shifting, and the good old ways don't work anymore. The good old times will never be back. And in the process, trillions of dollars will change hands.

Quite a shocking turn of events, considering how pretty the stalwarts of global industry were sitting a mere 50 years ago. How much power and prosperity, wealth and influence they had amassed in the centuries leading up to that. How impenetrable their corporate fortresses seemed, how unsurmountable their advantages. And yet, in the span of 50 short years, a blip in the context of human history, everything has changed. How did this come about? How did such a dramatic change come to pass? To understand this, it is helpful to look back in the rear-view mirror.

The history of commerce and transacting likely dates back to the earliest days of humankind as well. The earliest forms of commerce were structured around barters—the simple exchange of goods that suited the needs of both transacting parties. There is evidence of commerce in human civilizations dating as far back as 150,000 years ago.

As commerce took hold, humans uncovered the value and scope of benefits to be realized. They realized that it was far more efficient to trade for goods and services than enter into battle every time you needed something! Marketplaces quickly developed into major meeting spots in societies, where people could transact with each other, but also congregate, socialize and celebrate their barters. The unscripted nature of marketplace interactions, the spontaneous exploring and transaction matchmaking between buyer and seller brought its own chemistry and dynamic to a marketplace. The bigger the congregation, the exponentially greater the energy and innovation, and matchmaking opportunities on offer.

Bartering gradually evolved from exchanging finished products such as weapons, implements and property to measurable commodities such as grains, metals and livestock, as that made it easier for humans to trade equivalent value. This also enabled humans to exchange raw material or ingredients, bringing the economic benefits of trading to more and more levels of the food chain.

In the Stone Ages, trade took the form of obsidian and flint trading, triggered by the need of the era to manufacture cutting materials and tools. There is evidence that obsidian was traded and transported nearly 1,000 kilometres during this time, indicating the value society placed on its utility.

As humans developed into an agrarian society, the use of grain to transact became more and more prevalent. Around 10,000 years ago, the Sumerian kings in Ur and Uruk built granaries and accounting systems to quantify value and facilitate commerce. Shortly thereafter, societies started to use tokens with pictures of items traded to indicate value. Subsequently, tokens were marked with numeric value to represent or symbolize economic value.

The use of commodities to denote value spread to other regions of the world, such as Western and Central Asia, with the use of minerals such as gold and copper, which were commonly found in the region. By 3000 BC, this had evolved to the use of gold bars with standardized weights in places such as Egypt and Mesopotamia.

Accompanying the proliferations of monetary systems and the various forms of money was the proliferation of trade itself. The early marketplaces entailed transactions involving perishable products such as grains, fruits and vegetables. But trade across greater distances entailed higher value, non-perishable products such as jewellery, spices, textiles and precious metals. Trading centres frequently developed around sea fronts or inland waterways as that provided the easiest means of transportation of goods. Anatolia became a trading town for trading with Levant, Iran and Egypt. Afghanistan became a major trade source for lapis lazuli. Ebla became a major trading centre with Anatolia and Mesopotamia. Many of the biggest cities in the world developed, and in many cases, continue to thrive today on major trade routes. Cities such as London, Paris, Venice, Constantinople, Genoa, Dubai, Mumbai, Singapore, Shanghai, Tokyo, San Francisco and New York developed into major metropolises over the years as a result of being positioned squarely on the major trading routes around the world.

Also around 3000 BC, long-distance trade first started with the trading of jewellery and precious materials between Mesopotamia and the Indus Valley. The Phoenicians were the first seafaring traders, sailing across the Mediterranean up to England to trade for metals. Waterways provided the most efficient modes of transportation for goods, and some of the earliest trade routes were down the great rivers along which some of the earliest civilizations settled—the Yellow River, the Indus, the Tigris and the Euphrates, and the Nile. Trade advanced the economic development of societies and civilizations in pronounced ways, and traders grew into positions of tremendous power and influence from controlling this commercial activity.

Trading distances continued to increase as the economic value and power gained from trade gained further prominence. Around 2000 BC, a sophisticated network of transportation and routes appeared across the Central Asian steppes, called the Steppe Route. True to the terrain and fauna of the region, transportation was powered by horses, which brought a whole new efficiency to trade. For the first time, most of the continental land mass of Europe and Asia were connected, galvanized by the economic value to be had along its corridors. This lead to the flow of goods across vast regions—remnants of Chinese silk have been found in Egypt dating back to the 12th century BC.

As trade flourished, the sophistication of money also flourished. Another commodity became the standard of value in China around 1200 BC—the cowrie shell. This shell of a mollusc found in The Indian and Pacific Oceans developed into a universal standard in the region, and eventually became the longest standing currency in human history.

Around 1000 BC, Chinese society manufactured imitations of cowrie shells made out of bronze and copper to broaden their use and make them more universally available. They experimented with various shapes, including round shaped coins that were precursors to today's incarnations, and coins with holes for convenient stringing together.

The first true coins are believed to have been created in the kingdom of Lydia in Western Turkey in the 7th century BC. The initial coins came in all shapes and sizes, but did have standardized weights, and were made of electrum—an amalgam of gold and silver. The coins were typically inscribed on one side only and differed from their Chinese antecedents in that they were made out of precious metals rather than base metals. Electrum-based coins quickly took hold and spread to Greece and other parts of Europe.

Trade and commerce had a powerful draw for societies around the world, but they also needed to smoothen out transportation and money flows to flourish. This is why the two developed hand in hand as trade proliferated around the world. Much of long-distance trade developed around waterways, but two road-based trade routes opened up that became nothing short of legendary for their impact.

While the Steppe Route had continued to develop for over a millennium, the Chinese Han dynasty took it to new heights with its silk trade in the 3rd century BC. This gave this trading route its contemporary name, the Silk Route, one of the truly transformative land-based trading routes in the world. The Silk Route connected vast swathes of land, from the shores of the Pacific in Asia all the way to the Indian Ocean and the Mediterranean Sea, stretching across much of the landmass of Asia and Europe. Different stretches of the road network were maintained and upgraded by different societies and countries, each leaving its cultural, religious and commercial stamp on the Route. A wide variety of products traded over the Silk Route, ranging from silks and spices to metals and grains. Over the years, no less than the Arabs, Armenians, Bactrians, Chinese, Georgians, Greeks, Indians, Jews, Persians, Romans, Sogdians, Somalis, Syrians and Turkmen all traded on the Silk Route!

The 3rd century BC also saw the development of the Grand Trunk Road, connecting the Indian subcontinent with Central Asia. This road ran from Kabul in Afghanistan all the way to Chittagong in Bangladesh, first constructed by the Maurya Empire, and refurbished among others by Sher Shah Suri in the 16th century AD. The Road saw massive volumes of trade, and extensive cultural assimilation across its reach. Entire towns and societies developed along these trading roads, bringing wealth and prosperity to all in its path.

Early community marketplaces and fairs in various societies functioned around sellers merchandising their wares in transient stalls. This was not the most stable or economically efficient model for buyers and sellers, which led to the development of the first stationary shops in ancient Greece called the agora in 100 BC. Similar shops started to appear in ancient Rome called forums, with the Forum Romanum and Trajan's Forum consisting of vast expanses of stores created to efficiently sell a wide range of products to consumers. The Roman forums are the first known examples of true storefronts, as are shopping lists, first developed by Romans to make the most of their versatile storefronts!

As the volumes of trade grew, the need for more accurate and effective currency systems to keep pace with it also grew. The increasingly sophisticated use of coins continued to take hold, and then in the 7th century AD, the Tang dynasty in China invented paper currency. The original paper currency had credit notes written on it and served the purpose of quantifying value. Paper currency was far more efficient to carry and transact with than large numbers and volumes of coins, and quickly took hold in other parts of the world. Consumers began using paper currency and metallic coins to purchase products with greater efficiency.

The next few hundred years saw even greater commerce activity across global societies. While consumers primarily still shopped for products directly from farmers and manufacturers, more and more storefronts started to open up to make shopping easier and more predictable for consumers, especially in big cities. By the 13th century AD, more shops are known to have opened up, often selling multiple products to make the shopping experience that much more convenient and efficient for consumers. Shops were quite primitive, often opening up directly onto the street, and usually being dimly lit with minimal products on display. This made shopping a chore more so than a leisure activity.

That began to change in the 17th century AD, with the emergence of a middle class in Europe. Consumers started to buy essential commodities, but also luxurious international products such as silks, spices and sugar. With this, shopping began to become a more pleasurable leisure activity rather than a mundane chore. Produce and agricultural marketplaces began to evolve into shops and shopping centres increasingly stocked with more indulgent products. Shopping centres became popular destinations for consumers to mingle and socialize. Conspicuous consumerism became the vogue, in keeping with the intellectual writings of the time extolling the virtues of consumer self-interest and indulgence.

The 18th century saw an acceleration in these trends, fuelled by growing consumer wealth, an increasing supply of goods through manufacture and trade, and developing cultural mores around shopping becoming a recreational activity. The growing popularity of shopping saw the emergence of entire streets and districts devoted to shopping, such as the Strand and Piccadilly in London.

As shopping grew in popularity, shopkeepers came up with creative innovations to appeal to consumers. Large glass windows emerged to showcase wares to incidental shoppers strolling by, giving rise to the trend and term of window-shopping. Shopping centres began using large glass roofs and atriums to stream in natural light, giving rise to the arcade effect which further catered to consumer fantasies even when they couldn't afford to buy the featured products themselves. Shopping continued to become more and more of an experience, and more and more of a place to see and be seen. Shopping arcades transported consumers away from their daily humdrums to fantasy getaways, facilitating greater buying and consumerism. The Palais-Royale in Paris became the most famous early arcade in 1784.

As arcades evolved, shopkeepers and retailers began to dress up their stores, designed to entice consumers to drop in even when there was no actual need. The purpose of a storefront evolved beyond serving an existing need to creating a non-existing one. Arcades themselves began to add cafes, salons and bookshops to become more of a destination where consumers came in droves, and stayed.

The economic growth fuelled by the Industrial Revolution in the 19th century led to a rapid proliferation of goods and products on offer and drew in increasing numbers of enthusiastic consumers coming up the wealth curve. This prompted innovative shopkeepers and retailers to migrate from single product specialty stores to general-purpose department stores stocking wide ranges of products. Large department stores such as Harrods, Selfridges, Bloomingdale's, Saks Fifth Avenue and Bonmarche all opened up around the middle of the 19th century. These department stores grew way beyond mere retail outlets, and into full-fledged recreational destinations, replete with spas, libraries, cafes, concert venues and art galleries to create a holistic experience for consumers. The model became so successful, that many of these department stores became cultural icons, and continue to be shopping institutions to this day. The era of true retailing was born.

THE LUCRATIVE BUSINESS OF ADVERTISING

The middle of the 19th century also saw the emergence of another commercial force in the history of humankind—advertising. Advertising had been around in society for thousands of years. Commercial, political and community advertising artefacts have been found dating back to ancient Greece, Rome, Pompei and

Arabia. Advertising formats ranged from papyrus art in Egypt, to oil paintings in India, to oral poetry and music in China. In England and France, merchants of good and services used picture signs to advertise their wares and draw consumers into their stores.

But it was the 19th century that saw advertising arrive on the world stage in force. The confluence of the Industrial Revolution, rising consumer wealth, burgeoning department stores, and mushrooming media and publishing outlets produced a perfect storm for advertising. The earliest advertisements started to appear in English newspapers, typically promoting books, newspapers, health remedies, and surprisingly, tobacco! Advertising companies began to refine messaging, packaging and positioning, and the notion of branding began to appear. The trend quickly caught on as sellers were able to differentiate and extract premiums in the market on the basis of their advertising campaigns.

In June 1836, when *La Presse* first began to charge advertisers for advertising, it introduced a powerful business model that dominates the media business till today. The symbiosis between merchants and brands looking to promote their products, and publishing and media outlets looking to monetize their audience made for a natural and potent partnership. The model took off briskly, with magazines and newspapers around France, England and other parts of Western Europe adopting it in droves.

Advertising just made so much sense. Or so it seemed anyway. Major producers and manufacturers, flush with their post-Industrial Revolution successes and market power, just had to extend and reinforce their market positions. They needed to extend and solidify their brands with consumers. They needed to sharpen their messaging and positioning, create a visage in consumers' minds about what they stood for, what their products delivered and why consumers should buy them. And advertising presented the perfect platform to do so.

The fundamentals of branding weren't lost in these leading producers and retailers. They saw the opportunity to precisely position and define themselves exactly the way they wanted to be seen by consumers. And then they saw the opportunity to showcase their messages repeatedly to mass consumers through advertising. They controlled the messaging, and they controlled the medium. There was no fact-checking and no independent corroboration of advertiser claims. The business model that developed was that if you bought advertising space, you bought the right to say anything you wanted short of tangible falsification.

Advertising aided merchants in broadcasting their positioning and selling propositions, thereby reinforcing and extending their market advantages. In the process, large merchants were also able to drown out smaller competitors and innovators, thereby reinforcing their market positions. Advertising thus became a mechanism for merchants to consolidate or expand their market power and dominance, reducing competition in the process.

Advertisements began to show up everywhere. There were ads in newspapers and magazines. There were ads on store signs. There were ads on billboards. The great branding bombardment was underway!

On the other side of the fence, publishers and media companies were only too happy to take the advertising money from advertisers. It helped them increase their revenues. It helped them subsidize consumers by lowering or entirely eliminating subscription fees. All for the simple exercise of carving out a little bit of real estate on their media for advertisers to do their business. It seemed like a great free resource to dole out to advertisers and collect handsome fees for it.

Except it wasn't. Advertisers and publishers saw advertising space as a free resource to be negotiated and contracted between them. But in the process, they overlooked the third and perhaps most important constituent involved in the process—consumers. Magazines and newspapers in some ways overlooked the fact that there were also pre-existing contracts between publishers and consumers. And advertising began to encroach on this contract.

Marketers got more and more sophisticated and talented at advertising. The line of work attracted some of the best and brightest minds in the business world. The pictures got better and better, the copy or text of ads got finer and finer, and advertising quality began to equal or even surpass that of the endemic content of a programme or a page. Advertisers got increasingly skilled at engaging consumers with superior advertising creative and copy.

Except it was still encroaching on the consumers' experience. Consumers didn't consent to being marketed to. They did not sanction the use of their time and attention being occupied by a commercial message. But they had no choice. They had no voice. There was business being conducted between publishers and advertisers. There were contracts being honoured. And consumers were simply the product on whom the contracts were being implemented.

The advertisers' cause was aided by the lack of clear measurability in advertising. There were no precise tools to measure how effective the ads were at actually driving sales, how many consumers were engaging with them, or taking action after seeing an ad. This, combined with the conventional wisdom around the effectiveness of advertising lead to rampant use and proliferation of advertisements. Advertisers made hay, both individually and collectively. Companies were born, careers were built and performance bonuses flowed. Coming up with creative presentations for companies, publishing them at will on a vast acquiescing consumer base without any hard metrics to live up to felt like the best gig in town.

The business model of advertising became so successful that each subsequent rollout of a media format came with its own formatting for advertising. Twenty-seven years after radio technology was invented, it became a consumer hit in 1922. Radio stations started cropping up everywhere, and consumers started buying radios in droves. And the year radio commercials were launched? 1922. It took no time for radio to leverage advertising the same way print

had done up to this point. New York's WEAF radio station broad-
casted the first radio commercial for Hawthorne Court Apartments
that year. And the industry never looked back since!

A wide range of radio ads have been created since. Broadcasters
experimented with 15-or 30-second commercials. They experimented with sponsored programmes. They explored blending
commercials into radio programming by having broadcasters
become spokespeople for commercials. Radio advertisements
became pervasive. They sought to reinforce corporate messaging,
but they had to do it within the formats of the programming
around the advertisements. So they became more entertaining,
including dramatic effects and mini-skits. The jingle was invented.
Advertising developed into a form of entertainment, just with a
marketing or sales message embedded in it. Moving in the other
direction, radio programming began to creep towards commer-
cialism, as sponsorships and endorsements made their way into
programming. The lines between commercials and programming
started to blur. Advertisers and radio stations found great strategic
fit with each other and flourished around the world. There was still
that minor issue with consumer experience, but the conventional
wisdom was why let a little irritant with innocuous consumers get
in the way of a rollicking business party.

Advertising took another giant leap forward with the launch
of television into the consumer market. After the invention of the
first electronic television, a flurry of business activity ensued to
capitalize on its enormous potential. The Radio Corporation of
America, or RCA, which dominated the burgeoning radio business
in America with its two National Broadcasting Company networks
jumped in the fray with major investments to develop the television
business. In 1939, RCA televised the opening ceremony of the
New York World's Fair which became one of the earliest television
broadcasts. This was followed by the first televised baseball game
between Princeton University and Columbia University, and a
huge cultural phenomenon, televised sports broadcasting, was

born. In 1941, the Columbia Broadcasting System began televised news programmes, and one of the NBC networks was sold to create the new American Broadcasting Company.

On 1 July 1941, another behemoth was born. Just before the televised broadcast of a baseball game between the Brooklyn Dodgers and the Philadelphia Phillies at Ebbets Field in New York, the television station WNBT aired the first television commercial for the Bulova Watch Company. That set in motion one of the biggest trends of the 20th century—television advertising.

As with print and radio advertising, television advertising served the same purpose for advertisers and broadcasters, just on a new medium. Advertisers found a whole new channel to communicate with prospective consumers in a much richer way. And broadcasters found a whole new revenue stream to defray the non-trivial costs of television programming and production.

With three networks leading the charge in the United States, and others in Europe, television programming grew in leaps and bounds over the next several years. In 1946, only 0.5 per cent of US households had television sets. By 1954, that number increased to 55.7 per cent, aided in part by the introduction of colour television, first broadcast for a situational comedy called The Marriage by NBC. By 1962, television adoption had risen a whopping 90 per cent of US households.

Through the growth of television worldwide, television advertising also saw explosive growth rates. Major new companies were founded specifically to create and deliver the best advertising to consumers. At the turn of the century, Dentsu was founded in Tokyo in 1901. In 1926, in Paris, the Publicis Groupe was founded and became a multi-billion dollar corporation creating advertisements. In 1930, the Interpublic Group was founded in New York City. WPP, the pre-eminent leader in the space, was founded in 1971 in London, and grew into a multi-national behemoth. In New York City, the Omnicom Group was founded in 1986.

These companies led the charge in bringing insightful, creative, strategic advertising to advertising clients around the world.

Well-defined formats emerged, such as 15-second and 30-second commercials. Sophisticated targeting emerged, such as beer commercials during football games, and soap commercials during daytime drama serials. Elegant business models emerged, such as upfront ad sales and spot ad markets. And artful balancing between programming time and commercial time emerged. In the 1960s, a typical hour-long American show included 51 minutes of programming, and 9 minutes of commercials. By 2016, many hour-long shows had been reduced to 38 minutes of programming, and 22 minutes of commercials.

Easy money, right? Just dial-up the advertising quotient a tad bit year over year and reap the financial benefits both individually and organizationally. More opportunities for advertisers and publishers to make merry with each other. More good times. Likely at the expense of consumers, but they didn't seem to mind, did they?

Such was the draw of television that consumers would absorb the extra proportion of advertising being broadcast at them. Wouldn't they? Ratings were strong, especially for live sporting events and other mega broadcasts. Time to reap the benefits by extracting premium pricing for commercials during these broadcasts. Simple, wasn't it?

There were sophisticated analyses done to dial-up advertising times. There were satisfying accolades at having trained the consumer to accept commercials in increasing numbers. There were cute depictions of consumers taking snack and bio breaks around commercials—including in the very television programmes they were watching. It was all so innocuous, so quaint that they did that. And it couldn't possibly have any impact on the rollicking media and advertising symbiosis. Could it? Large, powerful marketers and large, powerful media companies could ride their alliances all the way to the bank and back. Couldn't they?

And then along came WWW, courtesy of Tim Berners-Lee in 1990. Pioneering websites started to appear on the Internet, and adventurous consumers started to visit them in search of information and entertainment. Powerhouse incumbent media companies took notice and began to hop on board—after all they couldn't sit out the dance as consumers started to get online.

As companies started to roll out websites, they realized that they also needed to make money! Luckily, there was a very successful model for publishers already established to make money in the print, radio and television worlds—advertising. All they needed to do was to adapt advertising to the new digital medium, the same way magazines, newspapers, radio and television had done, and they would be all set.

In 1994, the online magazine *HotWired* ran what would become the first banner ad—a very basic strip of text asking consumers to click on it. When they did so, the ad transported consumers to a primitive landing page from AT&T with some promotional messages. The ad saw a click-through rate, or number of times consumers click on an ad when they see it, of 44 per cent. Bingo! Monetization problem solved. Advertising had been adapted to the Internet and was all set for a heady ride as everything 'went digital'.

Publishers and websites large and small quickly jumped on the band wagon. Banner ads became ubiquitous, and publishers took full advantage of the easy money it offered. Different advertising formats were created, and later standardized to galvanize the market. There was the Internet Advertising Bureau formed in 1996 to coordinate, facilitate and spur the growth of advertising on the Internet.

As expected, Internet websites experimented with many forms of advertising. There were different sizes, different locations and different frequencies for advertisements. There were static ads and dynamic ads. There were screen takeovers and pop-up ads.

There were screen backgrounds and conquest ads. There was money to be made, and there was creative genius to put to use, and the industry thrived.

As Internet ads proliferated, a curious trend started to set in, however. The click-through rate statistic started to trend down from its imposing 44 per cent start. By 2000, this click-through rate for banner ads had fallen to 9 per cent. Analysts wondered what the reason was. But didn't see any major reasons for alarm—the amount of ad inventory was soaring, and most ads were paid per impression, or CPM as it's called in the industry—so the party continued undeterred.

Around the same time, at the Consumer Electronics Show in Las Vegas in 1999, ReplayTV and TiVo launched consumer digital video recorders (DVRs). These DVRs enabled innovative features such as time-shifting television viewing and skipping through commercials. Consumers lapped up the services, but media companies didn't take too fondly to their revenue-generating commercials being skipped over. Various levels of legal wrangling transpired between technology providers and media companies, but consumers showed a steadfast interest in watching the programming they found interesting and skipping past commercials at will. Given the option to skip through advertising, they did.

It seemed that something fundamental was changing in advertising. For the first time, consumers were empowered to click on an ad, or not. For the first time, they were empowered to view a commercial or skip it. Unlike with either print radio or television advertising, they had an explicit choice. And they were exercising it. The consumer revolution was starting to show up in the world of advertising.

Consumers were starting to raise their voices and be heard. They started to express their displeasures with advertising. Major media companies like Yahoo began to offer incentives to consumers to make their ads go away by paying for it in order to use their email service. Quite a shocking testimony to the value of a service where you would ask your customers to pay money to make it go away!

Still no one wanted to rock the boat. No one wanted to kill the golden goose. It was so convenient to look the other way. And pretend that consumers were just going through a phase—like a petulant child—until they were sufficiently trained.

By 2005, the average click-through rate had dipped to 7 per cent, and by 2009 to 4 per cent. Conditioned by decades of tradition, the industry response was to come up with different ad formats, more intrusive ads, roadblock ads, pre-roll video ads, ads you simply had to suffer through to get to the content you wanted to get to. In other words, tussle with consumers, jam advertisements down their throats, rather than adapt to the changed power dynamic.

Another developing trend that was viewed as a nuisance by the advertising industry was a technology called ad blocking—a tool that enabled consumers to shut out ads from their digital experiences. AdBlock, a leader in the space, started in 2009 and quickly became an Internet hit as consumers flocked for their tool to make those pesky ads disappear. The consumer revolution was catching its stride.

Over the next few years, a bizarre battle unfolded between producers and consumers. Publishers and advertisers collaborated to come up with bolder and more creative ways to get in front of consumers. Consumers fought back with more ad blocking adoption, and even lower click-through rates. The irony of this battle royale cannot be overstated. Producers are now collaborating to impose themselves on the very consumers they are in business to serve. The more insistent they are getting on being seen and heard, the more adept consumers are getting at dodging them. The warier they are about clicking on ads, the faster they are at shutting down ads.

For the first time, consumers are empowered to respond. And they are responding overwhelmingly. This raises a profound question. Were consumers ever welcoming of advertisements? Were they ever appreciative of having their entertainment or information pursuits interrupted by someone unwanted peddling unwanted wares? Or was this never a good idea, consumers just never had the means to express it?

As the consumer revolution rolls on in advertising, the evidence is becoming clearer and clearer. There are now 600 million ad blockers in the world. If billions of other consumers knew about ad blocking, they would likely take advantage of it too. The average click-through rate of a banner ad is now 0.06 per cent. The elephant in the room of advertising had been ignored far too long. And it is now starting to show up.

The consumer revolution is beginning to impose its will on marketers and publishers. For decades, advertisers and publishers were in charge of consumers. But not anymore. The consumer revolution is seizing market power back from producers. It is beginning to dictate terms. And it will not be denied. After all, it controls the purse strings that feed the entire food chain.

Advertisers are side-stepping and protesting, and contesting, of course. There are new levels of targeting being introduced, harnessing questionable levels of private consumer data. There are new native ad formats, designed to blend in better with the actual programming that consumers are after. But fighting the consumer revolution is a losing proposition. The revolution is much too powerful, much too smart and much too relentless to counter.

The fundamental battle between producers and consumers is about who is in charge. Who is in charge of the consumers' digital experience, who is in charge of their screen real estate, who is in charge of what they see and hear and when?

The answer is, it's the consumers of course. They now have a taste of their power and are exercising it. For decades, producers— media companies, publishers, broadcasters and their financial sponsors, the marketing companies—ruled the roost. They controlled and dictated what consumers would see and experience, and when. But no longer.

Since the onset of the consumer revolution, consumers are starting to assert their power. They are choosing when they will consume what media. They are searching and finding programmes they want to watch or listen to, not what broadcasters decide is best for them. They are dictating what they want to do with the web more than the producers dictating what they want consumers to see. They are taking charge while producers are losing their hold.

These optics help illustrate why search engines have become such a powerhouse on the Internet today. They provided the first major technology breakthrough since the dawn of computers, and the Internet itself that enabled the consumer revolution. They empowered consumers to get in the driver's seat, to initiate rather than be initiated upon by producers. By letting consumers specify what they were interested in via their search queries and surfacing the best matches from around the Internet to correspond to these queries, search engines flipped the power structure from being producer- or broadcaster-led to consumer-led. This galvanized the consumer revolution at a whole different level. Consumers seized their new-found power and flocked to search engines in droves. The technology caught on like wildfire of course, led by Google, and the rest is Internet history.

Search engines also enabled an entirely new generation of online advertising—search engine marketing—a close cousin but not to be confused with the more organic search engine optimization. For the first time in the history of marketing, advertisers had direct, real-time knowledge of individual consumers regarding their interests and requirements. They could use this information to serve those consumers matching ads that would be precisely matched to consumers' search queries. This was in contrast to traditional display or banner ads that could only serve banners based on less specific demographic and behavioural targeting criteria. The results, not surprisingly, were dramatically better. Serving consumers' interests as explicitly expressed via search queries, rather than by guessing at them with probabilistic targeting was turning out to be a far superior approach than traditional banner advertising.

Search engine marketing also introduced the pay-per-click model in advertising, where payment accrued every time an ad was clicked on. Up to this point, advertisements were primarily bought and sold on a pay-per-impression model where payment accrued every time an ad was displayed. The pay-per-click model was first introduced by Open Text in 1996 and GoTo in 1998. GoTo rebranded as Overture in 2001, and was acquired by Yahoo in 2003, bringing search engine marketing to the worldwide scale. Around the same time, Google introduced its search engine marketing solution through its AdWords program, and grew into a behemoth on the Internet.

Search engine marketing provided better returns to advertisers than traditional banner ads, and grew steadily, overtaking traditional ads for several years before slowing down in 2016 for traditional ads to catch up. Search engine marketing now makes up a significant share of the advertising market. In the process, a key point had been made—serving consumers advertisements that matched known search query keywords rather than probabilistic demographic targeting, produced far better consumer engagement and click-through rates. The proof was in the pudding—search engine marketing produced a 1–2 per cent click-through rate—a 20- to 30-fold increase compared to traditional display advertisements. This was more evidence of the consumer revolution at work in the most commercially important aspect of the Internet—generating money. Being on the side of the consumer revolution in advertising was leading to clearly better returns than not doing so. This was more evidence that producers won big by serving the consumers' interests, not dictating what they should watch or listen to.

Of course, with this success came hordes of advertisers and merchants, flocking to search engine marketing to harness its inherent advantages. On the one hand they found the channel much more productive, but on the other hand so did everyone else. Search engine marketing thus became more and more competitive as advertisers searched for a leg up on competition. Ironically, the biggest beneficiary of all this was the search engine itself, as evidenced by Google's meteoric rise in the Internet firmament. The point, however, had been proven. Consumers would engage with advertisements that were directly related to their query of the moment far more than they would with traditional, generic advertising.

As search engines became more and more pervasive, however, a curious bifurcation in consumer behaviour developed. Consumers were still flocking to search engines to search for content, or information on the Internet. However, when it came to commerce or buying things, they were preferring to start their searches on commerce sites instead. Search engines were thus at a significant advantage when compared with directory-based content browsing on the Internet, but at a significant disadvantage when compared with commerce site functionalities on the Internet.

This yawning gap in consumer traction between search sites and commerce sites, when it came to commerce searches, was best exhibited by Amazon. Despite being only one of 13 million commerce sites on the Internet, Amazon overtook Google as the number one site for commerce searches in 2011. The lead continued to expand, reaching 55 per cent share of product searches for Amazon alone, relative to 28 per cent share on search engines.

Not only were consumers frequenting Amazon for their shopping needs, they were also visiting other commerce sites such as eBay, Walmart, Macy's, Expedia, Priceline, Zillow, Trulia, Autotrader, CarsDirect, LendingTree and LendingClub at a healthy clip. It would appear that they were finding commerce sites more effective and efficient than search engines when it came to searching for things to buy.

Why would this be the case? After all, content search has become one of the standard bearers of consumer behaviour on the

Internet. To understand this, it is illustrative to look at shopping experience via a search engine, versus a commerce site. On a search engine, a consumer has to first do a natural language (which means approximate) search for a product or service of interest. This results in a list of dozens or hundreds of sites that match that approximate query to declining degrees of relevance and authority. The consumer then has to sift through the list of sites one by one, go to each one, and perform the exact commerce search on each to find the product or service of interest. This multi-step process is very inefficient and redundant for consumers. When you are trying to find out how long the Great Wall of China is, it is very efficient to find a series of sites that can provide the answer in varying degrees of depth and detail. When you are trying to find the right pair of jeans to buy, it is relatively useless to find approximate matches other than the ones that match your exact parameters.

On commerce sites, consumers can search or browse for the product or service they are looking for in a very efficient and precise manner. They can find products by specifying exact parameters, enabling them to quickly and efficiently find the exact product they are interested in, rather than a litany of approximate choices they have to sift through. Commerce sites reduce the friction and increase the shopping specificity greatly compared to content sites and search engines, producing a disproportionate advantage in serving consumers. Stated another way, commerce sites empower consumers to provide more specific needs and parameters than search engines. They empower consumers to express their requirements more precisely. And then they do a better job at serving the consumers' specific needs when it comes to buying things.

Commerce sites are thus more on the side of the consumer revolution than search sites when it comes to buying products or services. They give consumers more control and more power, and then serve it better. And they reap the benefits of doing so. It pays handsomely to be on the side of the consumer revolution!

What does this all mean for the world of advertising? On the one hand traditional ads are getting rejected more and more by consumers. They are installing ad blockers in record numbers, clicking through at record low rates, deleting ads as fast as they possibly can—letting advertisers know in every conceivable form that they are not welcome! And this is even before considering the far more egregious compromise of consumer trust at Facebook recently, with the unauthorized harvesting of consumer data to serve yet more unwelcome advertiser messages. Or the inconvenient slip at Google that allowed pristine brand name ads to be served up on vile and inappropriate Internet sites. All is clearly not right in the sprawling world of advertising.

Consumers are also showing that they prefer search ads to banners, and commerce experiences to search experiences. What does it all add up to?

This simply demonstrates that the consumer revolution is taking hold in commerce and advertising. There is a fundamental shift afoot in advertising, for instance. Consumers are rewarding providers who put them in charge. They are rewarding sites and apps that are consumer-centric. They are rewarding merchants and producers who facilitate their journey rather than get in their way.

The sooner major advertisers and their agencies internalize this fundamental shift, the better for them. In the throes of the consumer revolution, the way to lead is to follow. The way to leverage consumers is to serve them. After decades and centuries of pushing the agenda, promoting a message, taking the initiative, it is time for advertisers to take a step back, let consumers take the lead, and simply serve their needs. This is the shape of the post-consumer revolution world. Those that heed its churning wheels and respond will win handsomely. Those that don't will see their market presence dwindle.

The shift from advertising to commerce is synonymous with a shifting of power from producers to consumers—and there is no getting away from it!

Commerce sites however, which include traditional e-commerce sites that largely sell products, as well as their cousins that sell services or conduct other forms of transactions, have their own challenges with the consumer revolution. As with advertising, most commerce sites started their digital journey by putting their offline store online. Or started with online-only stores modelled after offline stores, the one established paradigm for its time. This meant that online stores by and large looked and functioned like physical ones. They had storefronts, retail displays and promotions, store sections, aisles of inventory, shopping carts and checkout counters.

As Internet technologies developed, commerce sites started refining their catalogues and product categorizations to help consumers find their desired products faster. They realized that it was a lot easier to reorganize digital stores than physical ones, and that could be used to serve consumers better. Building upon that, they introduced personalization—the ability to tailor the entire store front to an individual consumer's shopping needs and habits at an individual moment in time. This was the beginnings of using the digital environment to raise the quality of the store experience rather than simply matching that of physical stores. This was also the beginnings of the consumer revolution taking hold in the world of commerce. Consumers were rewarding commerce sites that catered to their individual needs and punishing those that didn't.

Next up, commerce sites began to learn from the search engine revolution overtaking the Internet and began implementing search-based browsing and shopping within their own stores. This put the consumer more in charge of the shopping experience— instead of the store organizing and presenting shopping options in traditional retailing style, consumers could themselves organize the store in the order most relevant to them, thank you very much. The consumer revolution in commerce was gathering momentum.

Using search technologies to shop for products and service had its limitations of course. Keyword-based search, by its very nature, is an inexact technology that can get consumers generally close to the shopping area of interest. Saying you want 'blue jeans' and landing in the blue jeans section of a commerce site is a good start, but doesn't complete the shopping process. You then have to pick the exact style, size, colour, brand and price you would like before you can complete your shopping transaction.

Search technologies did however make commerce more personalized in real time. This gave more ammunition to the consumer revolution, enabling consumers to take more charge of their shopping behaviour, to get in the driver's seat rather than being pitched to.

Other innovations followed in the realm of product merchandising. Commerce sites got more sophisticated and refined in serving consumers further by providing shopping tools. Consumers could see pictures and videos of hotels and resorts they would stay at, 360 degree views of a grill they would set up in their backyard, or try a video game out before they bought it. Consumers were demanding better shopping experiences to earn their business, and merchants were providing it to them. Consumers were taking charge of their own shopping experiences, rather than be mediated through a salesperson with vested interests.

As commerce sites continued to refine the shopping experience to serve consumers better, they also had to refine their marketing approaches to attract consumers. They started marketing themselves first with the tools and techniques available to them in the early days of the Internet—traditional banner advertising, directory listings and press releases. This was traditional offline marketing brought online, and the results were similar to those accomplished offline.

However, marketing online had some important structural differences. First, consumers could be tracked and targeted at an individual level. In the offline world, it is impossible to tell which individual saw a billboard ad and which didn't. In the online world this is no longer the case. Also, in the online world, every impression, every click, every sale could be tracked back to an individual consumer. In the offline world this is not the case.

This trackability made for a closed-loop system as opposed to an open-loop system in offline marketing. The consequences were profound. As marketing became more measurable, companies started seeking better return on investment for their marketing dollars. Initiatives that provided higher, quantifiable return began to increase, and initiatives that didn't started to decline. For the first time, conventional wisdom on the value of advertising and branding began to come under scrutiny. This fit in nicely with the emergence of search engine marketing.

Where traditional advertising was entirely advertiser or merchant led, search engine marketing was much better aligned with the consumer revolution. In the former, it was all about what the advertisers wanted, what their messaging was, what their branding was, with probabilistic targeting applied to try and reach likely customers. The endeavour was completely advertiser-centric, and consumers were simply inventory being targeted. Publishers, broadcasters and media companies were simply instruments in support of advertiser goals—they overwhelmingly regarded advertisers as their real customers, and consumers as simply products or inventory to serve their purposes. This mindset continues through today, and sometimes leads to catastrophic breaches of trust and faith, most recently surfaced by the Facebook data harvesting scandal at the hands of Cambridge Analytica.

SEARCH ENGINE MARKETING

Search engine marketing began to redress this balance in some measure. Advertising and marketing began to become a tad more consumer-led, flipping the age-old model in advertising. As consumers took more charge of their behaviour and experience, search engine marketing grew in leaps and bounds. Coupled with the measurability and trackability of advertising dollars, marketers were able to demonstrate great return on investment, or return on ad spend as it is commonly referred to in the industry, relative to traditional branding ads. Search engine marketing and direct response marketing budgets began to increase, and branding budgets began to shrink on a relative basis.

Search engine marketing, however, has now run into its own set of challenges for marketers. Its global scale and near-universal advertiser participation has made it exceedingly difficult a platform to create and sustain profits on. Advertisers are battling each other to eke out a living a search query at a time as search engines extract more and more value from their vantage point of being the market maker. The consumer revolution has made search engines vast in volume and traffic, but the hyper bidding amongst advertisers has made it very difficult to sustain high return on ad spend. Any modicum of advantage is quickly marginalized by other competitors swooping on any search query or keyword, requiring advertisers to constantly jostle and stay ahead of each other on a minute-by-minute basis to preserve their businesses.

Not the least of the challenges in search engine marketing is dealing with search queries or keywords. Keywords are the flip side of what makes search engines a mismatch for commerce. Not only is search an inexact way for consumers to search for things to buy, it is also an inexact way for advertisers to bid on what to sell. Because search is a natural language technology, there are many variations to expressing a search query, and consequently advertisers need to target that consumer in just as many ways. For instance, if you are interested in buying a pair of blue jeans, boot cut, size 6, made by Lucky Jeans. There are dozens of ways to express that query via search engines. Advertisers then need to target that consumer by bidding on each of the dozens of keywords the consumer might type in. If you add up the permutations and combinations of all attributes of all products and services a site might sell, you quickly end up with trillions of keywords that have to be bid upon on a daily or hourly basis. Clearly not a project for the faint of heart!

This natural effort barrier imposes a natural limitation on the utility of search engine marketing for most advertisers. A sort of natural plateau that while on the right side of the consumer revolution, can only take you so far before effectively tapping out.

As a result, as the number of sites on the Internet proliferates, it gets more and more difficult and expensive to bring consumers into the store. At the same time, as the number of sites proliferates, it gets tougher and tougher to convert site visitors to sales.

The average conversion rate for commerce sites is now a mere 2 per cent. That means an astonishing 98 per cent of traffic is lost without a sale—for each of 13 million commerce websites!

That is a staggering amount of economic waste in today's digital environment.

What can this stunning statistic be attributed to? How can some of the best companies in the world, the smartest minds in the industry, work on something this long and accomplish such an underwhelming result?

The answer, again, is the consumer revolution. It is moving beyond the current ability of producers and merchants to respond. It is moving faster than producers are able to adapt. It is fascinating to look at how consumers are taking charge of their experiences, forcing producers to scramble to meet their needs.

For instance, take a look at how consumers establish a need in today's world. Consumers decide what content or media they want to consume. If something strikes their fancy, or if they identify a need in their life, they can go from stimulus to action within seconds in the digital world. The value of bombarding them with 'entertaining' advertisements enough times to trigger an unrecognized need, or trigger a recall hours or days later about a spur of the moment need is declining rapidly. As the consumer revolution kicks in, and consumers orient themselves to demand what they want and when they want it, not only are 'brand impressions' losing their value, they are actually driving up nuisance value and consumer irritation. Advertisers are better served letting consumers initiate their shopping needs, and using their branding funds to improve merchandising, promotions and pricing rather than squandering them on empty branding calories. The chief marketing officer of Proctor & Gamble recently went on record saying the company slashed its marketing budget by $140 million and its revenues went *up* by 2 per cent! The link between traditional banner advertising, and return on ad spend is becoming weaker and weaker as the consumer revolution gathers momentum.

As consumers switch to the driver's seat, there is diminishing ability for advertisers to influence their utility functions with ads. Consumers no longer have the need for a circuitous dotted line from watching a show, reading an article, interacting with a friend, then seeing an ad—typically several times—then clicking on one, entering a shopping funnel and making a purchase. If consumers have an interest, they can take more direct paths to buying a product or service that matches their interests, bypassing traditional marketing routes. The walls between content, advertising and commerce are collapsing at rapid rates, and do not require mediation from advertisers.

Traditional brand advertising is a vestige of the old producer or merchant-led world. In that world, the consumer had to be educated, informed, induced, persuaded, charmed, goaded, teased, appeased and urged into action. It still has some value in creating soft perceptions, goodwill and bonhomie for companies. But its centrality in bringing consumers in is rapidly diminishing as the consumer revolution takes over.

Another fundamental tenet of marketing under duress from the consumer revolution is positioning and messaging. Consumers now have access to exponentially more information than ever before. They get their information not only directly from merchants, but also from their competitors, from neutral reviews, from commentators and pundits, from research sources and of course from each other. Consumers can consult with their friends or peers with the greatest of ease in the digital world. In the physical world, it is inconvenient to bring family and friends along for every shopping trip. It is also awkward to consult with strangers shopping at the same store. But in the digital world, it is easy and efficient to do both. So consumers are no longer beholden to merchants to provide them all information pertaining to their purchase. They can bring their own army of consultants with them.

This information needed for commerce is still quite scattered. Consumers are still figuring out how to use all the information available. But the information is out there to be harvested, synthesized and acted upon. This is changing market power dramatically—the friction for consumers getting information is going away. Why is this a profound development? Because it reduces the leverage for advertisers and merchants dramatically.

Prior to the consumer revolution, consumers simply did not have access to the information they now do. They were utterly reliant on merchants to inform them and educate them on the merits of their products, the differentiation and superiority of their services and even their characterizations of why consumers needed their offerings. In such an information vacuum, the value of product positioning and messaging was profound. If the entire consumer's framework for a product's value proposition was defined by the merchant, that provided tremendous leverage to the merchant. Positioning and messaging were paramount to the success of a business.

But with the onset of the consumer revolution, consumers define the positioning and ascribe it to merchants, not the other way around. Consumers define a brand, they define a value proposition, and merchants have to deliver actual value to get positioned the right way in the market. Merchants have rapidly diminishing ability to set the agenda, or to inform consumers in captive settings. Now they must do so in public, in full view, with cross-checking and fact-checking instantly available to all. In this environment, merchants are much better served spending their time and budgets on fine-tuning products, promotions, merchandising and customer service than trying to hammer consumers with a positioning or messaging.

The consumer revolution is changing consumer commerce behaviour in other fundamental ways too. In the offline world, not only did consumers have limited market intelligence on products and services they were interested in consuming, but they had significant friction in the actual shopping process itself. It took effort—both time and money—to go to a physical store, look for products and find the right ones to buy. Once in a store, it took effort to leave and go to another store. There was the time cost, but also there was the administration cost—how to track products in the consideration set, and how to compare products in different stores efficiently. There were also psychological and relationship costs—how to desert a sincere and helpful salesperson and leave for a competitive store.

There were thus significant switching costs in going from one store to another. Physical stores were optimized for this behaviour, resulting in walled garden mindsets. Stores did their best to bring consumers in the door, and then organized their in-store experiences to do everything possible to sell as many products and services to them as possible. Stores developed into two main varieties for the most part—specialty boutique stores and multi-category department stores. But in all cases, the core value ingrained in their DNA was to do their level best to draw consumers in, and then do their level best to sell them every conceivable product in as full-service a capacity as possible. The mindset was if you could draw a consumer in the store, you had essentially secured the sale. And if you lost a customer to a competitor, it was the end of the world.

Then along came the consumer revolution and the accompanying consumer empowerment that changed consumer shopping behaviour fundamentally. Rather than merchants and stores dictating shopping experiences, consumers started to. And one of the fundamental changes ushered in by the consumer revolution in commerce was the dynamic of shopping the market. Consumers are no longer beholden to a single store or a single brand for their shopping needs. They are starting to hold merchants accountable for delivering real value, and one of the primary ways to do so is to compare their products and services with others'. Brand loyalties are diminishing in appeal, and being replaced by cold, hard facts. Consumers are getting better and better at separating the wheat from the chaff, identifying what matters and what doesn't, and making incredibly informed purchase decisions.

With the consumer revolution, consumers are getting accustomed to brazenly comparing products, prices and stores. They can now go from store to store in the digital world in seconds, not minutes or hours. This has a profound impact on how they buy or shop. This frictionless shopping means that they can evaluate choices across stores, compare features, prices and experiences with total ease before making their purchase decisions. Every purchase from every consumer is akin to a business-to-business request for proposal (RFP)—a way to get competitive bids, usually reserved for large purchase made by large companies. Now every consumer is going through a mini RFP for every purchase. The walls holding in walled garden e-commerce are crumbling. Stores are not silos any more, they are becoming free-flowing thorough fares and conduits of commerce. The consumer revolution in commerce has arrived.

Switching costs between stores are falling drastically for consumers. Brand loyalties are plummeting in significance. Consumers are increasingly concerned about their needs being met, and care less and less who meets them. To them, the Internet is becoming one mega-network of products and services. Which node in the network services their needs is becoming incidental.

And therein lies the fundamental disconnect between consumers marching on to the beat of the consumer revolution, and merchants and stores stuck in the past. To consumers, the store is no longer an individual merchant's site, it is the entire Internet itself. One giant, interconnected, transparent megastore. The super mall that straddles the globe like a colossus. Merchants are now nodes in this network rather than standalone silos. Their success now depends on aligning with the consumers' journey and enabling it. They no longer have the mandate to direct consumers, they simply have the mandate to serve them.

The consumer revolution will demand that producers and merchants serve their shopping needs as they take charge. They will require commerce sites to take their shopping parameters with great precision and specificity, and surface products and services that match their requirements precisely. They will require commerce sites to also surface complementary products and services, if appropriate, anticipating consumers' needs using artificial intelligence and machine learning technologies.

But they will also reward commerce sites for reducing their friction on their shopping journey. This includes passing them on to other commerce sites with full shopping details handed off, so they can efficiently conduct their cross-site shopping process. Sites that understand and align with the consumer's comparison shopping demands will fare much better than sites that fight it. Counter-intuitive as it might seem, commerce sites are better off collaborating with one another to serve the consumer's need, rather than fighting it or pretending that consumers won't cross-check with competitive sites.

Why should commerce sites collaborate with their competitors? Take a look at the physical shopping world. Despite their silo mentality, physical stores often ended up co-locating with other physical stores, often in direct competition with each other. Why could this possibly be? In a world where stores compete in hand-to-hand combat with each other to lure consumers, why would they station themselves right next to each other, making the tussle even more challenging? Why would malls even exist?

The answer, of course, is proximity to prospective customers. It is far easier to bring the store to the customer than bring the customer to the store. Stores realized that it is much better to be in the flow of customer traffic even if that meant competing with alternatives, rather than be off on a homestead or ranch and be the only store in sight. Being in the flow of live customers trumps competitive dynamics. This is why malls exist. This is why downtowns exist. On a larger scale, this is why cities get bigger. And this is why cities are settled on railroads, waterways and roadways. Everyone wins by being close to the customer. And everyone wins by collaborating to serve the customer rather than throwing up barriers and friction on their journey. This requires merchants and storefronts to be on a commerce network or railroad where customers are passing through, rather than off on a silo or homestead struggling to get customers in the door. And it requires merchants to hand off customers to each other along with all their shopping requirements, to make the experience seamless and frictionless for them.

As consumers seize their power via the consumer revolution and adapt their shopping behaviours to their new-found powers, merchants will need to fall in line. They will need to bring consumers in to their storefronts of course. But new technologies are enabling them to bring active shoppers with predefined shopping parameters, rather than squandering their budgets on uninterested shoppers who will get irritated more than anything else by being bombarded with unsolicited ads. In other words, the most efficient way to get consumers into the store is off the commerce railroad, as they are already shopping, have well-defined needs, and can be delivered right to the store section with the right product prese-lected to service their need. This is far more capital efficient than to spend funds attracting less qualified consumers with less well-understood needs and letting them wade through the sites and leave.

Then, when the consumer's shopping is done, commerce sites are best served putting them back on the commerce railroad so their shopping journeys can continue—either for competitive or complementary products. Trying to block off the consumer's journey is a futile exercise on a network where all stores are readily accessible. On the contrary, new technologies are enabling merchants to benefit from handing off consumers with already defined shopping parameters to other merchants who are only too happy to pay for them.

The consumer revolution in commerce is driving average conversion rates of commerce sites down to 2 per cent across the Internet. There is not a whole lot that commerce sites can do about that. But in this environment, it is critical to monetize the other 98 per cent of the traffic by sending consumers off to other sites, and getting paid for that handoff. This is what will make or break the economics of a commerce site through the consumer revolution. Sites that excel at serving consumers with predefined shopping parameters coming off the commerce railroad, and at sending consumers with refined shopping parameters back on the railroad will win huge. Sites that don't will find themselves at a greater and greater economic disadvantage with both traffic in and traffic out. Being in an old school commerce silo will become akin to sitting on a distant homestead with your storefront battling for consumers while they are streaming in en masse to the mall in the heart of the city!

This is why the leader in the commerce space, Amazon, has itself moved to align itself with the consumer revolution. The com-pany's offerings include its own products, but also offerings from a wide range of third-party sellers and merchants. This has the self-reinforcing benefits of Amazon being able to serve an ever-increasing range of products to consumers, drawing them to the site in increasing numbers as its coverage increases and being able to monetize its non-converting traffic by sending off consumers to other sellers. For a fee, of course. There are many analyses done for the phenomenal success of Amazon. But one of the least understood and analysed is this—that Amazon is on the right side of the consumer revolution. It is equipped to support the consumer's journey the best, and is hence getting rewarded handsomely by the consumer revolution.

Putting it all together, the cumulative effect of power moving to consumers is that the entire Internet is becoming one giant store, with media and entertainment, and friends and family interlaced throughout this giant store. An Internet of one. The Internet is becoming consumer-centric, where everything organizes itself around the requirements and preferences of each individual consumer, at each point in time. Any company that can spur this transformation to service the needs of the empowered consumer with the right set of products and tools is going to become the big winner in the digital space.

Current behemoths in the digital space fall short of delivering on this vision in many critical ways. Google delivers an exceptional experience searching for information, but not for commerce, enabling a slew of other sites to emerge to fill that gap. Amazon delivers an exceptional commerce experience for its own site, but not for the millions of other sites and merchants beyond themselves. Providers of commerce aggregation and synthesizing services largely focus on specific industry verticals, and do not deliver on seamlessly interlacing their content with other sites. This all adds up to a disjointed end-to-end commerce experience for consumers, and opens up the opportunity for technologies to serve as the central backbone and glue for delivering seamless commerce to them. Such a platform can enable consumers to truly claim their market power, and merchants to collaborate to serve consumer needs, rather than compete with each other but lose the consumer in the process.

WHERE WILL THE CONSUMER REVOLUTION IN COMMERCE GO FROM HERE?

As in other domains, the consumer revolution will only get more powerful in the commerce realm. Consumers will be even more informed about their requirements, and especially about the competitive landscape for every product and service they desire. They will be able to fact-check every claim, cross-check every detail and have information parity with the merchant's human- or machine-based points of sale. Given this, merchants will be best served enhancing their product or service value—features, benefits, price points, merchandising, promotions and customer service. This is where the competitive battlefield will shift. The return on investment will be substantially lower investing in messaging, positioning and branding when consumers are so armed with information. The brand will be the product or the service itself, not its representation through clever taglines and advertising campaigns.

The consumer revolution is driving commerce to its true, authentic roots. Commerce at its core is about selling great products and services at great prices. Commerce is about providing great customer service to ensure consumers get the most out of their purchases. Everything else is secondary at best, and fluff at worst. The consumer revolution will force merchants and commerce to become more authentic.

Consumers will also amass massive buying power and leverage over merchants. The intrinsic information advantage sellers have enjoyed over buyers for centuries will fade away entirely. The friction to consumers getting product and pricing information is coming down dramatically. Consumers have unprecedented ability to keep merchants honest. Each sale will have to be earned the

old-fashioned way—on the merits of the product and the pricing
and the shopping experience. Consumers will be verifying value
right up to the checkout counter—cross-checking alternatives in
the market on their mobile devices for instance right up till the
moment of purchase. Every sale, every purchase will become a
real-time bid at the point of transaction, where the best bid wins.

The rise in buyer power will also enforce significant streamlining
in shopping experiences. Merchants and retailers that successfully
simplify their shopping experiences will win big. This can entail
reducing unnecessary complexity from the consumers' journey,
this can entail eliminating efforts and steps required for consumers
to go through, this can entail anticipating what consumers need
even before they reach that point. But in all forms and fashions,
reducing friction for consumers in the shopping process will pay
off handsome dividends.

In similar fashion, the consumer revolution will wreak havoc
with profit margins of businesses. Unlike in the physical world,
where the lack of transparency about features and prices, and
alternatives has for centuries enabled merchants to get away with
premium profit margins, in the era of the consumer revolution
those margins will dwindle away. With the consumer in the charge,
and this much information on merchants and competitors trans-
parently available, there is no option but for margins to compress.
There is no alternative but for prices to come down and be utterly
competitive, otherwise the consumer revolution will take its toll.

Consumers will amass yet more power by banding together.
They will come to shop with their posse in tow, able to discuss the
merits of a product, and the pros and cons of making the purchase
with their friends and family at will. Not only that, they will be
able to band together with total strangers, who come together
purely for the purpose of making a smart purchase decision, and
then disband.

All in all, power is shifting dramatically from sellers to buyers.
The more merchants invest in value and product differentiation,

the more they will win. The more they invest in messaging and branding, the more they will squander their resources.

The more merchants connect and collaborate to serve the greater good of the consumer, the more they will win. The more they stand apart in old school silos, the greater the barriers for consumers to shop in them, and the greater their loss.

The consumer revolution will also demand new generations of point of sale interfaces and tools. It will demand richer forms of interaction with merchants, starting with voice and moving on to videos, virtual reality shopping environments, holograms and more. Voice-based shopping is already here with Amazon's Alexa and others, but the consumer revolution will demand more in short order. It will require increasingly real shopping experiences, real trial experiences and real usage experiences as part of the commerce process. For instance, apparel shopping can entail 3D imagery of you dressed in the clothes you want to buy, in different settings you might find yourself in. Or car shopping can entail a virtual test drive, where you can experience yourself driving a car you are considering on your regular work route, or perhaps an exotic vacation excursion. Or vacation shopping can entail a virtual reality experience of the actual location before you decide to travel there for a week.

Merchants will be well served investing in experiential merchandising tools and core product value propositions, rather than excessively on positioning and branding. The consumer revolution is changing the entire rules of the game where it truly matters—consumers' purse strings. Merchants and retailers that make this transition to consumer-driven and consumer-centric commerce will win handsomely. Merchants that don't will slide into oblivion. And the gap between today's retailing and tomorrow's is so vast, that there will be entirely new merchants coming up to jump on the wide open opportunity before powerful incumbent merchants respond. The stakes are enormous, and there will be massive winners and losers created.

Another core differentiator in the emerging era of commerce is the calibre of shipping and transportation capabilities providers can offer consumers. With the skyrocketing emphasis on customer-centricity, merchants will need to compete more and more vigor-ously to deliver products to consumers with increasing reliability, precision and timeliness. Merchants will need to continue to inno-vate in delivery services such as drones and driverless cars to get products to customers better than others can. Merchants will also need to innovate further in return policies and procedures, substantially lowering the risk and anxiety in digital shopping.

Transportation services will evolve tremendously when it comes to transporting people as well. We are already seeing the impact of the consumer revolution in ride-sharing services such as Uber, Lyft, Didi and Ola, making it substantially more convenient and cost effective for consumers to move from place to place. The consumer revolution will only accelerate this trend, obviating the need to own automobiles when you can move around with such ease and convenience. Furthermore, consumers will push the frontiers further towards driverless cars and eventually pilotless planes, providing ultimate mobility on demand.

As with other realms touched by the consumer revolution, the technology providers and merchants that align with the consumer revolution will win enormously in the market. In today's world, Amazon has seized that pole position in the world of commerce and is devouring market share at a furious pace. Amazon has done several things to successfully align itself with the consumer revolution and serve its needs effectively. This ranges from its impeccable delivery and return service to frictionless checkout processes, not to mention its very successful cloud business which funds many of its consumer investments. But one of the most potent capabilities Amazon has developed is its marketplace for third-party products, which enables it to have the widest selection of products to offer to consumers and become the de facto super market to the world. This universality of products has enabled Amazon to overtake Google as the number one place consumers visit to search for things to buy. By purchasing the grocery chain Whole Foods, and by introducing a quantum leap in customer retail experience with Amazon Go, Amazon is racing ahead to anticipate and meet the needs of the consumer revolution.

As in other domains, the rise of a dominant technology provider to the consumer revolution is fraught with perils for the general public. As the power of Amazon multiplies at every stage, it is presenting mortal risks to the other retailers and merchants in the world. Furthermore, the increasing returns from the data that Amazon is amassing on consumers worldwide is giving it a disproportionate advantage over other retailers, widening its lead and competitive competency. The consumer revolution's powerful network effects are increasing Amazon's dominance in the market, not reigning it in, setting up for potential risks for the general public.

Open competition and maximum consumer choice can be severely curtailed by an online retailing juggernaut. There are huge costs to communities for stores shutting down, malls closing and local merchants shuttering doors. Taken to its extreme conclusion, you can envision a world with no stores in entire communities, just a giant online service delivering products and services to individual homes and secluded people. Not the best community future to look forward to!

As with other domains, the representatives responsible for safeguarding consumer interests—which means government officials—must step in aggressively and proactively to regulate a dominant marketplace platform and avoid risk of catastrophic failures. Free enterprise and incentive must be very carefully balanced with the public good so both can be accomplished. Leaving a profit-making enterprise to look out for the public interest of its own accord is a naïve fool's errand. Elected representatives must get ahead of this trajectory and put in the right regulations for Amazon, and other companies of its scale and scope that emerge. They must ensure the pure, unfettered access to sellers for buyers and vice versa. They must step up and safeguard long-term consumer interests.

Failing to do so will be akin to unregulated banks and the financial collapse of the early 21st century. There is ferocious market power being established by Amazon's marketplace, and left to its own profit-making priorities, there is phenomenal risk of abuse of that power. As with the financial crisis, regulators need to get involved as quickly as possible to put in safeguards, safety nets, and checks and balances to avoid a colossal collapse that could undermine the economic framework of society itself.

While government regulators step up to their responsibilities, the market will also push for better solutions and decentralization of Amazon's marketplace. The other 13 million e-commerce sites and apps on the Internet will look for ways to combat Amazon's dominance. They will realize that each of them individually is powerless to take on Amazon—the gap has already become too large.

So other retailers and e-commerce sites will realize they need to band together. The only way to catch up to Amazon now is through a network of commerce sites, and they need to be on it. A digital railroad that serves the same purpose as physical railways, roadways and waterways accomplished in historical times. If other merchants and retailers get on such a railroad, they can send and receive active shopper consumers without friction, serve their needs where they can and hand them off to the next retailer where they can't. No one merchant can serve the consumer on their own, but as a group they can.

Merchants that get on such a network will find themselves completely aligned with the consumer revolution, and soar with it. The network will become the super mall with the most products and services to offer. That is what consumers will flock to. Merchants that stay out of such a network will get crushed by Amazon and by networked merchants. The unit economics are so powerful by being on the commerce network that those off it will simply not be able to compete. It would be the equivalent of fighting with an army that is moving troops freely by rail, while sitting on a homestead unable to move your ammunitions!

The consumer revolution in commerce is upon us. Massive forces are now at work, giant structures are being put in place and there is unprecedented opportunity for existing merchants and new entrants to ride the consumer wave. And there is unprecedented responsibility on government officials to regulate the game so it serves the public interest rather than putting it at grave risk.

9

SOMETHING SPECTACULAR THIS WAY COMES

It is spectacular seeing images of cosmic phenomena unfold. Two galaxies colliding. A black hole devouring a star. The brilliant splashes of a supernova from an imploding star. It is the sheer size and scope of the energy released that boggles our minds. It is the sheer scale that stretches and rattles the limits of our comprehension. It is the sheer magnitude of it all that stirs our soul.

The consumer revolution is no less of a spectacle in the making on our own little planet. It is time to strap on our seat belts. To paraphrase Ray Bradbury, something spectacular this way comes!

The consumer revolution is nothing short of the socio-economic-political equivalent of such a cosmic phenomenon. It is the biggest development the human race has ever seen, and it is poised to change everything. Like many cosmic and natural phenomena, it won't emerge and make a dramatic appearance overnight. It might take years and even decades to play out in full glory. But its inevitability, size, scope and reach are astronomical. The human energy pent up to be released is massive. If harnessed correctly, it will energize an untold amount of creation, innovation and prosperity in our world. But if mishandled, it will lead to catastrophic results, and an annihilation of the very fibre of our society.

As the cliché goes, the biggest resource we have on our planet is our human resource. Humans have achieved incredible feats individually, or in groups that are small subsets relative to the entire human race. Just imagine what we could be capable of as a whole. Up until the consumer revolution, there could have been no endeavour or mission conceivable that could engage all of humankind. There could have been no mechanism to weave consumers together into a common fabric for a common cause. There has been no infrastructure available for humans to connect with one another, to trigger one another and to unleash their individual and collective energies.

This is why, up until this point, the human race has operated at a minuscule fraction of its true macro potential. A few leaders, champions and stars have ascended to the top and reaped handsome benefits from it. But for the rest of the world, much of the individual micro potential has been bottled up; its impact limited to small scale and local environs only. There has been far too much friction in the system to enable individual consumers to learn, congregate and unleash their collective energies upon the world.

This friction to information and connectivity has led to the human race being led by those who produce, govern and dazzle as stars. In a producer-led world, a few members of our race prospered enormously on the backs of the many. Few members of our race governed with great power at the acquiescence and the relative helplessness of the many. That we are at a generally prosperous overall state is testament to the competencies and compassions of our leaders and stars. But our overall human potential, the collective creative energy of 7.7 billion people, is far from tapped. There is incredible power waiting to be turned on, amazing energy to be uncorked and a fearsome force to be unleashed.

Anytime a juggernaut like this gets rolling, it shakes the earth and leaves big winners and losers in its wake. A major constituency that will be deeply affected by the consumer revolution is the producer world—companies, merchants, manufacturers, retailers, publishers, entertainers, service providers, financial institutions, health care providers, educational institutions, sports franchises and every entity that sells any product or service to consumers.

THE BUYER'S MARKET

While 'serve the customer' has been one of the core tenets of business since its inception, the caveats and nuances to that have been plentiful. The business principle largely meant 'serve the individual, scarcely informed, relatively helpless and naive customer with limited choices' up to this point. Now, the consumer revolution is upending the basic premises that most business operate under.

The consumer is no longer an isolated individual on a remote island trying to assess value in a vacuum. The consumer is now connected.

The consumer has an advisory council, a posse, a congregation to consult with at every step. The consumer is harnessing the collective expertise and collective judgment of other peers or confidants.

The consumer is also no longer ill-informed. The best information in the world is now available to the consumer in an instant. The information disparity, and the ensuing power dynamic, between buyer and seller is dissipating. In fact, the buyer may be now better informed than the seller, particularly when it comes to competitive products and services in the market. This has a profound impact at the point of sale. The power dynamic is completely flipped, with the seller having to earn each and every transaction based on pure value and merit.

The consumer also now has incredible choice. In fact, for every product or service consumed, the consumer has a selection of all the possible choices in the market available at their disposal. The barrier to hop from shop to shop has effectively gone down to zero. The consumer's ability to shop the market has gone up exponentially. The good old days of keeping consumers within a store's walled garden are long gone. Attempting to keep the consumer within a store and away from competitors is increasingly futile. This changes the dynamic for merchants, producers and entertainers utterly and completely. Each penny, each second of attention has to be earned by delivering true value.

These seem like very daunting times for producers to head into. For those stuck in their past habits, yes. For those willing to embrace the times ahead, not so much. The consumer revolution presents tremendous threats to business as usual for producers. But it also presents mind-boggling opportunities to be harnessed to those willing to adapt and truly serve their customers.

At their core, producers of all shapes and sizes need to redefine how they relate to their consumers. In a world where the consumer has so much power and information, how do they want to present themselves? How do they want to earn the consumer's business? How do they want to prove their value? How do they want to differentiate relative to competitors?

For merchants, how do they prioritize product features and benefits versus branding and messaging? How much do they talk to consumers, versus now listen? How should they invest in and harness artificial intelligence and machine learning to have one-on-one conversations with consumers, and deliver tailored products and services to each? How should they become intensely consumer-centric in their approach? How do they get in the consumers' good books? How do they price their products and services in a world where all prices are exposed to consumers all the time? How do they leverage differential pricing in a world of complete transparency? What should they do with their advertising strategy? In a world where consumers hate ads, and returns are increasingly difficult to prove, should they continue feeding the beast or retrench? How do they align themselves on the side of the consumer revolution rather than against it? How do they keep pace with industry leaders who have found the magic formula to ride the consumer revolution, and are soaring away with it? Where should they turn to for help in this new consumer revolution powered networked commerce economy?

For media companies, be it either movies, television, radio, concerts or sports leagues, the questions are just as vexing. Should they continue to broadcast or narrowcast? Should they persist with their packaging and bundling and programme compositions, or abandon them and let consumers decide? How should they compete with the splurge of content coming down the Internet, often with much closer associations and deeper relationships within friends and families? How should they monetize their content? How should they deal with the rising consumer distaste for advertising? How should they handle the tearaway leaders in media, such as search engines and social networking giants, who seem to be sailing away to glory on the consumer revolution tidal wave? How should they re-establish their value in the new world order?

For movie stars, musical celebrities and sports heroes, there are tough decisions to ponder as well. In a world where they are coming 'down to the level of the common person' to be relatable, and outperformers in the general populace are rising and shining with their own local networks, how do stars stand out on a consistent basis? How do they maintain their historical fan followings over time? How do they make the consumer revolution work for them, and not against them? How do they keep the consumer engaged in the main action on a sports field, and not derivative contests such as sports betting and fantasy sports? How do they handle declining viewership for premier musical and sporting events?

WINNER TAKES ALL

The answers to the above questions will determine the difference between dazzling success and abject failure. They will determine if businesses are pushing a boulder down the hill or up the hill. The sooner businesses adapt to the new market reality, the greater the distances they will be able to put between themselves and competitors. And such is the force of the consumer revolution, that leads will get amplified, advantages will get reinforced and victories will get larger for businesses that embrace the consumer revolution sooner rather than later.

In the best case, businesses that not only ride the consumer revolution but actually enable it, will win at a scale beyond our current imaginations. Networking systems, cloud providers, search engines, social networks, and marketplace providers will score epic victories by facilitating the consumer revolution. In fact, they will get so enormous and powerful that they will need to be regulated and managed by governing bodies in the interest of the greater societal good. These new age behemoths will need to decide how to address a curious problem—how best to handle their unprecedented power in the world. Should they continue to optimize for profits as their core foundations mandate them to do? Where do they draw the line between enabling consumers and exploiting them by delivering an essential commodity? How do they determine and negotiate the terms of regulations that are inevitable in the trajectory we are on?

POLITICAL MARKETING

Speaking of regulations, the next major constituency affected by the consumer revolution is the government. The consumer revolution is changing the very foundation of governments and governing institutions. There are a wide range of governing systems across the world, of course. These range from countries at the democracy and free-market end of the spectrum, to monarchies, to dictatorships and controlled economies. But all these government systems were designed for the model where the governed were essentially isolated individuals with limited access to information, access to congregation and access to collective might.

Monarchies have been able to flourish because subjects lacked the infrastructure to come together, have a collective will and coalesce the power of an entire populace acting as one mass of humanity. Monarchies put systems and processes together that wove their citizenry into some semblance of organization. But of course, along the way they ensured that they served their own purposes to propagate their authority and benefits. Monarchs could rule and enforce the laws of the land with a relatively small number of governors, administrators and soldiers because the rest of the population was so fragmented and separated into natural silos. Dissent and mutinies were extremely rare because organizing and mobilizing mass consumers was near impossible. Successful movements such as Mahatma Gandhi's Quit India Movement against the British Empire were exceedingly rare.

Dictatorship has been able to exist because of a similar dynamic. Absent the ability for consumers to organize effectively, it has been possible for an individual or a junta to control entire populaces effectively with minimal resources. Dictators have been able to throttle the flow of information, and the ease of congregation to subjugate entire masses of people. Most dictatorships have been self-serving in the extreme, exploiting their subjects in the process, but dissent has again been minimized by controlling consumer behaviour and access.

Even democracies are structured around the premise that consumers cannot easily congregate and collaborate. That is the entire basis for representative democracies. Since constituents could not get together every time a decision had to be made, they elected representatives who could do so for them. A whole set of systems and processes was created to govern societies and countries in the fairest and most effective ways possible. Elaborate voting systems were created, such as who could vote and how votes would be allocated into districts to ensure fair representations. Different countries went with different governance models, such as parliamentary, presidential or representative democracies. Sophisticated checks and balances were put in place, such as the division of authority between the legislative, executive and judicial branches of the government.

And yet, as with any models and artefacts put in place, they introduce their own baggage of behaviours induced by the models that often trump the original objectives themselves. Elections have become huge consumer marketing exercises, consuming enormous amounts of national time and money just to pick who would represent the voting populace the best. Parliamentary processes seem to have an endless array of procedures that sometimes seem to get in the way of the decisions the populace needs made. Elected representatives seem to be swayed by lobbyists and special interest groups much more than by the everyday consumer they are meant to represent.

All of this is because consumers couldn't up to this point connect and make collective decisions themselves in an effective manner. But now that they can, what risks and opportunities does that create for government officials?

As the consumer revolution takes hold, what should the role of government be in it? As consumers start to re-write rules, how should the government engage with the process? Government officials seem to already be getting behind the curve on digital governance. What rules and laws should they create to support and enable collective decision-making amongst consumers, not fight it? How should they orchestrate the transition of the governance model itself from a traditional, representative, artefact-laden, slow-moving model, to one that entails consumers reaching cloud-based collective decisions within minutes or hours? How should they define the place for government representation when representation itself is no longer needed? What should leadership mean, when they are increasingly left behind as consumers race ahead on issues that matter to them? How should they continue to be effective and relevant when the consumer revolution obviates their core working models?

Beyond redefining governance itself, how should government representatives handle core enablers of the consumer revolution? How do they rationalize a hands-off approach to regulation when it comes to dominant cloud providers, search engines, social networks and transaction marketplaces? Can they really entrust profit-making enterprises to self-regulate, and guarantee pristine and unadulterated use of the pipes and arteries enabling the consumer revolution? Do they have to put in checks and balances to ensure these enabler corporations override their core profit-making mandates, and serve the larger consumer interest instead? Or do they need to entirely take over these dominant enabler platforms as public utilities to safeguard the public interest?

This is all assuming a genuine dilemma, and honest conflict of interest for well-meaning enabler platforms. The implications of some malicious actor using the arteries of the consumer revolution to subvert it are nothing short of sinister. What should the role of government be in regulating and safeguarding against such excesses? How should the government protect its citizenry from such violations of trust and dangerous outcomes by misguiding or deceiving mass consumers?

And, of course, the central constituency impacted by the consumer revolution is consumers themselves. After millennia upon millennia of being on the receiving end, consumers are now taking charge. They are seizing authority and starting to dictate terms to producers, merchants, publishers, providers and governments. They are banding together at remarkable speed about things they care about, and then imposing their will. They are making this their world, they are taking charge of their own destiny. They are expressing themselves, they are ensuring that they are being heard. They are shaping the world in their own image.

The consumer revolution is arming consumers with everything they need to take charge. They can be informed on whatever they want. They can connect with whoever they want. They can be entertained however they like. They can transact whenever they want. They can demand services. They can require full satisfaction. They can set the agenda. They can determine the laws of the land. They can shape the world they live in—it was always meant to be theirs anyway. They are simply taking back what was always theirs.

The consumer revolution is nothing short of a nuclear weapon being armed for consumers. How do they maximize effective use of this fearsome power? How do they make the tools of the consumer revolution work for them, not work them over? How do they take responsibility for this powerful force, and direct it in the correct ways? How do they shape the processes of collective decision-making? How do they self-regulate—both for positive action, but also to identify and weed out bad actors? How does the silent majority speak up and not stay silent anymore? Because that is the only force that can counter and overpower malicious forces trying to subvert the consumer revolution for their own nefarious purposes.

Rolling on, how does the consumer revolution influence traditional government institutions? How does it dictate the terms of power sharing with elected representatives? How does it take the lead on the issues and representatives it supports? How does it balance venting and emotions with responsibility and governance? How does it prevent overreactions and hasty rushes to judgment? How does it develop a maturity and thoughtfulness to reach responsible decisions that benefit society as a whole? How does it ensure that all voices are heard in orderly fashion? How does it ensure that experts in a given field get adequate voice in actions affecting that field? How does it morph into the leader of society rather than a follower?

And how does the consumer revolution negotiate the massive changes in dynamic when it comes to dealing with producers? How does it use the powers of information and connectivity to take back control from merchants, advertisers, publishers and stars? How does it dictate the terms of engagement in an effective way? How does it express its will in cogent ways? How does it reward good behaviour and punish bad ones? How does it ensure a fair exchange with producers in each forum?

RIDING THE TIDE

As the consumer revolution gathers momentum, there are countless questions for all parties to ponder. Now is the time to reflect, organize and act. The genie is out of the bottle. The fire has been lit. The consumer revolution is barrelling down the runway!

Like most revolutions, the consumer revolution is not going to be very predictable. It has a mob psychology of its own, and it will take its own course through the various issues and objectives of the day. It will have competing agendas and objectives of its own. It currently has undefined rules of engagement, with unknown outcomes. It doesn't operate with one mind, but billions of minds. It can turn on a dime, or meander its way through its causes, or dissipate and morph into entirely new missions.

The consumer revolution is not going to be perfect. It has many inherent quirks and characteristics that will make it erratic and unmanageable at times. Like many natural phenomena, it will formulate and play out over decades rather than days. It will have bright days, and it will have dark nights. However, over time, the true nature of humanity will be revealed as it expresses its might and will like nothing else before it. Over time, it will reflect the true will of humanity, so it will always be 'right'.

The consumer revolution is accumulating such ferocious power that it is going to transform our very models of society. It is starting to re-write the fundamental rules of engagement and redefine interfaces with producers, manufacturers, merchants, advertisers, entertainers and government officials.

It is coming at us now with full force. We are all in its way and there is no escaping its folds. If we are unprepared for its unfolding, we will be demolished as a society. But if we can ride the tsunami, a glorious new world order awaits us. The choice is entirely up to us as consumers—to ride it or to be blown away by it. The stakes are the highest they have ever been. And the time to act is now!

ABOUT THE AUTHOR

The inspiration and perspective for *The Consumer Revolution: Tipping the Balance of Power* comes from Naren's 30-year career in the high-tech industry. He started his professional journey with a bachelors in computer science from the Indian Institute of Technology, Kharagpur, and a masters in computer science from the University of California, Santa Barbara. This provided him an intrinsic understanding of the high-tech industry at work since the dawn of personal computing.

From there, Naren moved to Stanford University for his MBA degree, which he completed in 1992. After Stanford, Naren was hired by Microsoft Corporation to work on its product strategy efforts for interactive television, and subsequently the Internet.

After Microsoft, Naren worked at Trilogy Corporation, an enterprise software and dot com incubation company in the late 1990s. After Trilogy, Naren held the position of president at cFares Inc., a travel metasearch company similar to Kayak, and subsequently, Founder at MetaRail Inc., a networked commerce platform company.